DUNFERMLINE ATHLETIC
Football Club

A Centenary History
1885–1985

John Hunter

Published by John Hunter

Dunfermline Athletic FC

A Centenary History, 1885-1985

John Hunter

For Jane (7), Karen (5) and Gillian (3) without whose help this book would have been finished much sooner; and for Irene without whom it would not have been finished at all.

Published and distributed by John Hunter,
7 Old Kirk Place, Dunfermline, Fife KY12 7ST. Tel (0383) 729699.

Typeset and printed by The Allen Lithographic Co Ltd,
40 Townsend Place, Kirkcaldy.

ISBN 0 951 0830 07

Contents

Acknowledgments

I would like to express my warmest gratitude to the following individuals and organisations whose help has proved invaluable in the compilation of this history: the chairman, secretary, manager and board of Dunfermline Athletic FC who have assisted in many ways, not least in making their records and facilities readily available; Information Technology Services of Edinburgh for the free loan of a microfilm reader; the Director of Libraries, Museums and Art Galleries, James K. Sharp, Chris Neale of the Reference Department and their colleagues of Dunfermline Public Library; Douglas Scott; Russell Shepherd; Paul Terris; George Simon, depute editor of the *Dunfermline Press*; Les Peters of the *Dundee Courier*; my colleague, Lachlan Campbell, for reading the proofs; contributors to the *Scottish Football Historian* and members of the *Association of Football Statisticians*; numerous typists who have deciphered my hieroglyphics; the staff of Allen Litho, Kirkcaldy, who have worked beyond the call of duty; and countless other individuals who have generously lent me material and given of their time.

I have been able to publish more than 260 photographs and I am deeply in debt to the agencies who have supplied me with photographs and who have all generously waived copyright fees: local photographer, Morris Allan; Douglas Spence of the *Dundee Courier*; Ted Molton, Tom Gormley and Steve Butler of the *Dunfermline Press*; the *Daily Record* and *Sunday Mail*; the *Evening News* and *Scotsman*; the *Glasgow Herald*; the *Daily Express*; and Dunfermline Public Library. I am also grateful to Davie Harrison, Margaret Thomson, Gerry Mays and many others who lent me photographs. I have made every effort to trace the ownership of photographs – my apologies to any agency whom I have unintentionally omitted. Thanks are also due to Hamlyn Press for allowing me to reproduce their League tables.

I am especially grateful to my sponsors who, through their advertisements, have helped to defray the considerable costs in publishing a book of this nature.

My final thanks must go to the players, management and fans, both past and present, of Dunfermline Athletic FC – without their efforts and endurance over the past century there would not have been a story to relate.

JOHN HUNTER
October 1985

Foreword

It is a great honour to be chairman of Dunfermline Athletic F.C. and to be asked to write the foreword to this history of the club. While one hundred years may not be a long time in the history of our famous town it is the whole life of our football team which has had literally an "up and down" existence since its formation all these years ago.

The thanks of all at East End go to John Hunter for all the work and effort that he has put into the writing of this book. Very few who will enjoy reading the contents will realise the time that has been spent researching and compiling this work and but for him this very important milestone in the history of our club might have passed without suitable recognition.

We all loved the thrill and excitement of the "glorious sixties" – and I would now like to acknowledge the debt the club owes to the late Jock Stein who did so much to put the Pars on the football map, not only in Scotland but in almost every country in Europe. He is sadly missed wherever soccer is played but nowhere more so than at East End Park. However, we must never forget that for the other ninety years there were those on and off the field who worked and worried without the satisfaction of success and glamour. To all who at any time have contributed to the very existence of our club I give my thanks – without you there would not have been one hundred wonderful years – and no history.

JAMES WATTERS
Chairman
October 1985

Cover design: Colin Lawson and Ken Forbes.

Back cover: *Jackie Williamson, Jimmy Stevenson and Jock Stein acclaim Dunfermline's cup triumph in 1961.* (Daily Express)

Introduction

In 1885 Queen Victoria was on the throne and Gladstone was Prime Minister. Britain was the "Workshop of the World" and was amassing a huge overseas Empire. Gilbert and Sullivan had just written *The Mikado* while Daimler and Benz were in the process of inventing the motor car. Beer was a farthing a pint; coal cost 8/4*d* a ton. In the same year Dunfermline Athletic Football Club was born and very quickly flourished to become a well-supported, provincial club.

The game of football has not stood still in the space of one hundred years: dress and equipment have changed, a few alterations have been made to the rules of the game, tactics have become more sophisticated and the financial attractions and glamour have never been greater. However, as the story of Dunfermline Athletic Football Club unfolds, it will be seen that some aspects of the sport never change. Throughout these pages certain themes keep reappearing proving that in football, as in life, there really is nothing new. Irrespective of the decade certain problems always perplex the fans, players and administrators: crowd trouble; the state of the pitch; reconstruction of leagues; dwindling gates; criticism of referees; excessive commercialisation; the prospect of winter shutdowns; financial problems; dominance of clubs from the West; lack of effort; and so on.

Looking through material for Dunfermline Athletic's official history are the author (seated right) and club chairman, Mr James Watters. Standing (l to r) are Mr William Braisby (director), Mr James McConville (hon secretary), Mr William M. Rennie (vice-chairman) and Dr John C. Yellowley (director and club doctor). (Dunfermline Press)

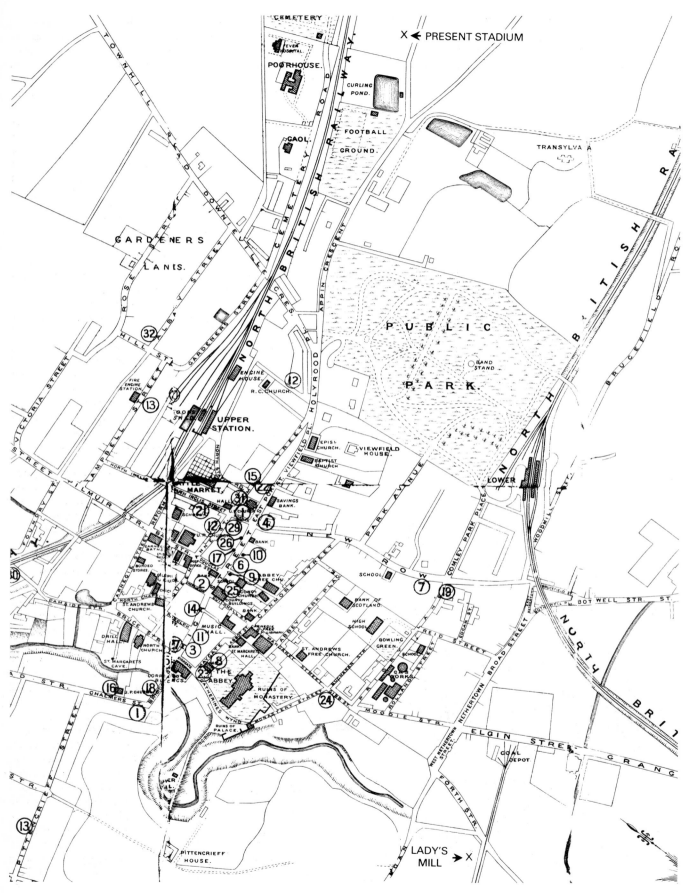

Early Years

Football has been around for hundreds of years but the birth of modern football, like that of other popular sports such as tennis, cricket and rugby, is to be found in the latter half of the nineteenth century. In 1863 a giant step was taken in the organisation of the sport when the English Football Association was formed. The formation of Queen's Park in 1867 marked the serious start of soccer north of the border. Other clubs soon appeared, such as Kilmarnock (1869), Dumbarton (1872) and Rangers (1872), mostly centred in the densely populated and highly industrialised belt of west and central Scotland. So great was the growth of football in the 'seventies that the Scottish Football Association was created in 1873 in an attempt to bring some order to this sporting explosion.

The epidemic swept eastwards to Edinburgh with the formation of Hearts and Hibs by 1875 and northwards across the Forth. In Dunfermline (population: 21,000) cricket was a very popular sport and it was one of its players, a Mr David Brown, who formally launched football in the town. In 1874 he witnessed a game involving Queen's Park in Glasgow which so fascinated him that before he left the city he purchased a football which he brought to Dunfermline that evening. The first organised football club consisted of members of the Dunfermline Cricket Club who played cricket in the summer and resorted to football in the winter to keep themselves fit and active. Their pitch was originally at the Town Green off Appin Crescent, just west of the present stadium, but later in 1879 they moved to Lady's Mill Park, now the site of McKane Park. Early SFA records show that they had 120 members and that they played in blue and white jerseys and hose with blue knickers.

Enthusiasm for the game grew, not just in the Auld Grey Toun where clubs like East End Swifts, Our Boys and Phoenix FC soon appeared, but throughout the county with the founding of many other clubs like Kingseat, Lassodie, Burntisland and Lochgelly. Arch-rivals Alloa and Cowdenbeath were formed in 1878 and 1880 respectively. To cater for and encourage this interest the Fifeshire Football Association was formed in 1882 with its own trophy, the Fife Cup.

So far, nothing has been said about Dunfermline Athletic and, indeed, the club would never have been formed had not a dispute broken out at Lady's Mill. At the Annual General Meeting of Dunfermline FC held on Tuesday 26 May 1885 in the Imperial Hotel, a letter was read out by the President, Mr Graham MacPherson, from the Cricket Club. The cricketers wanted the constitution of the football club altered in such a way that "no one be admitted a member of the football club unless he be a member of the cricket club". This demand was considered to be unacceptable to the committed footballers who decided that the best solution was for them to break away and form their own independent club devoted solely to football. An advert was accordingly placed in the *Dunfermline Journal* on Saturday 30 May announcing that a special meeting would be held in the Old Inn the following Tuesday 2 June.

Thus was born, in great haste, Dunfermline Athletic Football Club. In fact, the interim committee, comprising many members of the original football club, were able to report that "they had taken the East End Park and that there

Opposite: *Map of Dunfermline, 1893.* (Dunfermline Public Library)

Below: *Calendar of the Fifeshire Association, 1882-83.* (Public Library)

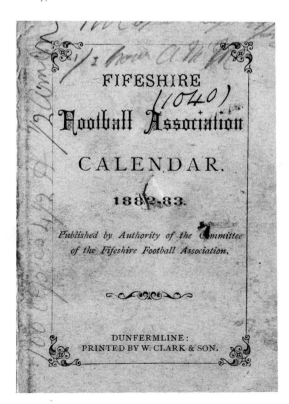

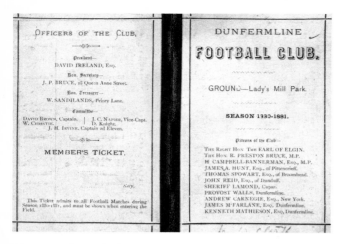

Above: *A season card for the original Dunfermline Football Club for season 1880-81. Amongst the club's patrons were a millionaire, an earl and a future prime minister!* (Public Library)

Below: *The first public mention of "Dunfermline Athletic Football Club".*

CRICKET MATCH.

SECOND EDINBURGH UNIVERSITY *V.* SECOND DUNFERMLINE, at LADY'S MILL PARK TO-DAY, Play commencing at Half-past One o'clock.

Admission, 3d.   Ladies free.

THE MEMBERS of the D. A. F. C. will Meet in the OLD INN on TUESDAY First, 2nd June, at Eight o'clock P.M.

Business—To draw up Rules, &c.
A. WESTWOOD, JUN., Int. Sec.

were already 60 members on the roll". The election of office-bearers proceeded as follows:

Captain - Mr E. Lennox; Captain of the Second Eleven - Mr A. Ramsay; Secretary - Mr A. Westwood; Treasurer - Mr D. Knight; Members of the committee - Messrs D. Johnston, D. Scotland, J. Brown, A. Hynd and W. Robertson.

From this small acorn a mighty oak was to grow. The new committee must have been a go-ahead concern because within 10 days after the meeting everything was arranged and East End Park, leased from the North British Railway Company, was formally opened for play. On Saturday 13 June, Dunfermline Athletic opened their account with a match against a side from Edinburgh University. The *Journal* noted that "it should be more comfortable for the spectators to witness a football match in summer than when the snow may be in full blast. The match will doubtless ensure the satisfactory floating of the Athletic". The first ever Athletic team, kitted out in maroon jerseys and blue knickers, lined up as follows: Niven, Reynolds, Smith, Westwood, Ross, T. Lyon, Sandilands, Toddie, Stewart and D. Lyon. The Athletic made a good start to their new enterprise by winning 2–1.

To foster interest during the summer and also to raise funds the club organised a five-a-side football competition in July. "The Elgin and City Band will be in attendance," noted the advert, "and dancing will be engaged." Two thousand spectators turned up on a sunny day to see the victorious side win by "one touch down to nothing". It was to be some time before the rules of football were standardised and before the influence of rugby was wholly discarded. Great efforts were made for the start of their first season. A trial match was held with the 'Probables' lining up against, rather discouragingly, the 'Improbables'.

Hurried though the birth of the club had been, the mid-1880s were a good time to launch a new football club. More and more industrial workers in the factories, mills and mines of West Fife were winning the right to a half-day on a Saturday and attending a football match was becoming the traditional way for the working man to spend his newly found leisure. This factor plus a rise in real wages and the availability of cheap public transport meant attendances at football matches were very healthy. At the same time newspapers began to carry advertisements for forthcoming games and to give substantial reports and comments on matches played.

In the early days of organised football there were no leagues with regular, pre-arranged fixtures each week. Like every other team Dunfermline Athletic was an amateur club whose secretary organised a series of friendly matches. No payments were made; each player turned out for the love of the game and since league tables did not exist, points were not awarded. As the fixture list for 1886 shows, Dunfermline's opponents were small, unpretentious clubs like themselves, easily reached without too much travel. Many of these clubs have, of course, disappeared from the football scene over the years.

The club's first football advert.

Admission, 3d.   Ladies free.

GRAND OPENING FOOTBALL MATCH.

EDINBURGH UNIVERSITY *V.* DUNFERMLINE ATHLETIC, at EAST END PARK, TO-DAY (Saturday).   Kick-off at Four o'clock.

Admission 3d.   Ladies free.

CARNEGIE SWIMMING CLUB.

GRAND SWIMMING ENTERTAINMENT, for Volunteer Bazaar Fund, will take place at the BATHS, on MONDAY Evening, 22nd inst.

For particulars see Posters.

Prizes on View at Mr HARLEY's, Jeweller, High St.
C. E. STEWART, Hon. Secy.

Dunfermline, 13th June 1885.

LODGE UNION, No. 250.

A SPECIAL MEETING will be held in the

GRAND FOOTBALL COMPETITION.

THE DUNFERMLINE ATHLETIC FOOT-
BALL CLUB will hold a FIVE A-SIDE
COMPETITION, on MONDAY, 20th July, in the
EAST END PARK.

SILVER BADGES, value 15s and 7s 6d will be
given to the 1st and 2nd Teams.

The ELGIN AND CITY BAND will be in
attendance, and Dancing will be engaged in.

Admission to Field, Threepence.

Football Competition to begin at One o'clock.

Entries—2s 6d each Team—to close with A.
WESTWOOD, Jun., 14 Reform Street, Dunfermline,
on Wednesday, 15th inst.

Above: *An attempt to foster interest in the developing club.*

Below: *Fixture list for season 1886-87.*

DUNFERMLINE ATHLETIC FOOTBALL CLUB.

LIST OF FIXTURES.
FIRST ELEVEN.

Date, 1886.		Club.	Ground.
Aug.	21	Clyde	East End Park
„	28	Camelon	Camelon
Sept.	4	Burntisland Thistle	East End Park
„	11	S.C.T.	
„	18	Dunfermline (F.C.T.)	East End Park
„	25	E.S.T.	
Oct.	2	Broxburn Thistle	Broxburn
„	9	Norton Villa	East End Park
„	16	Alloa Athletic	Do.
„	30	Bellstane Birds	Do.
Nov.	13	Cowdenbeath	Cowdenbeath
„	20	Caledonia	East End Park
Dec.	18	Cartvale	Busby
1887.			
Jan.	1	Shettleston	East End Park
„	3	Dumbarton Union	Do.
„	15	Bellstane Birds	Queensferry
„	29	Alloa Athletic	Alloa
Feb.	12	Norton Villa	Edinburgh
„	19	Armadale	Armadale
„	26	Cowdenbeath	East End Park
Mar.	5	Broxburn Thistle	Do.
„	12	Burntisland Thistle	Burntisland
„	19	Govanhill Athletic	East End Park
„	26	Armadale	Do.
April	2	Queen's Park Strollers	Do.
„	16	Camelon	Do.
„	23	Cartvale	Do.

SECOND ELEVEN.

Date. 1886.		Club.	Ground.
Sept.	4	Burntisland Thistle	Burntisland
Oct.	2	Broxburn Thistle	East End Park
„	16	Alloa Athletic	Alloa
„	23	Strathforth	East End Park
„	30	Bellstane Birds	Queensferry
Nov.	6	Alloa United	East End Park
„	13	Cowdenbeath	Do.
„	20	Clackmannan	Clackmannan
1887.			
Jan.	15	Bellstane Birds	East End Park
„	22	Strathforth	Inverkeithing
„	29	Alloa Athletic	East End Park
Feb.	12	Clackmannan	Do.
„	26	Cowdenbeath	Cowdenbeath
Mar	5	Broxburn Thistle	

Being members of the East of Scotland Association and the Fife Association, Dunfermline generally played clubs from within the county and from the Lothians with the occasional visit granted by a west of Scotland club. Occasionally the sparkle and excitement of one of the many cups broke the monotony. In pride of place was the Scottish Cup, bought in 1873 by the SFA for £56 12s 11d. Little did the people of Dunfermline then imagine that one day their club would win the trophy in dramatic fashion.

Initially the early rounds were played on a regional basis. On 12 September 1885, the Athletic played their first ever cup game against Crieff (away), beating them by a handsome 8 goals to nil, though on the same day Arbroath did considerably better in disposing of Bon Accord by a record score of 36–0. Their joy was short-lived as they lost 10–0 in the next round at Dunblane. Ten years later the growth of football forced the SFA to institute the Qualifying Cup which only allowed those few clubs reaching the later stages of the competition to gain entry into the first round proper of the Scottish Cup where they could meet one of the giants.

The Athletic's first success came in 1887 when they won the Fife Cup. In the semi-final when they were drawn away to Lassodie it is recorded that "at least 300 enthusiasts travelled, partly on foot, partly in vehicles". Ever since these early days Dunfermline has always carried a loyal support to away matches. The game of football, as played in the 1880s, was significantly different from today. Before starting the cup-tie at Lassodie, Dunfermline's captain

The goal of every club – the Scottish Cup.

"lodged a protest against the state of the ground which was in a very bad condition, besides being totally unfenced". During the match a goal claimed by Dunfermline was disallowed – there were no nets and a spectator had kicked the ball back into play. Fighting broke out amongst the players and when the players withdrew to the dressing room further fighting ensued with the officials joining in as well. The Association ordered the game to be replayed at Kingseat where a 5–1 victory put Dunfermline into the final to meet Burntisland Thistle at Lady's Mill Park, kick-off at 4.15 pm. Almost three thousand spectators turned up to see Dunfermline go into a one-goal lead after which fighting broke out both on and off the field. The referee was obliged to leave the field, followed by the players. The local reporter noted that "if rough play and scenes such as that of Saturday are to be allowed to go on, the national game should wither like a decaying thistle in the country". The tie was awarded to Dunfermline but, after hearing a protest, the Fife Association decided the game should be replayed at Cowdenbeath

The advert shows how footballers dressed in the early days. (SFA Handbook)

for which the *Journal* carried the following advert – "A Brake will leave the Commercial Hotel today at 2.45 for Cowdenbeath. Fare 1/- return."

Dunfermline finally won 3–1, causing the *Journal* to observe that "the beautiful passing of the Athletic compared favourably with the great kicks of the Thistle" – a comment on early tactics! Interestingly, during the game a Burntisland player touched the ball near the goal but was penalised merely by a foul – penalties were not introduced until 1890. The Athletic team returned to Dunfermline by a special train to be given an enthusiastic welcome at the station. From there they visited the Commercial Hotel to have the cup filled and then moved on to the Old Inn, their unofficial headquarters, where badges (as opposed to medals) were given to the players. Rejoicing continued throughout the week.

Football violence and hooliganism is certainly not a modern phenomenon. The records contain many reports of crowd trouble, break-ins and fighting on and off the park. The lack of proper fencing (a mere rope sufficing), the absence of nets and occasionally crossbars and the appointment of club linesmen (or "umpires" as they were originally termed) all made for controversial incidents and decisions. In October 1888, during an East of Scotland Cup-tie, Dunfermline were losing 3–0 to Leith Athletic when an Edinburgh player kicked his Fife opponent in the stomach; the crowd broke in and the game was abandoned. Despite winning the replay Dunfermline were forced into a third game (which they lost) when Leith successfully protested that "the ball was not in a fit condition for a cup tie". In those early days when administrators were trying to standardise the rules and apply them uniformly, protests were common and often successful.

Occasionally the game was abandoned not because of disturbances but because the Dunfermline players had had enough. In January 1889, Dunfermline were playing at Armadale for a place in the semi-final of the King Cup. The visitors were at a disadvantage from the start since only ten men turned up. With 16 minutes to go and 5–2 down the Athletic decided to withdraw from the game to give themselves time to catch the next train home. Later, while playing at Grangemouth, Dunfermline were losing 4–0. When torrential rain poured down they simply left the field. Sometimes it was their opponents who called it a day. In 1886, both Alloa and West Calder left the field when trailing 4–2 and 7–2 respectively. In the same year, severe weather conditions prevented Burntisland from fulfilling a fixture at Dunfermline whereupon the home side took the field, kicked off and scored, and claimed the match.

It was not uncommon for Dunfermline to be a man short. Sometimes players from the other clubs in Fife would step into the team at the last minute. On occasions a spectator or even a player from the opposing team would fill the vacant position. Players could find it difficult getting away from work on a Saturday and since they relied totally on public transport it is not surprising that many games started late. Some games finished in the dark while others were restricted to 30 minutes each way.

Not surprisingly injuries resulting from either rough play or accidents were as common then as today although the treatment often differed. In 1887 when one Dun-

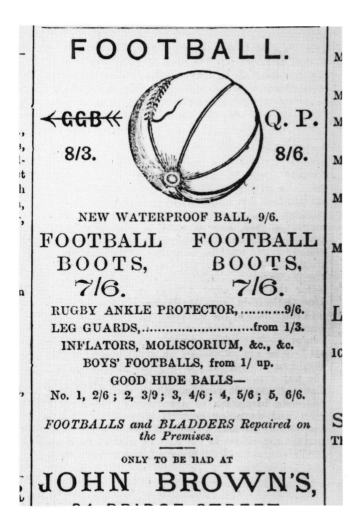
Above: *By the end of the century football was becoming big business.*

Right: *The forerunner of the teleprinter and teletext – the telegraph wire.*

doubt as to which club would represent the town. Rivalry, however, continued until matters were brought to a head when a semi-final tie involving Lassodie and Townhill was to be played at Lady's Mill on 14 April 1888. When the Athletic arranged a counter attraction at East End Park a protest was lodged which resulted in the East Enders being suspended from the Fife Association for more than a year, a severe blow to the developing club.

Much more testing, however, were the games organised against teams from the west of Scotland who were generally reckoned to be the best in the country. In July 1887, the crack-side, Renton, soon to gain the accolade of World Champions, came through and won 9–1. In the following year, a 3–1 victory over Third Lanark was heralded as "almost as good as winning a cup". In their first visit to Ibrox in 1887, Dunfermline were only allowed to play the reserves, the Swifts, and even then lost 2–0.

Some games were played for sheer pleasure and enjoyment. During October 1888, Dunfermline paid their first visit to Aberdeen where, due to competition from rugby, football had been slow to develop. The players left the station at 8.15 am determined to enjoy their day out. Lunch was taken at Queen's Restaurant followed by a three-hour ramble through the city. When the players arrived at Channonry ground they found a couple of games in full swing and had to wait an extra 45 minutes. After a pleasant game (a 2–2 draw) it was back to Queen's Restaurant for "a capital supper" and then home on the last train. On a return jaunt the visitors from the Granite City arrived early and paid a visit to the Abbey from which they saw in the distance the construction of the new Forth Rail Bridge. Dunfermline lost 9–2 on this occasion.

The Aberdeen games illustrated how essential rail travel was to the development of Dunfermline Athletic. The opening of the Forth Rail Bridge in 1890 cut journey times even more. Rail travel meant fairly easy access to almost any part of the country for both players and eager fans although it did have its problems. Dunfermline opened the 1888-89 season in a competition at Wemyss Castle where

fermline player broke his arm the trainer and a police sergeant set the limb there and then. The report stated that "it is setting as well as can be expected". Two years later it was noted that player Bell, suffering from a broken leg, was taken by an ambulance wagon to the Commercial Hotel where his leg was treated. In an attempt to root out wild tackling the SFA ordered this notice to be posted at East End Park and all other grounds in 1887:

"Rough play as specified in rule 10 is tripping, ducking, hacking, jumping at a player, pushing and charging from behind."

It was more than a year before the two Dunfermline teams faced each other, neither side wishing to give up ground advantage. When they eventually met in September 1886 in the Fife Cup, the Athletic trounced their rivals 5–0. They met again the following week in the Edinburgh Shield before a crowd of 3,000 and the Athletic ran up an even more emphatic score of 15–1. When drawn together in 1886 in the Scottish Cup, the older established club did not even turn up and thereafter there was never any they won first prize – marble clocks valued at 20/- each. After the presentation there was little time for congratulations and none for dressing. Volunteers assisted in carrying the prizes and equipment to the station which was a half-hour walk away. The party arrived there just in time, if a little breathless, boarded the train and then found they had to change at Thornton. In the following season their first away game took them to Camelon which involved a train to Larbert followed by a two-mile walk and a scramble over a railway embankment to reach the pitch. A few minutes later they took to the field (and managed a 4–4 draw). Occasionally an older means of travel was used. When Bo'ness came to play at East End they hired a special steamer which took them straight across the Forth to Charlestown whence they travelled by special train into Dunfermline. Increasingly, the club made use of the telegraph to "wire" clubs in advance of cancelled games. By this means also results were relayed across the country and displayed in a shop window in Dunfermline on a Saturday evening.

Off the field, the club was keeping its head above water. Near the end of the first season the AGM was held in the Inglis Street Hall where A. R. Shearer, Esq, presided. A local journalist noted:

> "The Secretary's report showed a satisfactory record of work done during the season, the number of matches won and the goals scored being in favour of both first and second teams. The Treasurer's report showed that the club, financially, was in a sound position."

In fact, gate receipts amounted to £80 which was considered unprecedentedly high in local football. By the end of the second season the president could report a membership of 150. Of the 32 matches played 19 had been won, 9 lost and 4 drawn with 100 goals for, 62 against. Expenditure amounted to £176 19s 11d with income slightly more at £179 4s 3½d, a balance of just over £2. For many years the admission charge was kept at 6d though it was said that some supporters could only afford 3d and were duly admitted. In the days before high walls many preferred to peep from outside the ground. For an attractive fixture a good crowd in the region of three to five thousand could be expected to turn up.

Even in those early days it would be a mistake to imagine that the team survived solely through gate receipts. But for various fund-raising activities the club would have been bankrupt very early on. Before the season started, successful five-a-side tournaments and sports days were held to raise money; during the winter, evening concerts, soirées, music hall entertainment and lotteries were held which all proved not only to be financially profitable but also to be successful social gatherings. At the first annual soirée in St Margaret's Hall in 1887, the club president cautioned the young team that "there was a way of players losing a game of football and at the same time upholding the honour of the club". At the next one, Provost Donald claimed that he "saw no reason why football should convert a Christian into a savage. Every mouth wasted on mouthing and vapourising is so much strength gone and means that less energy is applied to the game".

Most of the surplus cash raised was used to finance the building of a new pavilion. The original one was wooden and dilapidated. After much effort a new one, made of corrugated iron and beautifully lined with varnished wood, and measuring 30 ft by 12 ft by 8 ft, was formally opened by Provost Donald on 29 October 1887. The building consisted of two dressing rooms, a bathroom and a meeting room; as it stood on bricks 2½ ft above the ground there was ample storage space beneath it. It cost the princely sum of £80. A challenge match against Mossend Swifts followed the official opening but sadly the team's ability did not match its new structure, an 8–1 defeat being sustained.

The following year, the pitch was drained and black ash was laid down to provide a firmer standing area. Since the Athletic now had one of the best parks in the district, it was often chosen as the venue for local cup finals and for the staging of inter-county matches, in which a number of Athletic players always starred. Even then, sad to relate, complaints were often filed about the muddy playing surface and numerous games were unavoidably postponed in inclement weather.

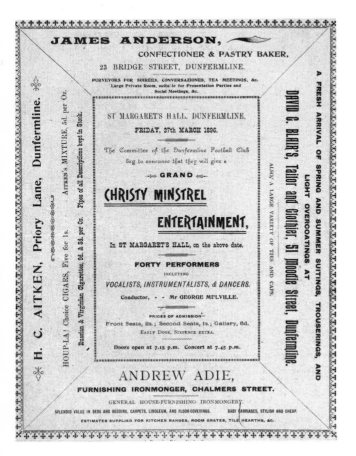

Left: *An early form of fund-raising.*

League Football and Professionalism, 1890–1914

At its formation in 1885, Dunfermline Athletic was strictly an amateur club. In that year, professionalism was legalised in England and the drain of Scottish talent over the Border began with the result that many clubs and administrators in Scotland were beginning to press for professionalism. Interestingly, the original Dunfermline Football Club had caused Heart of Midlothian to be suspended from the SFA in 1884 for paying two of its players in a Scottish Cup-tie (which they won 11–1). Dunfermline Athletic, not unlike certain Olympic committees of today, began to pay their players' travelling expenses, hotel accounts and even lost time at work. It was not long before the SFA finally agreed to professionalism in 1893. As Mr J. H. McLaughlin of Celtic put it when the matter was being debated – "You might as well try to stop the flow of the Niagara with a kitchen chair than endeavour to stem the tide of professionalism!" At a more local level the *Journal* stated that "the days of ornamental football have gone and the man that scores the most goals is the best player now".

The advent of professionalism had a strong effect on the development of the game in Scotland. Since Dunfermline Athletic and other clubs now had to pay their players each week they needed a guarantee of a game each Saturday which the system of friendlies often failed to provide. What this simply meant was the growth of league football and more emphasis on competition. The top clubs had already formed themselves into the First Division in 1890 while Dunfermline Athletic had to be content with one of the many provincial leagues. An 11–1 drubbing at home by Hibs in the third round of the Scottish Cup that year illustrated the vast gulf between city and country clubs.

Initially, in 1891, Dunfermline joined the Alloa-based Midland League along with Dunblane, Camelon, Clackmannan, Cowdenbeath, Grangemouth, Alva, Alloa, Raith Rovers and Bridge of Allan. Mr J. Brown of Dunfermline Athletic served as vice-president. The Athletic, with only two of the previous season's players in their side, crashed 11–1 to Dunblane in the opening game and later by an all-time record scoreline of 17–2 to Clackmannan. Though they went on to beat Clackmannan 8–1, their league campaign was far from sound, Raith Rovers eventually winning the title. During the season, goal nets were used for the first time now that points, and not just pride,

The Dunfermline Athletic Junior team of 1894 when they won the Fife Cup, the Dunfermline Cup and the Fife Shield.
Back row: Dunn, Macpherson, Nicol, Ross, Izatt. Middle row: Hay (secretary), Beattie, Keir, Lonie, McKee, Black, Sommerville. Front: Beveridge and Torbet.
(Dunfermline Press)

were at stake. Friendly matches and charity games, however, still continued.

In the following season, 1892–93, Raith left to join the friendly circuit as did Cowdenbeath and Clackmannan while King's Park, from Stirling, joined the league. This season proved to be no more successful than the previous one. In 1893, with professionalism now in full swing and a new Second Division established (which Dunfermline were not invited to join), the club's fortunes took a tumble. The committee had a weekly wage bill to meet in addition to guaranteeing part of the gate to the visiting club. The result was that the Midland League fell apart and the Athletic let their Senior team fall away, concentrating instead on its recently formed Junior (and presumably cheaper) team. In fact, in 1894, the Junior team was to do well, winning the Dunfermline Cup and the Fifeshire Shield.

For season 1896–97 the Senior team was reformed (with new colours – maroon and white) and played in the newly-formed Central League along with St Johnstone, Lochgelly, Kirkcaldy, Fair City and Cowdenbeath. The Seniors won the Fife Cup beating Clackmannan 3–2 (gate receipts – £17) and they also beat Cowdenbeath in the recently instituted Cottage Hospital Cup which raised funds for the new infirmary.

The cost of professional football continued to take its toll and the Central League collapsed during the following season, 1897–98, due to too many unfulfilled fixtures. Once again the Senior team was wound up with the Juniors left to carry the torch. At the end of the century football in Dunfermline was at a low ebb and it seemed not unlikely that Senior football in the town was gone for ever. Even the local newspapers found little to write about in their sports columns. Continuing crowd riots and break-ins did nothing to help an already depressing picture.

A number of citizens, led by Councillor R. Philip, refused to let the club disappear. A public meeting was called on 24 July 1899 in the Co-op Hall in Randolph Street where the arguments for and against a Senior professional

The original Dunfermline FC continued to do well, reaching the final of the Scottish Junior Cup in 1897, only to be beaten 3–2 by Strathclyde (and 2–0 in the replay, after a protest). Back row: Melville, Donaldson, Blair. Middle: J. McPherson, D. McPherson, Ford, Allan, Moultrie. Front: Cameron, Toshack, Donald, Taylor, Morris. Seated: Bowman, Turner.

team were debated. When it came to the vote those in favour of running a Senior team won the day – but only by one vote and despite their efforts football remained in the doldrums. The *Press* had the following advice for some of the club's more fickle supporters – "It has been the practice of a very large number of alleged enthusiasts to withdraw their patronage when the team happens to sustain defeats for two or three successive weeks. A little more practical sympathy would make all the good in the world."

In season 1902-3, Dunfermline joined the Northern League which comprised Dundee Wanderers, Victoria United and Orion (both from Aberdeen), Aberdeen, Arbroath, Forfar, Lochee, Montrose, Cowdenbeath, St Johnstone and Lochgelly. Although the league provided a great incentive for Dunfermline who recruited a squad of 20 players for the new challenge, the best the team could manage was a place half-way down the league table. At the end of the season, Dunfermline, along with other Fife clubs, withdrew from the East of Scotland Association and concentrated on their own Association which then organised its own league, the Wemyss League, for Fife clubs.

August of 1903 witnessed a great landmark in the club's development with the opening of a new ground in Halbeath Road, slightly east of their original ground and almost on the site of their present stadium. On Wednesday the 19th, Glasgow Celtic, fielding a strong team, played in a challenge match to commemorate the occasion and won 5–0. Gate receipts came to a welcome £25!

After two unimpressive seasons the Athletic's fortunes took a turn for the better. The *Journal* noted:

"Perhaps at no time in the history of the present Senior club have prospects been so bright as they are for season 1905-6 . . . It is calculated that sufficient men have been signed on to last the season."

Results on the field confirmed this promise. In the Qualifying Cup, Hearts of Beath were overcome, though only at the third attempt. In the second round it took two games to dispose of Kirkcaldy United. A bye in the third round gave Dunfermline a place in the fourth round of the Cup for the first time. Although they were unlucky to lose 2–0 to Beith in Ayrshire, Dunfermline nonetheless had done enough to

The oldest surviving programme with Dunfermline's name on it.

NORTHERN LEAGUE—Results to Date.

	Played.	Won.	Lost.	Drawn.	For.	Against.	Points.
Montrose,	18	14	4	0	43	23	28
Aberdeen,	19	10	5	4	50	29	24
Cowdenbeath,	20	10	7	3	37	32	23
Stenhousemuir,	21	8	7	6	43	41	22
Arbroath,	15	8	2	5	32	21	21
Dundee A,	20	8	7	5	45	34	21
Wanderers,	20	8	7	5	39	34	21
Dunfermline,	21	7	10	4	31	39	18
Lochgelly United,	20	5	9	6	48	49	16
St Johnstone,	17	7	9	1	41	46	15
Lochee,	18	4	12	2	20	51	10
Forfar,	19	4	14	1	27	57	9

Points since Re-Institution.

	1895-96	'96-7	'97-8	'98-9	'99-00	'00-1	'01-2	'02-3
Dundee Wanderers,	15	20	18	21	*18	15	17	17
Victoria United,	—	17	*19	10	17	15	17	22
Aberdeen,	14	9	11	13	16	24	27	15
Arbroath,	20	15	14	17	15	24	20	26
Forfar Athletic,	*21	17	15	16	14	10	23	19
Orion,	10	*21	12	*21	13	.28	21	26
Lochee,	12	3	11	12	10	10	8	14
Montrose,	11	12	10	2	5	6	9	21
Dundee A,	—	—	—	—	—	*28	31	*38
Fair City,	7	—	—	—	—	10	—	—
Raith Rovres,	—	—	—	—	—	—	*‡31	—
Cowdenbeath,	—	—	—	—	—	—	29	28
St Johnstone,	—	—	—	—	—	—	23	22
Dunfermline,	—	—	—	—	—	—	—	22
Lochgelly,	—	—	—	—	—	—	—	23

* Champions. ‡ After playing a deciding match with Dundee A.

Plan of the dressing rooms in 1903. (Dean of Guild)

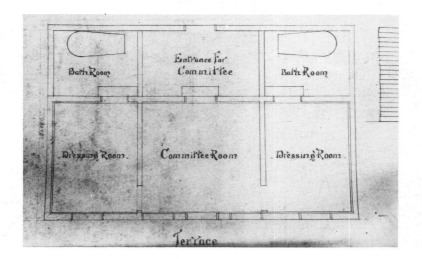

15

qualify for the first round proper of the Scottish Cup. On 27 January 1906, the team journeyed northwards to meet Aberdeen, formed only three years earlier, to play in their first ever Scottish Cup-tie since the competition was re-organised into its modern format in 1895. Despite giving a good account of themselves, Dunfermline lost 3–0.

During the season, a Fife publican, George Penman, presented a new trophy to give local teams something to aim for at the end of the season. Dunfermline were often to win this cup during the next sixty years. The Loftus Cup, donated by a Tayside businessman for neighbouring clubs, provided Dunfermline with another challenge.

In the league, Dunfermline had their best season ever and had they taken all their chances they would have done better than third position, only two points behind champions, Aberdeen. Encouraged by their relative success, Dunfermline applied to join the Second Division and although two new clubs were admitted, the Athletic were not one of them; Dumbarton and Ayr Parkhouse finding favour with the officials in Glasgow. To make matters worse, Raith Rovers, Cowdenbeath and East Stirling had already been elected to the more challenging and lucrative Second League while Dunfermline languished in the Northern

League which was proving to be a disaster for the club financially. Long trips by train to the northern clubs very quickly devoured the meagre gate drawings. It was no surprise that at the AGM in 1908 the treasurer could report a balance of only 16/7d. It was often left up to the committee chairman, Mr Tom 'Hatter' Robertson, to make a round of the shops to raise enough money for train fares. Occasionally he had to persuade the stationmaster to issue 15 third-class return tickets "on strap", i.e. on tick. If a good away gate did not materialise, the chairman was left to foot the bill.

The Athletic were delighted, therefore, when a new Central League with its headquarters in Dunfermline, was set up for season 1909–10. The league comprised East Fife, Lochgelly United, Dunfermline, Kirkcaldy United, Bo'ness, King's Park, Arbroath, St Johnstone, Alloa, Stenhousemuir, Broxburn and Cowdenbeath. Much less travelling was involved and Dunfermline liked the new financial arrangements whereby the home clubs kept their own gates. Dunfermline were no match for league champions, Bo'ness, in the first season, but for season 1910–11 it

Dunfermline's team for 1907-8. Back row: Herd, Innes, Spittal, McLaughlan. Front: Pitblado, Livingston, Grier, Brown, Anderson, McDougall, Fraser.

was reported that "not for so many years have the club's fortunes appeared so bright". President James Farrell was not to be disappointed. Amidst great excitement and before large crowds the Fife Cup was won in Kirkcaldy against Raith Rovers 'A'.

More importantly, the club had a good run in the Qualifying Cup (amassing over £100 in receipts) and to crown it all, they captured the Central League thereby gaining the Calder Cup. Throughout the season they never lost a game at East End Park and the crowds loved it, contributing around £40 per game which was excellent for that period. The club applied again for entry to the Second Division but their bid was rejected.

Greater success was to follow in the next season, 1911-12. Ploughing some of their financial gains back into the team in the form of new players, the committee secured a more mature and experienced side backed up by power and muscle. New faces included Maurice Slavin, a goalkeeper

Left: *An early example of commercial sponsorship in football.*

Above: *Jim Brown, Dunfermline's outstanding captain before the War.*

from Bathgate; Ballantyne, an inside forward from Partick Thistle; and Fred Gibson, a left winger from Raith. All told, however, it only cost £38 to put the team together and the weekly wage bill came to a mere £20.

Dunfermline made an excellent start in the defence of their league title but interest was greatest as the team progressed through the early stages of the Qualifying Cup, a trophy of great prestige and financial reward. In the first round, the Athletic beat Kirkcaldy 1–0 (Gibson scoring), and disposed of Hearts of Beath by the same score in the next round (Ronaldson scoring). Excitement mounted in the town when the third round kindly gave them a bye into round four where, in a thrilling game, they defeated King's Park 1–0.

The rhythm of the team was slightly upset at this time when, in a league match, goalkeeper Slavin was found to be drunk between his posts and had to be ordered off by his captain, Jim Brown. Dunfermline lost 7–2. Slavin was duly chastened but was back on duty the following week to perform his customary heroics. In round five, Dunfermline were lucky to be drawn at home against Leith Athletic whom they thrashed 4–0 in front of 5,000 fans who forked out the remarkable sum of £120 at the gate. As a bonus, two barrels of apples were donated to the players. In the semi-final, Dunfermline again had the good fortune to be drawn

Above: *The side that won the Scottish Qualifying Cup in 1911. Back row: T. A. Robertson (vice-president), A. Liddell, W. Crichton, R. Philp (secretary). Third row: E. Millar (treasurer), J. Philp (trainer), D. Donaldson, D. Izatt, J. Brown (captain), A. Wilkie, J. Thomson, T. Ballantyne, J. Bewick (secretary).*

Second row: G. Anderson (vice-president), J. Murray, M. Slavin, F. Gibson, G. Newlands-Robertson, J. Farrell (president). First row: J. McLaughlan (trainer), C. Duncan. The Loftus Cup and the Calder Shield are also displayed. (Dunfermline Press)

at home; Motherwell supplying the opposition in front of another 5,000 crowd. The game produced an exciting struggle, Dunfermline scoring first, then going behind 2–1. By the final whistle they had worthily beaten the visitors 4–2 to march into the final against another crack side, Dumbarton, the Second Division champions.

The game was played at Gymnasium Ground, Edinburgh, the home of St Bernard's, on 25 November 1911, in front of 8,300 fans, half of whom had travelled from Dunfermline. Both sides had chances and escapes but eventually it was the Englishman, Gibson, who scored the only goal of the tie for Dunfermline to win the Cup. Great jubilation followed, first in Edinburgh and then in Dunfermline when the team arrived home. Seated in a large carriage and accompanied by a motley set of musicians calling themselves the Braxy Band, the team was driven through the streets in a three-horse brake with President James Farrell holding the Cup aloft. Congratulations were heaped on the team from far and wide, even from ex-patriots in Alberta, Canada.

Their success in the Qualifying Cup gave them entry to the Scottish Cup itself where, in round one, they were drawn against the mighty Celtic, managed by the legendary Willie Maley. On 27 January, three special trains transported supporters to Glasgow where the home crowd received the shock of their lives. The game was not the walk-over they had expected and the Celts had the greatest difficulty in shaking off the Cup-holders through a very questionable goal. In these days, with club linesmen permissible, Maley and Farrell officiated. After a goalless first half and with no signs of Dunfermline weakening McAtee broke away on the Celtic right and ran the ball out of play, some said by as much as a foot. No signal was made and from the resultant cross outside left Brown of Celtic scored the winning goal. This was to be the first of many famous cup meetings between these two sides. Celtic went on to retain the Cup.

Despite this setback, Dunfermline went on to complete their most successful season ever – winners of the Central League (for the second year running), the Loftus Cup, the Fife Cup and the Penman Cup. So great was the silverware that season that no one noticed that the jewellers had not returned the Loftus Cup after engraving it. It lay "lost" for some time. *The West Fife Echo* noted that:

"their consistency most assuredly marks the club out for promotion when the time is opportune. That time cannot now be long delayed. The gates drawn at present are equal, if not bigger than, anything taken at provincial football in Scotland".

The time, in fact, was now right because in June 1912 the Second Division was extended from 12 to 14 clubs and Dunfermline, along with St Johnstone, were admitted. "It behoves every football follower in Dunfermline and district," the *Echo* continued, "to support with renewed vigour the colours of Dunfermline Athletic." Thus the new season of 1912-13 saw Senior League football at East End

Park for the first time ever. The committee kitted their team out in colours which have remained, almost without interruption, ever since: black and white striped jerseys with black shorts. Significantly, it is at this time that the local newspapers start referring to Dunfermline Athletic as *The Pars*, a nickname which has stuck to them over the years. What the nickname alluded to was the fact that after almost 30 years of playing football the local team, having left the minor leagues behind and having now gained access to the top drawer of Scottish football, were equal to, or on PAR with, the best in the land.

Besides Dunfermline, the Second Division comprised Cowdenbeath, St Johnstone, Albion Rovers, Leith, Abercorn (from Paisley), St Bernard's, Vale of Leven, East Stirling, Dundee Hibs (later United), Arthurlie, Johnstone, Ayr and Dumbarton. The league campaign began with an away draw (2–2) against Cowdenbeath; the first league game at East End Park resulted in a 2–0 victory over St Bernard's.

However, it was the Qualifying Cup which once again thrilled the fans. In rounds one, two and three Dunfermline disposed of Lochgelly, Cowdenbeath (over three games before 20,000 fans) and St Andrews. Little wonder the *Echo* observed – "Football is booming in the city just now as it never boomed before." In round four, St Bernard's lost to the champions (again over three games) but in round five, Dunfermline surprisingly fell at home in a replay against Abercorn during which Slavin had the misfortune of being ordered off. Having qualified for the first round of the Scottish Cup, Dunfermline found themselves drawn away

Above: *The medals won in 1911-12 by Jim Thomson. Top left: Loftus Cup. Top right: Qualifying Cup. Fife Shield. (Courtesy of John Thomson)*

Below: *Another popular way of raising funds – a bazaar.*

DUNFERMLINE ATHLETIC FOOTBALL CLUB.

A GRAND BAZAAR

WILL BE HELD IN

ST MARGARET'S HALL, DUNFERMLINE,

— ON —

THURSDAY, FRIDAY, AND SATURDAY,

13TH, 14TH, AND 15TH FEBRUARY 1913.

THE object of the Bazaar is to provide the Club with a fund to enable it to acquire either the ground on which it at present plays or some other suitable pitch in or around the town.

The sum required approximates £1500.

While the Club has now been in existence for many years, at no time in its history has it occupied the position of importance in the football world which it at present holds, and the Committee, in order that nothing may be wanting to enable it to acquire and retain a foremost position in the game, earnestly invite the co-operation of the Citizens of Dunfermline, and all others interested in the prosperity of the Club, so that the object they have in view may be achieved.

Cheques or other monetary contributions should be sent to the Secretary and Treasurer of the Bazaar Committee:

MR P. M'LEOD, SOLICITOR, 1 ABBEY PARK PLACE, DUNFERMLINE.

DUNFERMLINE ATHLETIC FOOTBALL CLUB.

THE TEAM.

GRAND BAZAAR

13TH, 14TH AND 15TH FEB. 1913

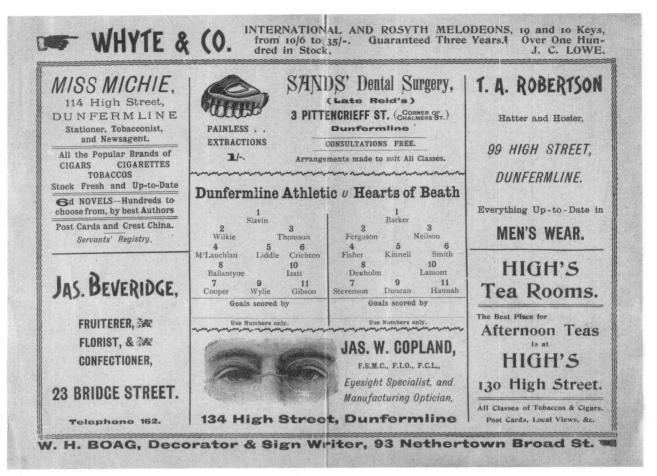
The oldest surviving Dunfermline programme. The adverts always make interesting reading.

again to one of the leading clubs, Hearts. Interest in the game was high and 25,000 turned up to witness the battle. Despite putting up a gallant fight in the first half the Fifers crumbled in the second half, losing 3–1 but picking up a magnificent cheque for £255 for their outing.

Due to their progress in the Qualifying Cup, Dunfermline found that whilst they had only played four league games, some of the other participants had played as many as 19 games! Dunfermline made up the backlog, performing remarkably well in the process in that they never lost at home and finished up in second position. Today this would have meant automatic promotion to Division One, the more especially since that league was being increased from 18 to 20 clubs. However, the Scottish League did not operate a policy of automatic promotion and relegation. John Bewick, club secretary, sent a letter to the League offices in Glasgow to press Dunfermline's case:

"The city is situated on the main line Glasgow and Edinburgh and the north, and is easily got at from any part, being only 60 miles from Glasgow and 30 from Edinburgh. The ground is situated between the two stations and the Dunfermline and district trams pass it every 10 minutes. The Tramway Company contemplate extending their route to the other side of the city, linking up Rosyth, Inverkeithing, Limekilns, Charlestown, Crombie, Valleyfield and Blairhall.

Our population within a 6-mile radius is 100,000 which will be greatly increased in another year or two, especially to the south and west, seeing our close proximity to the Naval Base and the Crombie Naval arsenal and the large coalfields that are opening out at the places I have mentioned above."

Unfortunately Dunfermline's appeal was rejected and the west of Scotland clubs won the day. The two "relegated" clubs in Division One – Partick and Queen's Park – stayed put while Ayr (Division Two champions admittedly) and Dumbarton (lying sixth) were promoted. This decision, when announced, was considered so important that it was flashed on the screen of the Opera House. Dunfermline did have something to cheer about when ex-Provost Macbeth opened a new stand and pavilion on 23 August 1913. These buildings were to survive two world wars, a tribute to either the soundness of their construction or the poor financial state of the club in later years.

The last season before the war saw Dunfermline continue to make their mark in league football, keeping up with the leaders for most of the season. Cowdenbeath eventually ended up as champions, their game against Dunfermline at North End Park pulling in a 7,000 crowd. Dunfermline came a disappointing third. Perhaps it did not really matter since neither the champions nor the runners-up, Albion Rovers, were asked to step up. In any event a far greater struggle lay ahead.

World War One

When the Great War broke out in August 1914 many people believed "it would be over by Christmas". Perhaps because of that wishful thought or possibly because the authorities wanted an entertainment to distract the nation from greater fears, football was allowed to carry on with "business as usual", at least in the first season. However, many "weel-kent faces" were missing both from the team and the terraces as the young able-bodied from Dunfermline district, as from all over Britain, rushed to enlist to fight the Kaiser. Somer players joined the "Sportsman's Battalion" of the Royal Scots.

Division Two functioned as before although Dunfermline, experiencing the loss of so many of their established team, failed to fulfil the promise suggested in the previous seasons. By the end of 1914 the Athletic had played 18 games but won only eight. With hostilities ever increasing and no likelihood of an early cessation the Scottish Cup was put in mothballs until season 1919-20. Dunfermline finished their first war-time season lying sixth in the league. Thereafter, the Second Division was abandoned in view of the grave military situation in Europe. Like the other clubs, Dunfermline suffered financially because of the disruption to their programme, so much so that at a special meeting in February 1915, the committee unanimously agreed to investigate the possibility of forming the club into a limited liability company though this adventurous step would have to wait until the war was over.

To make matters worse the military authorities commandeered East End Park whose well-kept, level turf proved too attractive a base for keeping horses and heavy transport wagons. This was the only senior ground in Scotland to be thus affected. A branch of the Royal Army Medical Corps was stationed at the ground and provided the opposition for a few friendly games.

A temporary home for the club was found at Blackburn Park, situated behind Milesmark School and within minutes of the Milesmark tramcar terminus. The team had to change in the neighbouring Red Lion public house which was owned by the chairman. At this ground the Pars played their games in a new league which was set up to keep interest going during these dark years. The Eastern League, as it was called, comprised another 11 clubs – Lochgelly, St Bernard's, Armadale, East Fife, Broxburn United, Leith, East Stirling, Cowdenbeath, Bathgate, Dundee Hibs and Kirkcaldy United. Each club retained its own gate. The league also organised a new Eastern Cup but

Above: *Soldiers marching down the High Street.* (Public Library)

Below: *Dean of Guild plan of the 1913 stand which survived until 1962. Indeed, certain parts of it were incorporated into the present stadium.*

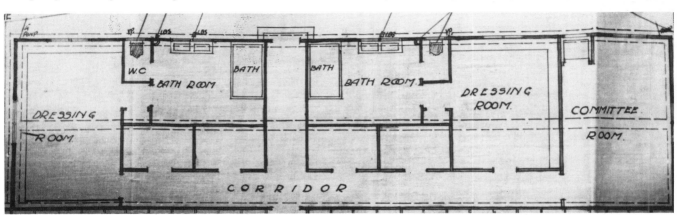

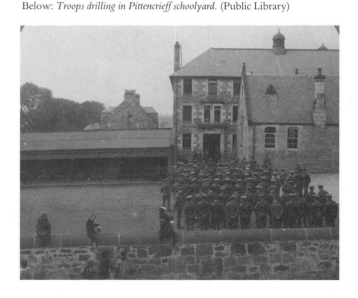

Dunfermline had no success in either of these new competitions, finishing third bottom of the league.

Players were being continually called up for war service as battles like the Somme and Passchendaele demanded more and more cannon fodder; those unaffected by conscription often found their war work was too important to miss for a mere game of football and, in any case, the vagaries of public transport frequently meant that players were unable to turn up at the right place at the right time. A settled team was an impossibility. Blackburn Park proved even less of a success with relatively small gates. In the past, certain supporters from the western end of the town had complained that East End Park was too far away; the club was more than happy to re-occupy their original ground when the army eventually surrendered it. One recruit to the Dunfermline team at this time was Eddie Dowie who was to serve the club both on and off the field for more than 40 years. His playing career was cut short following a leg break against Lochgelly in March 1915.

The Eastern League continued to provide the basic fare throughout the war years although it gave Dunfermline fans little about which to enthuse. In 1916, Leith and Kirkcaldy were forced to drop out through financial and administrative difficulties as were other clubs the following season; by 1917-18 only seven clubs were left. It is a tribute to the committee, players and fans of the club that the Pars were one of the few clubs able to survive these testing years. In the absence of more glamorous competitions the Fife Cup continued to be a crowd-puller. In 1918, Dunfermline beat Raith 3–1 in the replayed final at Kirkcaldy in what was described as "one of the fastest and most exciting games witnessed at Stark's Park sinced pre-war days". Shortly afterwards, competition of a different nature was served up at East End Park in the form of an England-Scotland International involving players based at Rosyth Dockyard, then a bustling work-place. For the record, England won 2–1, the proceeds of the gate going to the local VAD hospital.

Citizens and players alike heaved a sigh of relief when the Armistice was signed in November 1918 though it was to be some time before the troops could be brought home, especially as the war in Russia was still continuing. Football was in a state of limbo as administrators, players (stationed throughout the Empire) and fans awaited the return to normality in season 1919-20. In March 1919 the club appealed to the Scottish League to be admitted into Division One when the new season started. Despite putting up a strong case the committee's pleas were rejected.

Between the Wars 1919–1939

Andy Wilson – undoubtedly one of the best centre forwards of his generation.

If normality meant a return to the pre-war set up with no automatic promotion and relegation between the Leagues, Dunfermline and other ambitious clubs were having none of it. Proof of Dunfermline's ambitions was demonstrated when a group of supporters realised that a voluntary committee running the club was not a realistic or sound proposition in the new, modern, post-war age that was about to dawn. Instead, they floated a limited liability company in 1919 with £3,000 capital raised through £1 shares; from the shareholders was elected a new board of directors empowered to raise money, by borrowing if necessary. The new Board comprised:

> President - local joiner, Alex Mitchell; Secretary - William Whyte; J. Bewick, J. Belloch, J. Cousin, W. Simpson, J. Low, T. Burns, J. Anderson, J. Ritchie and G. Brooks.

The Board secured a long lease on their ground and planned to make it into one of the best in Fife.

Rather than revert to the unsatisfactory Second Division, Dunfermline and other aggrieved clubs formed themselves into the Central League, a body totally outwith the jurisdiction of the Scottish League and rivalling the Eastern League which they sponsored. Other teams lining up beside Dunfermline for the new 1919-20 season were: King's Park, Hearts 'A', Bathgate, Alloa, Bo'ness, Stenhousemuir, St Bernard's, Armadale, Broxburn, Clackmannan, East Fife, Falkirk 'A' and East Stirling. Since Dunfermline belonged to this "rebel" league they were able to attract players of merit to the club without any transfer fee being paid. This situation led to one of the greatest "transfer" coups of the century when Andy Wilson, then the country's finest centre forward and valued around £2,000, signed for Dunfermline without a penny being paid. Today this would be like the Pars signing a Denis Law or a Kenny Dalglish for nothing.

From Newmains in Lanarkshire, Wilson originally played for Cambuslang Rangers before being transferred to Middlesbrough in 1913. During service in the army with the 6th HLI during the war he was badly wounded at Arras, shrapnel tearing into his left arm. Although he lost the use of that limb it did not prevent him from later becoming a very skilled billiards player at the Netherton Hall and he also represented England at bowls. While stationed in Scotland he played for Hearts but when the war ended and the Athletic heard that he might be available, President Alex Mitchell, using his own resources, managed to secure the forward's signature. The signing was the talk not just of Dunfermline but of the whole of Scotland. Mitchell also helped him to establish a sports shop in Guildhall Street.

Starved of top class competitive football throughout the war, the public of Dunfermline flocked back to football in their thousands, glad to be rid of the heartache of war and willing to be entertained once again on a Saturday afternoon. Dunfermline got off to an excellent start, beating Hearts 'A' 7–1, Wilson netting four of them. Lining up with Wilson was a glittering array of talent not seen since the successful days of 1911-12; only two of their pre-war players, Jackie Baird and Hardie, were still there. The squad was: Paterson; Baird, Callaghan; Bennet, Main, Robertson, Hardie, Gow, Dick, McQueen, Lawrence, Heard. Football in the town was booming. A local reporter noted

The team that lost to Cowdenbeath. Back row: Gordon, Baird, King, Robertson, Low. Front: Stalker, Croall, Strachan, Wilson, McInally, McGowan. (Dundee Courier)

"queues of considerable dimensions were forming, many ladies seemingly having caught the fever". A crowd of 5,000 turned up to see the Hearts match; next month 8,000 fans turned up to see Dunfermline play at home in the Qualifying Cup against East Fife. Wilson did not play for fear of being cup-tied, and Dunfermline lost 1–0.

Dunfermline continued to do well in the league and the crowds kept turning up in their thousands. It was once said that "gate receipts could be comfortably carried in vest pockets" but not any more. By the end of the year, Dunfermline were leading the league though they were made to work all the way as the publicity and the glamour attached to Wilson made him a marked man and every game produced a cup-tie atmosphere.

By February, Wilson had scored 35 goals, including a double hat-trick, despite missing eight penalties. On one occasion he delighted the crowd by scoring with a header while lying on the ground. Wilson was seldom out of the headlines and his natural goal-scoring talent was recognised by the SFA when they chose him to play for Scotland even though he played in one of the lesser leagues. That season he was capped against Wales, Ireland and England, honours which were to be bestowed again during the following season to give him six full Scottish caps, a record for the club.

Dunfermline had an excellent season and were only just pipped for the championship by Bo'ness, leaving the Pars to rue the three points they lost to wooden spoonists, Clackmannan. However, they did have the consolation of beating Cowdenbeath 3–1 in the Fife Cup final before a crowd of 10,505 at East End Park.

By the start of season 1920–21 Dunfermline had seven ex-Scottish League players on their books, the most notable being Jimmy Gordon (ex-Rangers and Scotland internationalist), Bob Mercer (the Hearts and Scotland centre forward), Arthur McInally (from Aberdeen) and John Low (Hearts). The arrival of Hugh Strachan, Stalker, Croall and Jimmy Smith, also strengthened the playing staff, valued at around £10,000.

Further evidence of the football boom can be seen from the Cowdenbeath-Dunfermline first round Qualifying Cup match at Central Park which attracted 18,000 fans, over half of them from Dunfermline. Despite being 2–0 up at half-time, the Pars lost 3–2. The crestfallen Athletic supporters were subjected to further humiliation when their faces were covered with coal dust which a high wind whipped up from the ash terracing.

Confidence in the team was so high that the directors bought their ground and another three acres of land to the east for £3,500 in order to build, in effect, a new stadium. The pitch was moved further east and laid in the centre of the new field surrounded by a cinder track. The embankments (terracing would be too grand a description) on the north, west and east sides had space for up to 64,000 spectators, or so the plans suggested. To meet the cost the old company was converted into a public limited liability company with a capital of £12,000 divided into £1 shares. A shareholder had to own £50 in shares before he could offer

Certificate No.

No. of Shares.

241

1

Dunfermline Athletic Football Club, Limited.

(INCORPORATED UNDER THE COMPANIES ACTS, 1908-1917).

CAPITAL - £12,000

DIVIDED INTO

12,000 ORDINARY SHARES of £1 each.

This is to Certify that *Walter Millar, Junr.*

Townhill Road, Dunfermline is a Registered Holder of

one ORDINARY SHARES of One Pound each, fully

paid, numbered from *3290* to inclusive, in DUNFERMLINE ATHLETIC

FOOTBALL CLUB, LIMITED, which are held subject to the Memorandum and

Articles of Association of the Company.

GIVEN under the COMMON SEAL of the said Company this

Seventeenth day of *April* One thousand Nine

hundred and *Twenty five* years.

John Fraser Director.

William Knight Secretary.

This Certificate must be deposited at the Company's Office, with any Transfer of the whole or any portion of the above Shares, before a new Certificate can be issued.

Below: A Scottish Select side which toured North America in 1921. They won 24 games and drew one. J. Low is seated on the extreme right and A. Wilson is third from left.

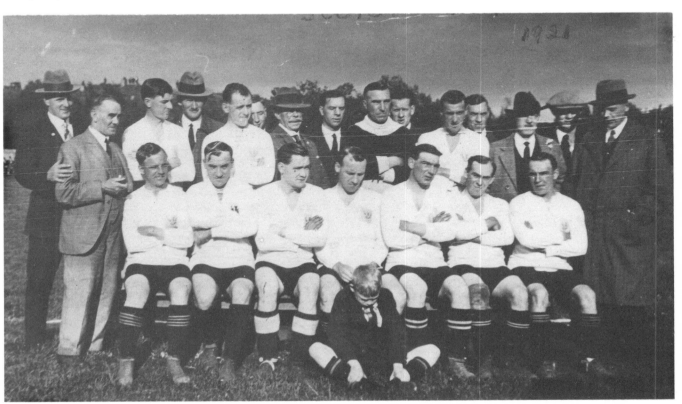

The Dunfermline team, 1922. Back row: J. Ritchie, Baird, Brown, J. Lowe, Mercer, W. Simpson, Sinclair, J. Fraser, Cruickshank, W. Knight, Dowie. Middle: Strachan, Smith, Patterson, Gordon, Gilmour. Front: McMillan, A. Mitchell, Donaldson.

himself for election to the Board. Over the years the club seldom paid dividends or directors' fees, the main object of the company being to promote the game. The new project, the *Journal* noted, "would give employment to all the local people who are either idle or on short time".

On the field, Wilson continued to excel and win further admiration. When he played against England (and played his part in the 3–0 win) it was reported that, of the 85,000 crowd, "quite a number of Fife football enthusiasts 'hoofed it' to Hampden, the majority of these being strikers from Cowdenbeath and other mining centres".

The overwhelming success of the Central League finally persuaded the governing officials to give way and to concede the principle of automatic promotion and relegation. For season 1921-22, therefore, the Second Division was resurrected and the Central League scrapped. Sadly for Dunfermline all their illegally signed stars had to be surrendered. Wilson returned to Middlesbrough, although before doing so, in a close season tour of Canada with a Scotland Select, he scored 23 of his side's 36 goals. His beautiful ball control, his bullet shot, his guile, his dynamism and his

goal–scoring feats (100 goals in two seasons) were to be sadly missed not just by Athletic fans but by afficionados of the game throughout Scotland. In 1923, Middlesbrough transferred him to Chelsea for £6,000, a very high sum in those days. He ended his playing career as the first British player to join a French club, Nîmes, for whom he played from 1932-34.

Denuded of much of their talent, Dunfermline made a poor start to their new league campaign of 1921-22, falling to the bottom spar after only five games. The energetic chairman pulled off another surprise signing by bringing in a new goalkeeper, Arthur Halliwell from Canada, which caused quite a sensation in the days when overseas travel was rare. During a match against St Johnstone, Dunfermline players became so incensed by adverse refereeing decisions that after the match the referee was jostled and barracked off the pitch. It was reported that "for safety the referee made his way to town later by way of the railway". The SFA took a dim view of the whole matter and shut Dunfermline's ground for one month from 5 December.

Now that Dunfermline were in the "big time", the Qualifying Cup, which had provided so much excitement and cash, became a memory of the past and the club automatically gained entry into the first round proper. In the opening round, the first Scottish Cup-tie since the disruption of the war nine years earlier, the Pars were drawn away to Steven-

son United. However, the Ayrshire club, enticed by the prospect of a fat gate cheque, were persuaded to surrender ground advantage and play at East End Park. Despite trailing 1–0 at half-time the Pars stormed back to win 3–1. Their joy was short-lived when they lost 2–1 to East Stirling in the next round. It is interesting to note that after this defeat, William A. Knight, a publican from Rumblingwell, and the son of one of the original founders of the club, was appointed 'Manager' of the club, the first person to be so designated. Previous to this the day-to-day running of the club and team selection rested with the secretary and the Board although they had surrendered some of their powers in January 1921 when they appointed a full-time trainer, Dick Vickers.

Also at this time a new Supporters' Club (reckoned now to be the first of its kind in Scotland) was formed, in part to help pay off the £3,500 debt on the new ground. At a well-attended inaugural meeting in the Co-op Hall, Dr Bell was elected chairman and soon 719 members had signed on. In spite of these efforts the team could only finish eighth in the league and the club's financial statement noted that the club lost £1,600 4s 3½d over the season. Visiting clubs to East End Park took away cheques to the value of £1,749 while Dunfermline only received £1,333 from their away matches.

For the following season, 1922-23, new players were added to the staff – Tommy Donald, Andrew Campbell,

Left: *Dunfermline's first manager – Willie Knight, 1922.* (Dundee Courier)

Below: *Halbeath Road in 1924 with the ground's dilapidated fence on the right.* (Public Library)

Three of Dunfermline's top players in the 1920s – Bobby Skinner, Hugh Strachan and Jimmy Stein. (Dundee Courier)

Peter Gaffney, Willie Miller, Tony Harris and Jimmy Blair – but they were unable to stop their team ending up in 13th position in the league. They made some amends by having their best ever run in the Cup, reaching the third round. In the first round they surprisingly beat Dumbarton 1–0 at Boghead and followed this with a home victory (1–0) over Clydebank. Round three paired them at home against Raith Rovers, then playing well in the First Division. In spite of a brave fight they went out 3–0 to the much superior side who had the peerless Alec James in their ranks. Twelve thousand supporters turned up that day and 2,000 tons of ash from Townhill were used to make the embankments less uncomfortable.

The following season, 1923-24, brought little better cheer. The supporters blamed the chairman for the lack of success and the high debts and Alex Mitchell resigned, pointing out the club's liabilities would have been even larger but for his generosity over the years. A first round exit in the Cup at the hands of Arbroath by one goal to nil at home was coupled with very indifferent league form – seventh position. Spectators were heard to mutter that "they dinna want promotion; they're quite content to bide in the Second Division so long as they can get oor bobs [shillings]". To make matters worse, local rivals, Cowden-beath, gained promotion and it was feared that the increased drawing power of "the Miners" would lure fans away from Dunfermline. Hindsight was to show, however, that the club made some excellent signings during the season for their future promotion bids – Jimmy Dickson, Joe Sutton, Watty Richardson, Reid, Frank Henderson and Chris McCleary. Bobby Skinner later signed from Ayr

while Tommy McMillan and goalkeeper Bill Paterson (who was able to lift two balls with his open hands) left to play in America.

An added worry for the 1924-25 season was the introduction the previous season of a Third Division, comprising minor teams and reserve teams, into which a struggling Second Division side could now tumble. For some time, indeed, it looked as though this might be Dunfermline's fate when only three points were secured from the opening seven games. Attendances were dropping alarmingly and when the club's overdraft reached £3,450 panic set in. The chairman, Mr John Fraser, had to call a special public meeting in St Margaret's Hall at which he urged supporters to buy £1 shares to keep the club afloat. A special committee was set up to canvas for prospective purchasers. The club's financial plight was not in the least aided by a repetition of last season's cup failure - dismissal in the first round by Arbroath. If it is true that the darkest hour comes before the dawn, this season must rank as one of the club's darkest. The final league table recorded the Pars in 13th place.

The new dawn was to be a spectacular one – promotion to Division One for the first time ever with a record-breaking performance in season 1925-26 which secured them their first, and sadly only, league championship in their first 100 years. They began with a 4–1 home victory over Niths-dale Wanderers, from Dumfriesshire, and never looked back for the rest of the season. Several factors accounted for this scintillating performance. The club appointed a new manager, Sandy Paterson, from Cowdenbeath FC whom he had just steered into Division One. To be fair, however, it was mostly the players signed by outgoing manager, Knight, who played in the promotion winning side. One such player was Bobby Skinner who signed for the club in November 1924 for £75 and who made the football season all his own. His speed, quick acceleration and lethal finishing brought him no less than 53 league goals in 38 games that season, a club record which still stands to this day and is unlikely to be broken. Perhaps fortunately for Skinner, the League had just changed the offside rule to require two and not three defensive players between the advancing player and the goal. The team generally operated in top gear, scoring no less than 109 goals throughout their league campaign, surpassing the previous record held by Falkirk by four goals and beating every other club in Britain. Other prominent players were Jimmy Stein, the club's left winger who ran up 21 goals; Jock Wilson, right back, who added strength and solidity to the defence; Andy Herd, half back;

The earliest surviving accounts date from 1923-24. Here are a few snippets:

Home gate drawings £4,300
Players' wages £1,778
Entertainments tax £1,033
Referees' fees £58
Policing £33
Teas and lunches £137
Rates £48

The team which took Dunfermline into the First Division as champions for the first time in 1926. Back row: T. Burns, R. Wyllie, E. Miller, G. Turner. Middle: E. Dowie, Bain, Mitchell, Herd, Gibb, Wilson, Clark, Masterton. Front: Paterson (manager), Ritchie, Sutton, Skinner, Dickson, Stein, J. Fraser, and J. Farrell (linesman). (Dundee Courier)

and Joe Sutton, inside forward. Throughout the season, Dunfermline never lost at home and were undefeated in their last 15 games. Perhaps it was just as well they were knocked out of the Cup in the first round at Shawfield where they lost 3–0 to Clyde who, incidentally, were also promoted with Dunfermline. Raith were relegated from the First Division.

A shadow was cast over the club's rejoicings when the news of two bereavements was announced: director and former president, Alex Mitchell, the man who put Dunfermline on the football map by signing Andy Wilson; and former player, Bob Mercer, an old Tynecastle favourite. A loyal servant, Jackie Baird, was transferred to Montrose, having served the club well since 1913. A few players were added to the team: Shingleton (a goalkeeper from Clyde), Jack (Stenhousemuir) and McLean (Lochgelly).

At last, 41 years after their foundation, the club had joined Scotland's top league in which the supporters could anticipate visits from Rangers, Celtic, Hearts, Hibs and other glamorous names. Interest in the town was high as reflected in the 5,000 attendance at a pre-season club trial game from which the West Fife Hospital benefitted. From being top dogs in the lower division, Dunfermline now found the going extremely tough amongst Scotland's élite. Skinner was suspended from the first two games and his absence was highlighted in the club going down at Cappie-

low and Ibrox, 3–0 and 2–0 respectively. A period of eight weeks passed without a win being recorded and during six of these not a goal was scored. The goal-happy side that had scored 109 goals in the previous season had struck rock bottom.

The position on New Year's Day, 1927, did not provide seasonal cheer for the supporters. The statistics of won 4, drawn 2, lost 15 – placed Dunfermline at the foot of the league. The Scottish Cup provided some relief – victories over Bathgate 5–2 in a replay and over Airdrie 2–1 put them into round three. There they were beaten 2–0 by East Fife who went on to reach the Final. The crowd of 12,000 set a new record then for Bayview.

The last few months of the season saw a welcome improvement but the position was still desperate. The climax came in the last league game of the season. Dundee United were already doomed but the question of who would join them remained to be answered. Dunfermline had 26 points, Clyde 27 points and Morton 28 points. Dunfermline travelled to Edinburgh to play Hearts in front of a 20,000 crowd. The Pars' slender hopes appeared to vanish just before the interval when Hearts scored but before the whistle sounded Skinner burst through the Hearts' defence to score a fine solo, equalising goal. That is how it stood until ten minutes from the end when Skinner shot at the goal. The Hearts' keeper thought he had successfully scooped the ball away, but the referee awarded a goal, enough to give Dunfermline victory. Then, from across the country, came the word that Morton, who by a strange twist of fate were playing fellow strugglers, Clyde, had just lost at home by 2 goals to nil. Dunfermline and Morton were equal on points but by the smallest decimal fraction the Pars escaped on goal average.

Skinner again topped the team's goalscoring list, notching 24 league goals. Raith were promoted and for the first time Fife had three clubs in the First Division for season 1927-28. Some well-known faces were missing – Andy Herd moved to Tynecastle, Jock Bain to Dundee United, Tim Williamson to Crystal Palace and Joe Sutton to Luton Town. Newcomers to East End Park were Dand (Hearts), Morris (Hamilton), White (Kelty), Clark (Hibs) and Moffat (East Fife and Everton). For Dunfermline this time, however, there was to be no miraculous escape. In the first game of the new season, Dunfermline lost 4–0 at Motherwell. After five games they had yet to win a point. This they managed to achieve in the sixth game, against Celtic at East End Park, where they secured a very creditable draw before suffering three defeats. Fans had to wait until October for their team's first victory, against Cowdenbeath. After 16 games, Dunfermline could only boast seven points and they were firmly anchored at the foot of the First Division. To make matters worse for their loyal supporters, the Board, perhaps realising even then they were doomed, transferred Skinner, who had not long since been capped against the Irish League in Belfast in recognition of the 127 goals scored for his club, to Airdrie for £2,500 to bolster the club's ailing financial position. In his first match against Aberdeen, Skinner broke his leg, a blow from which he never fully recovered.

By the end of the year their points total still remained at seven. It was no surprise when Celtic hammered Dunfermline 9–0 at Parkhead on 14 January 1928. What was surprising was that Celtic's famous forward, Jimmy McGrory, scored eight of them (as well as having two others chalked off for offside) and set up a Scottish record. It was skill and ability like this which also put McGrory into the record books as the only British player to average more than a goal a game – 410 league goals in 408 games.

Out of this gloom, however, came Dunfermline's best ever run in the Cup. In the first round they beat Clydebank 3–0 (away), followed by an easy 3–1 win over Leith at home. It was the third round that produced the real shock when the Athletic were drawn against Dundee, then a strong First Division side, at Dens Park. A remarkable goal, hit from a free kick in his own half by full back Jock Young, and a second goal from the other full back Jock Wilson, also from a dead ball, were enough to give Dunfermline a surprise 2–1 victory. Dunfermline were now in the fourth round for the first time but their luck ran out when Hibs brought a strong team to East End Park and won 4–0. The gate of 16,000 was a record for Dunfermline.

The season ended, inevitably, with relegation. Of the 38 games played the Pars won only four and with four drawn games their pointage came to a mere 12. The 'goals against' column revealed the loss of 126 goals with only 41 scored. For forward Jimmy Dickson, however, honour came when he was chosen to play for Ireland against Wales.

The decade which had started in a blaze of publicity for Dunfermline and which gave the club its first sample of football in the highest grade ended with the club in the doldrums. At the same time as the Great Depression hit Britain with high unemployment, poverty and decline in heavy industry, so too did a depression hit Dunfermline Athletic, sinking them into a football malaise and threatening the club's very existence. Government cuts had put Rosyth Dockyard into mothballs and an air of gloom settled on the community, relieved only occasionally and fitfully by the excitement that a game of football could generate. A cut in players' wages was imposed and sometimes they were even given shares in the club as payment.

There was little to cheer about in season 1928-29. Inevitably players were sold to help balance the books. Jimmy Stein, for example, was transferred to Everton where his dangerous low crosses gave 'Dixie' Deans a bagful of goals. The successful promotion side was slowly disintegrating.

Road developments in 1926 brought a double track for the tramcars – and a new brick wall for the club. (Public Library)

The contract that bound player and club to each other.

One new signing, Bob Syme from Blairhall, a strong centre forward with a dynamite shot, proved a good buy and was to provide one of the season's few highlights when he scored three hat-tricks in five days against Albion Rovers, Arthurlie and Stenhousemuir, over the New Year holiday programme. Later he scored four of his side's eight goals against Bathgate.

Even he, however, was unable to save his club from a first round Cup exit at the hands of Cowdenbeath (3–1) in front of a 7,000 crowd which, for these depressed times, was an excellent gate. The team was: Harris; King, Hall; Dand, Hamilton, Patrick; Paterson, Miller, Syme, J. Dickson, T. Dickson. Indifferent league form destined the club to another season in the lower division. The best that can be said is that the club managed to keep going which is more than can be said for Bathgate and Arthurlie who both resigned from the league. More good players left the club – Strachan to Edinburgh City, Hall to Sunderland and Harris to Manchester City.

The following season, 1929-30, saw no improvement in the club's fortunes – a first-round defeat again in the Cup (at Airdrie by 3–1) and a place half way down the league, despite being able to inflict a 10–1 defeat over Brechin (Syme and Paterson scoring four goals each). The average attendance fell to 1,300 and East Fife, by scoring 114 goals, beat Dunfermline's record of four years earlier. When Armadale announced that they were returning to being an amateur club a few observers wondered if Dunfermline might be next. Some clubs contemplated severing their links with the Second Division and resurrecting the successful Central League.

The close season brought more financial trouble for the club. Chairman John Fraser failed to be re-elected and Mr William Whyte took over the reins. It was then revealed that the club had lost £710 during the last season and that the overdraft at the bank had reached its limit of £3,000. The Inland Revenue were demanding payment of tax arrears and had instructed a sheriff's officer to sell off some of the club's assets by public auction. At the eleventh hour, the club sold Syme, who had scored 42 goals the previous season, to Manchester City for £750 and Dickson to Leicester for £200. The club was again safe – for the time being. Sandy Paterson resigned as manager and was replaced by Willie Knight who thus began his second spell in the hot seat, and the team adopted, for a time, a new strip – maroon and yellow jerseys. A few new players were signed: McCrorie, Sclater, Gallacher, and a set of brothers, Jamie and Willie Rarity. A player could expect to be paid about £2 per week while his full-time job, for example, as a miner, brought in four times as much. After a match the players received a free tea at Dick's Co-operative Institute.

The changes certainly did bring about some successes. On 27 September 1930, the team ran up the club's record league win – an 11–2 victory at home against the luckless Stenhousemuir. With the entrance charge standing at one shilling, spectators could boast that each goal had cost less than a penny. A few weeks later an unusual ceremony took place at East End Park – a minute's silence was observed for the victims of the R101 Airship which had recently perished. A bugler from the Royal Navy, standing in the centre of the field, played the *Last Post*.

Later, for the first time in 22 years, the team managed to beat Bo'ness away from home. While playing Armadale at Volunteer Park, the kick-off had to be delayed 30 minutes to allow time for three Dunfermline players to arrive. (They finally won 2–0.) This good form away from home, "aided" by a first-round exit in the Cup from Airdrie (by 6–1 in the replay after a 2–2 draw at home), put the Pars in a strong position for promotion. After an 8–0 win over Brechin in March, the club was in second top position. However, in the final run-in they faltered and allowed Third Lanark and Dundee United to escape into the higher division. The Depression, meanwhile, claimed another victim – Clydebank – who resigned from the league.

Dunfermline failed to keep the momentum going and in season 1931-32 slipped into 10th position in the league although some compensation was to come in the Scottish Cup. In the first round they disposed of East Stirling (the eventual league champions) by 5–2 at East End Park. There was great excitement when the second round draw paired

The team that took Dunfermline back into Division One in 1934 as runners-up to Albion Rovers. Back row: J. Low, E. Dowie. Middle: Laidlaw, R. Drever, Currie, Rarity, Steele, Rodgers, R. Wylie, J. Anderson, W. Knight. Front: Reid, Dobson, Paterson, McKendrick, Watson, Weir, Garland. (Dundee Courier)

them at home with Dundee of the First Division. Once again Dunfermline proved to be the Dens Park bogey side by beating them 1–0. Lady Luck stayed with Dunfermline in round three by giving them a bye into round four where, as the only Second Division side left, they met Kilmarnock, again at home. Slips in the home defence gave easy goals to Killie who won 3–1 and went on to the final, losing to Rangers.

During the season, an interesting incident occurred at Tynecastle. At the end of the previous season, East Fife had been relegated and had scrapped most of their reserve side. The reserve cup draw, however, offered them a lucrative tie against Hearts and rather than forego it the Bayview side temporarily signed eight players from the Athletic (who had a vacant day) and won 3–1. As a result of this and similar incidents the authorities later tightened up on the registration of players.

In an effort to boost their flagging finances, the Board allowed a company to set up greyhound racing on the track surrounding the football pitch. After a slow start the sport became very popular and provided much appreciated revenue to the club.

Dunfermline supporters must have thought that the 1932–33 season was to be theirs. Many new faces – Rodgers, Archibald, Allan, Currie and Paterson, to name a few – appeared in the side and from the start of the season the team hit top form, being seldom lower than fourth top in the league table. Celtic, however, showed them just how far off they were from the First Division by crushing them 7–1 at East End in the first round of the Scottish Cup.

Undeterred, they maintained their challenge for promotion and by the end of April they were lying third, only two points behind second placed Queen of the South and with a game in hand. Disaster struck on 29 April when they surprisingly lost at Stirling to King's Park which meant that for the second time in three years the club had failed to gain promotion by practically the last kick of the season. Interestingly, the Pars, along with all other sides in the lower division, played four games less than scheduled that season. During November, Bo'ness United were expelled for being unable to meet the £50 match guarantee and in the following month Armadale resigned. One can only surmise what might have happened had the full quota of games been played. At the end of the season, Dunfermline made their first trip overseas when they visited Ireland and played out a no-scoring draw with Derry Celtic.

The team that had performed so well the previous season was given a vote of confidence for the new challenges ahead. Right from August the team got into their stride and were well up amongst the pace-setters. After a month they were at the top of the table. In December they did well to beat second top Stenhousemuir 3–0. On New Year's Day they beat East Stirling 10–3 and fans thought that promotion, if not the championship itself, was secure. Undisturbed by a first-round cup defeat by Ayr at Somerset Park (2–0) the side battled on and eventually gained promotion. Had it not been for a defeat by Albion Rovers on 17 March, their first home defeat of the season, they would also have pipped the Coatbridge side for the championship. It is interesting to note that Sir Harry Lauder, who was currently starring in the Carnegie Hall, appeared at East End Park to kick off that particular match.

By a statistical anomaly the 44 points which the Pars had attained were actually three fewer than the total which had kept them in third position the previous season. The successful team was: Steele; Rodgers, McKendrick; Rarity, Reid, Currie; Dobson, Paterson, Watson, Weir, Garland. Paterson was top scorer with 16 goals. Local rivals, Cowdenbeath, who had done so well in the top division for the past decade, were relegated.

At least one lesson was learned from the club's last sortie into the top grade in 1926 – a winning Second Division side is no guarantee that success in assured "upstairs". The club, under the chairmanship of Mr Martin Porter, wisely decided that experienced players would have to be bought. To that end they signed from Celtic, Alex Thomson, the player who had laid on so many goals for McGrory. Other signings included Gene McFarlane (Celtic and Middlesbrough), Brown and Pollock (Chelsea), Murdoch (Dundee) and Johnmann (Motherwell). A "Shilling Fund" organised by the *Press* helped to finance these purchases. The Supporters' Club pledged their assistance and saw to the building of a new enclosure opposite the stand as well as installing a new gas-powered hot water system. They even bought the club a new flag pole in anticipation of greater honours. The directors enlarged the car park to accommo-

date 200 cars, a sign of growing affluence in part of the club's support.

Despite these preparations, the Pars made a poor start, losing 7–1 at home to Rangers in front of a 14,000 crowd. Not till the third game did they win their first point, at Dundee. This did not prove to be a turning point. After 10 games they still had only one point and rested firmly on the bottom rung of the league ladder. The management searched high and low for new players and secured Stewart Chalmers (Manchester United), Dickie Boag (a Junior internationalist with Lochee Harp), 'Tiddler' Murray, Jimmy Warden, Bob McGowan, Bobby Bolt and old favourite, Bob Syme, signed on a free transfer from Burnley. The story goes that manager Knight was awakened out of his sleep at 4 o'clock in the morning by a policeman who brought the news that Syme had just returned to his native Blairhall from England. Knight covered the journey in record time to secure the forward's signature.

The re-vamped team recorded their third victory in 13 games on 20 October with a 2–1 victory over Hibs but two shattering away defeats to Motherwell (9–3) and Rangers (8–1) meant that relegation stared the club in the face. By the end of the year their 23 games played could only muster a meagre 11 points. In the New Year came one of the club's greatest revivals. Victories over Albion Rovers, Kilmarnock, Hearts (at Tynecastle in front of a 17,000 crowd) and Queen of the South showed that the new players were beginning to click. An exit in the first round of the Cup at home to Hamilton Accies (2–1) simply meant that the club could concentrate all its resources on avoiding relegation. Slowly but surely the club climbed the table although in April they were still one of the five clubs who might take

The path trodden by thousands of fans over the years. The turnstiles, essentially unchanged today, date from 1921. "The Fife Motor Co" is next door. (Public Library)

the plunge. In a thrilling finish to their programme they gained three good victories over Partick Thistle, Airdrie and Motherwell, to secure their position in the top league – a fitting 50th birthday present.

Prospects for the new season looked promising. The team had all re-signed and, with a few new additions, lined up as follows: Steele; Johnmann, Warden; Bolt, Crawford, Donald; Dobson, Thomson, McGowan, Chalmers, Murray. A reserve side, the 'A' team, was entered for the East of Scotland league. In anticipation of bigger crowds, wood from the broken up *Mauretania* in Rosyth was used to terrace the East banking. New advertising stances were quickly filled up. The team got off to a fairy-tale start. Victories in the opening games put them at the top of the First Division beside Rangers. A creditable draw at Tynecastle in front of a 25,000 crowd brought them a record cheque, £540. In their game at Ibrox, the Pars shocked the home side by going into a 2–0 lead after only 15 minutes but they could not keep up that pace and lost 6–2. In December, they were able to shock one of the Old Firm by beating high flying Celtic 1–0 at East End Park. A young chauffeur, Morrison, scored on his debut for the Pars.

Their fine League form was matched by a good run in the Scottish Cup when, for only the third time, they reached the last eight. Round one saw them beat Brechin 6–2 at home, round two took care of Galston 5–2, also at home, while a bye took them into round four to meet Falkirk. The presence of 3,000 Pars' fans at Brockville could not prevent a 5–0 thrashing. Thereafter their league form slumped and they finished in 10th position.

Season 1936-37 was almost a disaster for the club. Before the first ball of the season was kicked, a financial crisis erupted. The sale of the rights of the very profitable greyhound racing for £2,500 helped stave off bankruptcy but it meant there was little money in the kitty to buy new players. The chairman, Mr James Anderson, and his Board

Left: *Hugh Farquharson, goalkeeper.*
Right: *Jimmy Warden, left back.*
(Courtesy of G. Baird)

Above and opposite: *A real collector's item – a programme from 1936.* (J. Scobie)

resigned and the shareholders appointed Mr Martin Porter, the proprietor of the East Port Bar, as the new chairman. This in turn led to the resignation of manager Knight whose place was taken by David Taylor who, after leaving Rangers, had won a FA Cup medal with Burnley and had previous managerial experience with St Johnstone and Blackburn. New signings included former Junior internationalist goalkeeper, Hugh Farquharson, from Hull City and Felix McGrogan who also returned from England.

On the field, the team, clearly upset by the backroom upheavals, played five games before recording their first victory. By the end of the year, their poor run had placed them at the foot of the league with only 11 points from 22 games. There was to be no joy in the Scottish Cup either as Arbroath put them out of the competition in a first-round replay at Gayfield 1–0.

This time no revival was to be mounted and the club slipped helplessly towards relegation. Throughout the whole season only five games were won and 21 points secured. After a brief spell of three years in Division One, Dunfermline (along with Albion Rovers who had been promoted with them) returned for what was to be a long spell in the lower division. The unsuccessful team was: Farquharson; Warden, Bourhill; Bolt, McAllister, Syme; Dobson, Jamieson, Morrison, Chalmers, McGrogan. To secure the finances of the club for the future, each director had to become a guarantor for the sum of £200, a figure which was to rise steadily over the years.

Almost inevitably most of the club's good players now left – Bob McGowan joined Kilmarnock, Bobby Bolt went to Falkirk for £1,120 and Alex Thomson was given a free transfer. Although the team did not play particularly well at the start of the new season they did manage to stay up with the leaders and by the turn of the year they were third top. As an added incentive each player was offered an extra 10/-

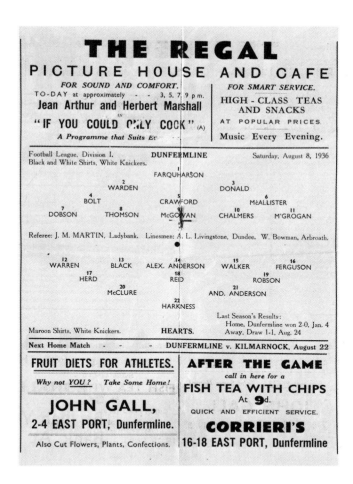

Football League, Division I.   **DUNFERMLINE**   Saturday, August 8, 1936
Black and White Shirts, White Knickers.

1
FARQUHARSON

2   3
WARDEN   DONALD

4   5   6
BOLT   CRAWFORD   McALLISTER

7   8   9   10   11
DOBSON THOMSON McGOWAN CHALMERS M'GROGAN

Referee: J. M. MARTIN, Ladybank. Linesmen: A. L. Livingstone, Dundee. W. Bowman, Arbroath.

12   13   14   15   16
WARREN BLACK ALEX. ANDERSON WALKER FERGUSON

17   18   19
HERD   REID   ROBSON

20   21
McCLURE   AND. ANDERSON

22
HARKNESS

Last Season's Results:
Home, Dunfermline won 2-0, Jan. 4
Away, Draw 1-1, Aug. 24

Maroon Shirts, White Knickers.   **HEARTS.**

Next Home Match - - - **DUNFERMLINE v. KILMARNOCK, August 22**

per game if promotion was achieved. However, a 4–1 defeat in the New Year by Raith Rovers, one of their main challengers, set the club off on a calamitous run. In the Scottish Cup in January, St Mirren, despite playing three-quarters of the game with only ten men, put an end to Dunfermline's unbeaten home record by recording a 1–0 victory. The *Press* recorded that "St Mirren would not allow cheap admission to the unemployed", an innovation which the Pars had pioneered to boost the crowds at home games during the depression.

On several occasions the manager protested at the barracking the home crowd inflicted on his players; fans were heard to ask if the team really wanted promotion. By the end of February all promotion hopes and a quick return to Division One were gone. Taylor resigned in April to take up a post in Carlisle and the club drifted towards the end of an unsuccessful season.

For the historian, however, the season did have something to offer – the minutes of the meetings of the Board of Directors date from this period (the previous ones having been unfortunately lost during the Second World War) and what an interesting insight they offer into the affairs of the club. Most of the material they deal with is of a very mundane nature – paying bills, answering countless appeals, writing letters, signing players, looking after the fabric of the property and generally overseeing the daily business life of the club. Here, the researcher can discover the true transfer fees of players which are often at variance with the wild

estimates conjured up by the press. The Board usually picked the team with voting often required to fix a particular position; the manager, who also acted as secretary, simply looked after the team on a Saturday afternoon. The directors also acted as scouts, travelling widely across not just Central Scotland, but sometimes to the North of Scotland and into England in their search for new talent.

In May 1938, a new manager was appointed – Peter Wilson (32) from Beith, in Ayrshire. Noted as an outstanding half back with Celtic and Hibs he continued to play for Dunfermline until a bad ankle injury kept him out of the side for a while. His salary was fixed at £6 per week with a bonus of a £1 for a win and 10/- for a draw. One of his best signings was Charlie Johnston, of Motherwell, a left winger of great ability who went on to have a very long and successful career in Scottish football. Another good signing was goalkeeper Willie Stevenson from Clyde.

Despite promises of good bonuses the team failed to find promotion-winning form and had to be content with fifth top position. In the Scottish Cup, their first-round match against Morton at East End Park had to be abandoned with the score at one goal each. Before the kick-off the pitch was icebound and waterlogged and when torrential rain and mist made the game a complete farce, the referee had no option but to abandon the game. Two weeks later, a fine 5–2 victory saw Dunfermline safely through to the next round. In round two, a 2–0 home victory over Duns brought Alloa to East End Park for the next round. The expected hard-fought game resulted in a 1–1 draw but what was remarkable was the size of the crowd – 16,611, a record for East End Park which brought in takings of £370. The Pars lost the replay 3–2.

The Supporters' Club, however, did give themselves a treat in the form of an outing to the Scotland-England game at Hampden. After the game, tea was taken at Lewis' Royal Polytechnic followed by a visit to the pantomime at the Princess Theatre.

The AGM at the end of the season revealed a loss of £800,

Here are a few snippets from the 1937-38 minutes:

transfer fees ranged from £20 to £100 with a signing on fee of £10 to £20; the manager earned £5 per week with a £50 bonus offered for promotion while a player received £2 to £3 per week (£1 during the close season); goal-nets were £4 a set. Season ticket prices were: stand 25/-, ground 12/6, ladies and youths 6/-, schoolboys 3/-. Gatemen were paid 2/- per match.

Correspondence received included a letter from a soldier in Palestine asking for a trial.

Complaints were made to the greyhound company about the damage done to the playing surface by dogs cutting the corners (though the rent of £135 p.a. was most welcome).

Directors offered to use their own private cars to transport players and hampers.

Very few cautions were handed out by the football authorities.

Above: *Manager Peter Wilson*

there being no transfer of note during the season to offset the loss. The Supporters' Club helped out by donating £105 and by carrying out improvements to the ground which was badly in need of a major facelift. The *Journal* noted that "East End Park is no credit to the town and bad as an advertisement in our city". An insurance certificate of that period offered a mere £1,300 in compensation for the buildings and the fixtures in the event of disaster. The Supporters' Club launched a fund which would restore the Pars to the First Division. "No single sports organisation in our city," their pamphlet noted, "has a broader appeal. All classes of the community share this interest." The Chairman announced that they "were in favour of (League) reconstruction as they thought it would strengthen the club financially if fewer and better clubs took part in the League games". The manager reported that his side had suffered from a large number of injuries throughout the season but he "was looking forward with confidence to next year's struggle".

Little did he then realise that the struggle that was to dominate the minds of everyone in the future related not to competition on the football field, but to the hostility which was engendered by the rise of Hitler's Germany and which led to the outbreak of another world war.

Below: *The team for season 1938-39. Standing: Hogg, Thomson, Stevenson, Callan, Whyte, Hart. Front: Farmer, ?, Hynds, ?, Johnston*

World War Two

Throughout the summer of 1939 preparations for the new season continued as usual despite the rantings and ravings of Hitler in the background. Dunfermline Supporters' Club published their Official Handbook with a full fixture list to be fulfilled. By the time the peace of Europe was shattered in early September by the German invasion of Poland, the Pars had played four games and were joint second top to Dundee.

Because of its proximity to the military bases at Rosyth, Donibristle and Pitreavie, Dunfermline was designated a "sensitive area" (along with Dundee, Edinburgh, Glasgow and Clydebank) and, in view of possible air attack, the congregating of large crowds was forbidden. The possibility of the club playing elsewhere, for instance in Cowdenbeath, was discussed but quickly dropped as being impracticable. In September, Company 907 of the Royal Army Service Corps took over part of the terracing for a car park, and then asked the Board if they might use the field for training on Wednesday afternoons; the request was granted "subject to the pitch being kept in condition by the RASC Co to the satisfaction of the trainer". The £50 annual rent from the army, however, proved to be most welcome. At the same time, manager Wilson, with nothing to do, returned to his home in Beith and severed his connection with the club. The contracts of the players were cancelled though their registrations were unaffected.

As the autumn passed without any real signs of hostilities during this period known as the "Phoney War", the authorities relaxed restrictions and allowed friendlies to take place. When a reserve side from Ibrox came to East End Park on 7 October to keep football ticking over in the district, the following advice was given:

"The Management request that all spectators carry their gas masks."

Director George Robb was given the task of liaising with the ARP officials and he was instructed that all gates must be kept open during matches in case of an air raid.

Further relaxations allowed a new competition to be set up, the Eastern League, which included Aberdeen, Raith Rovers, Cowdenbeath, St Bernard's, Dundee, Hibs, East Fife, Hearts, Falkirk, King's Park, Arbroath, St Johnstone, Alloa, Stenhousemuir and Dundee United plus Dunfermline.

(Courtesy of R. Fothergill)

Civil Defence squads in Dunfermline try out their gas masks.

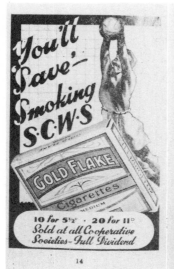

FIXTURES FOR SEASON 1939-40				
DATE	CLUB	Won	GOALS Lost	Pts.
Aug. 12	Stenhousemuir A			
„ 19	Queen's Park H			
„ 26	Leith Ath. A			
Sept. 2	Brechin City H			
„ 9	East Stirling A			
„ 16	Dundee (H)			
„ 23	Edinburgh C. A			
„ 30	East Fife (H)			
Oct. 7	Dundee Un. A			
„ 14	Forfar Ath. H			
„ 21	King's Park A			
„ 28	Montrose (H)			
Nov. 4	Raith Rov. A			
„ 11	East Fife A			
„ 18	Dumbarton A			
„ 25	Airdrie H			
Dec. 2	Leith Ath. H			
„ 9	Morton A			
„ 16	Montrose A			
„ 23	Stenhousemuir H			
Dec. 30	Brechin City A			

G. MURRAY
12

PRINCIPAL FIXTURES
1939-40
INTERNATIONAL MATCHES
1939
Oct. 21—Scotland v Wales—In Wales.
Nov. 22—Scotland v Ireland—in Scotland.
1940
April 13—Scotland v England—In England.

INTER-LEAGUE MATCHES
1939
Aug. 30—Scotland v Ireland—In Ireland.
Sept. 20—Scotland v England—In Scotland.

AMATEUR INTERNATIONAL MATCHES
1940
Mar. 2—Scotland v England—In Scotland.
April 24—Scotland v Ireland—In Ireland.

SCOTTISH CUP
1940
Jan. 20—1st Round.   Mar. 9—4th Round.
Feb. 10—2nd Round.   Mar. 30—Semi-Final.
Feb. 24—3rd Round.   Apr. 20—Final.

QUALIFYING CUP
Sept. 16—1st Round.   Oct. 14—3rd Round.
Sept. 30—2nd Round.   Oct. 28—4th Round.
Nov. 11—Semi-Final.
Nov. 25—Final Tie—North v. South.

13

Above: *Extracts from Supporters' Handbook*

Right: *Willie Kelly.*

In October, the Pars appointed a new manager, Sandy Archibald, then manager of Raith Rovers. Archibald, from Crossgates, had been a Rangers' player of some note and in his 666 games for the Light Blues he scored 162 goals, none more important than the two goals in the 1928 Cup Final which brought the trophy to Ibrox for the first time in 25 years. He was also capped eight times for Scotland, four of them against England. He was paid £4 per week and his duties included many general administrative jobs in addition to looking after the team. For the players under him, football became even more of a part-time recreation as each was required, in some form or other, for more vital "war" work. A maximum weekly wage of £2 was imposed by the government to discourage able-bodied men from devoting too much energy to this pastime when more urgent work

had to be tackled. Dunfermline started off with the following squad, though war service was soon to deplete it: W. Stevenson, J. Hogg, S. Hynds, A. Barnes, H. Hart, J. Whyte, S. Murray, G. Brooks, W. Kelly, W. Black, D. Callan, C. Johnston, G. Murray.

The Athletic made a good start to the new league, beating both Hearts and Falkirk, two of Scotland's leading clubs. Their victory over Falkirk was especially noteworthy: from 3–0 down, the Pars stormed back to win 4–3. Travelling difficulties, enlistments and shift work often meant that the manager was unable to field the side he would have wished. In the New Year, the Scottish Cup was put in mothballs with a new national cup taking its place. Dunfermline received a bye in the first round and were defeated by Clyde at Shawfield in the second round. When the league was decided in the spring, Dunfermline did remarkably well to finish in third position.

At the AGM in July 1940, the chairman reported that "the war had upset all our anticipations" which resulted in a loss of £81. To their credit the Board decided to keep the team going and not to follow the example of Cowdenbeath who shut down for the duration of the war. Cowdenbeath had received £100 in gate money from Dunfermline but withdrew before their neighbours could get their share from the lucrative return fixture.

Football in Dunfermline fell into a state of limbo during 1940–41 while the nation struggled for its very existence during the Battle of Britain and throughout the early days of the Blitz. During 1940 the gates of East End Park were closed for a while when a Polish transport unit occupied the ground. A league was formed in the west of Scotland but Dunfermline were not considered good enough to be asked to join. With transfer regulations relaxed many Athletic players freely joined other clubs, usually more suitable for them in view of the transport problems and evening black-out restrictions; others simply played with local Junior clubs. Under these arrangements Johnston went to

Rangers, Dougan to Hearts, Hart to Dumbarton and Hogg to Falkirk. The Board still found the time to organise a competition at East End Park for local clubs in order to raise money for the Plane Fund.

A revival in football took place in season 1941–42 when the SFA Secretary, Sir George Graham, organised a new competition, the North Eastern League, comprising only eight clubs: Dunfermline, Leith Athletic, Rangers 'A', Raith, Aberdeen, Dundee United, East Fife and St Bernard's. With clubs now only shadows of their former selves due to the mass exodus (and influx) of personnel, it was difficult to work out form and forecast results. Since there were so few clubs the first series of 14 games was played before Christmas with a second series coming in the New Year. The team which started the season for Dunfermline saw a number of new faces (and a number of changes throughout the season) – Such; Hogg, O'Neil; Smith, Hart, Jannett; Callan, Nailton, Kinnell, Smeaton, Birrell.

Such were the inconsistencies of the new set-up that in one game the Pars beat St Bernard's 7–3, only to lose the next game, 8–0, to East Fife. In the first series, Dunfermline finished fourth. The administrators then organised a Supplementary Cup in which the top four clubs were paired off, matches to be played on a home and away basis. In their first appearance in this competition, Dunfermline lost both their matches against the much stronger Aberdeen. Dunfermline were never to win this cup though they often qualified for it. The authorities noted how popular this "league trophy" was and it helped to provide the inspiration for the post-war League Cup, now an established part of the football calendar.

Throughout the war years, many established players "guested" for Dunfermline when war service or business

Below: *Bert Kinnell.*

Right: *Willie Forbes.*

brought them into the area. Names included goalkeeper Jock Wallace (from Blackpool, father of the Rangers' manager), Connolly (West Bromwich and Newcastle), Jackie Hunter (Morton), Jimmy Logie (Arsenal), Walker (Sheffield Wednesday), McGilvray (Dundee United and Motherwell), Dougan (Manchester United), Harley (Liverpool) and many others who helped brighten an otherwise gloomy scene. Willie Forbes was signed from Ashfield for £40. Johnston was permanently transferred to Rangers for a welcome £350 and went on to win international honours. In spite of these arrangements war-time football for the Pars was a demanding and depressing affair. Players would turn up straight from work in their dungarees; minutes before the kick-off, manager Archibald would be seen standing outside the ground scanning the road for late players. Passions certainly seem to have been quieter as only one player was ordered off during the entire season.

Bill Harrower.

Aided by their new "imported" players, Dunfermline had their best spell in 1942-43 when they came second to Aberdeen in the first series of the league. In the second series, an interesting experiment was conducted: when Dunfermline scored more goals than they conceded against an opponent in their two matches a bonus point was awarded to stimulate attacking play. During one of their games against Aberdeen, a local reporter noted that "this was the best refereed match I've seen this season. The referee was always up with play." He was referring to Bobby Calder from Rutherglen who, a few years later, was to become manager to Dunfermline – an unusual twist of fate.

A further setback occurred early in 1943 when the Army even requisitioned the club's pavilion for military use. By the spring, the club's overdraft stood at £398 3*s* 10*d*, a huge sum for the times. Despite these problems the team did well to reach the final of the Supplementary Cup, even though they lost 9–3 on aggregate to Aberdeen. In 1943-44, the authorities conducted another experiment, that of awarding three points for a victory, thus anticipating the English League's recent innovation by about 40 years. In 1944, the Pars could boast of their own record by having two sets of brothers on the books: Willie and Jimmy Harrower and Willie and Colin Syme. The star of the side in 1944 was undoubtedly local boy, Billy Liddell, who had gone straight from Lochgelly Violet to Liverpool FC in 1938. Equally talented with either foot the burly forward tormented defences and delighted the crowds with the sparkling form that was to win him 28 caps for Scotland. While guesting for Dunfermline in a game in November 1944, he supplied the crosses from which Jackie Hunter scored five goals against Dundee United.

Another future internationalist was also on the club's books for a brief spell at this time – left back Willie C. Cunningham, signed from Hearts of Beath for £20. He later had a very successful career with Preston North End. Archibald completed another very astute piece of business when he signed a young "Bevan Boy", the talented Jimmy Baxter, for a mere £5, also from Hearts of Beath.

Each year the club's AGM told the same story: financial losses, partly offset by generous gifts from the Supporters' Club; inadequate training facilities and the uncertainty over player availability. Even the purchase of a new strip was complicated as in these days of rationing the requisite number of clothing coupons had to be saved up. Eventually the club made do with a utility strip – maroon, white and blue. Above all others it was Archibald, through his energy and enthusiasm, who kept the team going. At one stage he even hired a sandwich-board man for 10/- on a Saturday to parade the streets with an advert for the forthcoming game. With an eye to the future in 1944 he signed seven young players for £200 to build up a new team. To help recoup some losses, Willie Harrower was transferred to Third Lanark for £350, followed later by his brother who went on to win international honours.

The Board, which continued to meet regularly throughout the war, were always keen to stage a game to aid the war effort. In 1942 they organised a match in aid of "Dunfermline Warship Week" and later they allowed the ground for the promotion of a boxing match for "The Help To Russia Fund".

When the second series of the league finished in the spring of 1945 the North Eastern League was wound up. The war in Europe was all but won and the administrators were making plans for a full-scale revival of League Football throughout Scotland in August. The SFA had already started coaching courses, a sure sign that a new era was approaching. Dunfermline were ready to resume the challenge of national competition. The Army had formally given up the ground in January 1945 and granted £329 in compensation for rebuilding a damaged wall, for resurfacing the terracing which had been damaged by heavy vehicles and for demolishing an ammunition compound. A group of boys was paid £10 to clear the terraces of weeds. A new car park was laid out with a railing to separate it from the field. Archibald gave up his job at the Dockyard to become full-time manager of the club on a salary of £8 per week plus 5% of the transfer deals.

Above: *The winning team at the five-a-side football tournament at East End Park, July 1944. Standing: J. and W. Harrower, W. Penman, Andrew Watson. Seated: J. Ellis and W. Syme.*

Below: *Football was a popular pastime with the workforce at Rosyth Dockyard, a hive of activity during the war. A number of players shown here went on to sign for Dunfermline.*

The Road to Hampden

Until they arranged their own house in order and until normality returned to the country, the footballing authorities decided on a Victory Season for 1945-46 and set up two provisional leagues, 'A' and 'B' Divisions, between which there would be no movement for the first season. Dunfermline, considered to be one of the smaller fry, were consigned to the lower division though they raced off to a flying start by beating Dundee United 7–1. The Taysiders surprised everyone by wearing numbers on their jerseys. After four games and 18 goals scored (with only two conceded), they stood at the top of the league with seven points. To make ends meet, however, it was necessary to sell one of their best players, Jimmy Baxter, to Barnsley for £2,000.

When 8,000 fans turned up to see Dundee play a league game at East End Park it seemed like old times. The large crowd could hardly believe its eyes when both sides appeared in white jerseys. The referee, who had officiated at the Scotland–England match at Hampden in the April, had duly checked the boots in the dressing-rooms but had failed to notice the near identical strips. Dunfermline lost 6–0 though some pride was retrieved when they thrashed Raith Rovers 8–1 in December.

When the league finished in January 1946, Dundee ran out easy winners with the Pars coming a poor ninth out of 12 teams. A Supplementary Cup was organised in which East Fife easily disposed of Dunfermline. In the absence of the Scottish Cup proper in these unsettled days, a Victory Cup was played for, ties to be decided on a home and away basis. Dunfermline were drawn against Third Lanark and did well to beat them 2–1 at Cathkin

The nine Dunfermline players who made the trip to Barnsley. Standing: W. Aitken, T. Docherty, J. Ellis, W. Cunningham, W. Forbes. Front: W. Kelly, W. Allan, Ritchie, J. Calder.

Park. In the second leg, Thirds managed to win 2–0 and thus clinch the tie on aggregate. On Thursday 11 April, Dunfermline played their first game in England when they met Barnsley in a friendly game which had been organised when Baxter was transferred. The team, which gave a good performance despite losing 4–0, comprised: Allan; Calder, Cunningham; Forbes, Kelly, Ellis; Maule (Raith), Aitken, Ritchie, Till (Raith), Docherty.

When the first post-war AGM was held on 12 August 1946, the club was reported to be in a good financial state, largely as a result of transfers. The manager was thanked for "his untiring efforts in trying out young players". It was also wistfully noted that the club "could do with a new stand so that enthusiasts could bring their wives with them and watch the game in comfort".

Significantly, the Dunfermline chairman, George Robb, was also vice-president of the Scottish League and it was largely through his efforts that the leagues were reconstructed along the lines in which they had existed before the war. Automatic promotion and relegation were reinstated. A third league was also created and, as a mark of egalitarianism, they were simply called leagues A, B and C. Dunfermline, allocated to the middle division, made a poor start to the new season by losing 3–0 away to Dundee United in front of a 13,000 crowd.

Before the league was fully underway, the Pars took part in the newly organised League Cup. League teams were drawn into sections of four clubs and played in a mini-league on a home and away basis, with the winners going forward to the quarter-finals, also decided over two legs. In the Cup's first season, Dunfermline were drawn alongside St Johnstone, East Fife and Alloa with the Bayview side winning all their games and thus qualifying for the next round. Kelly and Cunningham joined Airdrie for £4,500 and £3,000 and later Forbes was sold to Wolves for £1,500. Former Rangers' winger, David Kinnear, signed from Third Lanark for £300.

Dunfermline's fortunes suffered a tragic setback with the death of Archibald at the end of November 1946. His enthusiasm, judgment, ability and drive were to be sadly missed, not just by Dunfermline but throughout Scottish football. Perhaps his guiding hand could have prevented the 6–2 drubbing which East Fife handed out at Bayview to Dunfermline on 25 January in the first round of the Scottish Cup, resurrected for the first time since 1939. On 13 February 1947, the Board appointed Mr William McAndrew from Hamilton, as the new manager on a salary of £500 per annum plus the free tenancy of a house, specially bought at 23 Shamrock Street for £1,500. As a player he had spells with Queen's Park and Clyde though for the last 20 years he has been associated with Hamilton Accies. Sadly, the impetus and fervour which a new manager often brings could not prevent the Pars from suffering their worst ever League defeat – losing 10–0 at

The Balance Sheet for 1945-46 presented at the AGM in St Margaret's Hall on 12 August 1946. Mr George Robb was chairman.

ABSTRACT ACCOUNTS and BALANCE SHEET for Year ended 30th April 1946.

PROFIT AND LOSS ACCOUNT.

To Share of Gates to Visiting Clubs, S.F.A. and League Levies		£2011 4 5	
„ Players' Wages and Bonuses		2352 2 5	
„ Players' and Officials' Expenses and Travelling		668 0 6	
„ Entertainment Duty		2696 8 7	
„ Referees' and Linesmen's Fees		104 3 0	
„ Gatemen		65 14 6	
„ Police		30 3 0	
„ Teas, Luncheons and Refreshments		301 10 9	
„ Printing, Stationery and Advertising		66 5 5	
„ Manager's and Trainer's Wages and Expenses		612 0 0	
„ Miscellaneous Expenses		75 18 8	
„ Interest on Bank Overdraft		26 3 6	
„ Local Rates		89 17 9	
„ Insurances		63 5 0	
„ Hiring		173 2 9	
„ Heating and Lighting		15 1 3	
„ Footballs, Boots and Repairs		40 19 5	
„ Telephone Rent and Calls		46 16 2	
„ Postage, Telegrams and Commission		11 19 11	
„ Subscriptions:—			
S.F.A.	£0 10 6		
League	1 0 0		
Fife Association	0 6 3		
		1 16 9	
„ Audit Fee		10 16 6	
„ Trainer's Expenses		38 13 3	
„ Ground Upkeep		48 5 8	
„ Laundry		11 2 4	
„ War Damage Contribution		5 14 10	
„ Income Tax		61 12 6	
„ Depreciation		35 0 0	
„ Net Profit for year—Carried down		1367 15 0	
		£11,031 13 10	
To Balance—Brought forward		£5767 19 3½	
		£5767 19 3½	

By Gate Drawings, Stand and Enclosure Drawings, and Share of Away Gates and League Levies	£9392 2 10
„ Transfer Fees received, *less* Signing and Transfer Fees Paid	1435 0 0
„ Rents	163 10 0
„ Subscriptions and Donations	41 1 0
	£11,031 13 10
By Net Profit—Brought down	£1367 15 0
„ Profit on Loans Repaid	250 8 6
„ Balance—Carried forward	4149 15 9½
	£5767 19 3½

Above: *Dunfermline Athletic, October 1947. Back: Jack, Donaldson, Kinnell, Michie, McDonald, Copeland. Front: Kerr, Whyte, Noble, McIntyre, Kinnear.* (Dundee Courier)

Right: *Manager Bobby Calder.*

Dens Park on 22 March. Thankfully, the press reported that the visitors' trialist goalkeeper, 'Newman', had a good game and kept the score down! Dundee centre, Juliussen, entertained the 14,000 crowd with seven goals and helped create another record. In their previous game Dundee had also scored 10 goals against Alloa (Juliussen bagging six) – the first time a senior club had scored double figures in successive league games. On form like that Dundee were duly promoted while Dunfermline could only manage eighth place.

With Europe slowly settling down to normality again, matches against foreign opposition became an attractive proposition as the famous Rangers-Moscow Dynamo game of 1945 illustrated. Dunfermline were offered a tour of Norway but turned it down, believing that the arranging of it would have been too complicated and unrewarding. During the season the ever faithful Supporters' Club were busy installing a loudspeaker system and erecting concrete pillars and tubes in places of the old wooden fences around the field. The acquisition of 93 clothing coupons allowed a new strip to be bought for the players.

The next season, 1947-48, brought little more cheer to

Dunfermline. The war team by now gradually faded away, giving way to: Michie; Whyte, Coupland; Ferguson, Rooney, McDonald; Irvine, Wright, Kinnell, Noble, Kinnear. Other players in the side were Roberts, Donaldson, Aitken, Jack, Pope, Kerr and Hickie. In the League Cup, Dunfermline were drawn with Raith Rovers, Hamilton and Alloa and only one victory from six games ensured that the Pars made no further progress in the tournament. After a 6–1 thrashing by Raith at the end of August, McAndrew was obliged to resign and the former referee, Mr Robert Calder from Rutherglen, was appointed to take his place. The former railway signalman was a highly popular and well-respected figure who did much to build up the team's flagging spirits, especially with several excellent signings. Keith was signed from Clyde and became a prolific goal-scorer; Jimmy Clarkson, one of the tallest men in football at 6 ft 3 in, was bought from Arniston Rangers for £40 and made the centre half position his own for many years; Bobby Kirk was also signed from the same junior club for a similar fee and became a talented full back; Tommy Wright was signed from the junior ranks and proved to be a clever forward. Calder was one of the first managers in Scotland to wear a track-suit instead of the customary suit at training sessions.

However, Calder's results were little better. Following a bye in the first round of the Scottish Cup, Dunfermline were beaten 2–1 at Shawfield. After being reprimanded by

the Board for talking to the press he too resigned, after only six months in the job. After lecturing in America he eventually became Aberdeen's top scout and recruited many excellent players for the Dons. For over a year no appointment was made. Vice-chairman, Mr Sandy Terris, owner of the baking firm of William Stephen, took charge of coaching. To ensure that players were as fit as possible lights were installed at the ground for training purposes, the facilities in the Carnegie Baths were utilised and a ground in the west of Scotland, at Cambuslang, was hired as a centre for mid-week practice by the large contingent from the west. In an effort to improve the comfort of spectators "the Board approved the purchase of three huts, one 72 feet and the others 36 feet, being bought and erected as covered enclosure on the north terracing". Other building projects were rejected by the Ministry of Works, ever careful to preserve precious materials for more vital structures.

On the playing side, an astute piece of business was carried out when Kinnell was sold to Partick Thistle for £6,000, part of which was used to bring Gerry Mays from St Johnstone and Jimmy Cannon from Blantyre – and two

Team of September 1948 photographed with Directors, Tom Gibson (left) and Sandy Terris. Back row: Whyte, Kirk, Michie, Clarkson, McDonald, Noble. Front: Naismith, Cannon, Roy, Wright, Kinnear. Due to the disruption caused by the war many players carried on playing into their late thirties and beyond. (M. Allan)

Above: *J. Cannon in action at East End Park.* (M. Allan)

Below: *Gerry Mays scoring against Queen's Park.* (M. Allan)

excellent forwards they turned out to be. To give their large playing squad more match practice, the Board entered the reserves into Division C, a place they occupied for six seasons.

Despite their preparations the team's League Cup performances against Raith, Stirling and Cowdenbeath were disappointing. Their six games, in front of 53,000 fans, produced three wins, sufficient to gain only second place behind Raith. Their best form was to be reserved for the league which saw the Pars experiment with a novel idea. Sandy Terris had been bewitched by the sparkling displays of the famous Moscow Dynamo team which had recently toured Britain and he had become a staunch advocate of intensive coaching and of playing to set plans, an approach which would raise few eyebrows today but which caused a great storm of controversy amongst supporters and fellow directors. They thought that the team should play "ordinary football with strict instructions to keep the ball on the carpet". A central feature of "The Plan" (as it became known) was the deployment of two centre forwards – Keith and Cannon – serviced by a link inside forward – Tommy Wright. Only one defeat in the first 14 league games suggested that the new tactics were paying off. The Pars were never far from the top of the table and looked a good bet for promotion. Recognition of some sort came when, for the first time ever at Dunfermline, the BBC broadcast sound commentary from the last half-hour of their game against East Stirling. The fee of £2 12s 6d was sent to the League Benevolent Fund as were subsequent fees for many years to come. In November, the club paid out a record fee of £2,000 to promotion rivals, Stirling Albion, for George Henderson who went on to score 22 goals that season.

Not until the New Year in 1949 was the team's away record smashed when Cowdenbeath convincingly won

4–0. Their cup hopes also took a knock that same month when Stenhousemuir ousted them 2–0 in a first-round replay at Larbert. However, despite these setbacks and despite boardroom disagreements over tactics, Dunfermline still seemed set for promotion by the time the spring came along. In the most exciting finish for years, any two teams out of three – Dunfermline, Raith and Stirling – could have been promoted as the league table demonstrated:

	P	W	D	L	F	A	Pts
Stirling	30	20	2	8	71	47	42
Dunfermline	29	16	9	4	80	54	41
Airdrie	30	16	9	5	76	42	41
Raith	29	19	2	8	76	44	40

It all hinged on the last Saturday 30 April, when the Pars, leading Raith by one point, travelled to Kirkcaldy to meet their rivals before a crowd of no less than 22,000 (a record for Fife clubs). The Dunfermline team was: Michie; Kirk, Roberts; McSeveney, Clarkson, Noble; Mays, Cannon, Henderson, Keith, Kinnear. The Raith defence was well marshalled by Harry Colville and Andy Young who were later to serve Dunfermline so well.

Disaster struck Dunfermline when, after only 11 minutes, goalkeeper Michie clashed with Willie Penman and had to retire with a broken arm. In the days before substitutes this meant the Athletic had to play out the game with only 10 men. Keith went into goal and no one was surprised at the final score – a 4–0 victory for Raith. This was only Dunfermline's second away defeat, but it was enough to rob the club of the promotion which they so richly deserved.

An interesting footnote appeared in the club's records – of the 27 players on the club's books only nine could be said to be local. Even then, just after the war, a club like Dunfermline cast its net far and wide for new talent.

The Board decided they needed a manager after all and, failing to obtain Bobby Ancell from Dundee, appointed Mr Webber Lees as manager-secretary in July 1949 on a salary of £500 per annum. As a young man, Lees had seen action in the First World War at the Battle of Jutland and later began an association with Albion Rovers that was to extend over 23 years. Indeed he was manager of the club on no less than three different occasions and each time he took the club into the top division. One of his first signings was the Aberdeen goalkeeper, George Johnstone, who also acted as coach, an acknowledgment that detailed planning was required after all. Other new signings included: 'Tiger' Houston, McLean, Gilchrist, McCall, Kerr, McGairy, Shaw, Dunlop, McKay and Kelly. Keith was transferred to Stirling for £1,000. Approaches from Arsenal for Kirk were rejected. At the same time, long-serving director, James Anderson, resigned as did Sandy Terris. Messrs John Spears and David Birrell were elected to the Board and Peter Jamieson was later co-opted as a member.

Lees was to have almost instant success when his team reached the final of the League Cup. When the teams were drawn out of the hat no one gave Dunfermline's chances a second thought – Queen's Park, St Johnstone and Kilmarnock were tough opposition. Ironically their campaign started where it was to finish – at Hampden Park. In their opening match, Dunfermline scraped home 1–0. In the second game, the Pars suffered a home defeat (2–1) at the hands of St Johnstone but made amends for this with a

Left: William Webber Lees, Manager.

Below: Joe Houston in action. Nicknamed "Tiger" after the Moscow Dynamo goalkeeper. (M. Allan)

dazzling 5–1 home victory over Kilmarnock, Henderson scoring three goals. Another victory (3–0) over the Amateurs put the Athletic in a strong position and additional away wins over St Johnstone (3–2) and Kilmarnock (4–2, including another Henderson hat-trick) ensured that Dunfermline had easily qualified for the later stages. The successful squad was: Johnstone; Kirk, Roberts; McCall, Clarkson, McLean (McSeveney); Mays, Cannon, Henderson, Dunlop, McKay.

The quarter-final draw brought together Dunfermline and Airdrie. In a real classic game at Broomfield, Dunfermline emerged triumphant with a 4–3 victory. In the return leg, neither side scored and the Pars were through to the semi-finals where they met the much fancied Hibs at Tynecastle. On 8 October, four special trains brought the biggest exodus of supporters that had ever travelled with the club outside the Fife border. The pre-match news was not encouraging. Dougie Roberts, who had played in all the previous games, called off at the last minute due to illness. McLean took over the full back position and Andy Whyte was brought in at wing half. Stirton Smith replaced McKay on the wing. Hibs were without Gordon Smith who was injured, but had an impressive line-up nonetheless which contained six internationalists: Younger, Govan, Shaw; Gallacher, McNeill, Cairns; McDonald, Combe, Reilly, Turnbull, Ormond.

The 31,622 crowd (receipts £2,932) saw a real surprise when the underdogs, despite losing the first goal, more than contained the favourites. The majestic Clarkson held Scottish internationalist Reilly in check and Kirk gave Ormond little room to manœuvre. Johnstone was an inspiration in goal but the real hero of the day was Mays, dismissed like Clarkson from Easter Road on a free transfer, whose two goals gave the Pars a 2–1 victory and a place in the final. Dunfermline was truly on the football map at last.

Sadly, there was to be no fairytale ending at Hampden on 29 October. Their opponents, East Fife, winners of the trophy two seasons earlier, had already been at Hampden twice in 1949. The talented Methil side had lost to Rangers in a Scottish Cup semi-final and had then beaten the same side in the League Cup semi-final. The Bayview team, ably managed by Scot Symon, were in Division A and were having one of their most successful runs in their history. Before the match, Roberts, the regular left back, had to

The team of August 1949 who helped Dunfermline on the way to Hampden in October. Back: B. Kirk, J. McCall, G. Johnstone, J. Clarkson, A. McLean, D. Roberts. Front: G. Mays, J. Cannon, G. Henderson, W. Dunlop, W. McKay. (M. Allan)

Two views of Mays' first goal against Hibs. A good example (above) of the early use of the telephoto lens by local photographer, M. Allan.

Above: Mays scoring his second goal against Hibs from an apparently impossible angle. Shaw, Younger and Govan are the despairing defenders.

withdraw through injury; Johnstone's father died and though he decided to appear he understandably did not play to his true form. The teams were:

Dunfermline: Johnstone; Kirk, McLean; McCall, Clarkson, Whyte; Mays, Cannon, Henderson, McGairy, Smith.

East Fife: McGarrity; Laird, Stewart; Philp, Finlay, Aitken; Black, Fleming, Morris, Brown, Duncan.

Two quick goals from East Fife, the first when Kirk was lying injured on the ground, gave them a flying start which a seasoned defence would not surrender easily. East Fife scored a third goal after 20 minutes and ran out worthy winners by 3 goals to nil. The crowd, 39,744, was the biggest the Pars had ever played before and also set a record, unlikely to be broken, for a game between two Fife clubs.

After the final, Dunfermline's promising team fell away: Johnstone left the club and Henderson was transferred to St Mirren for £5,500. Not long afterwards a Mr Andy Dickson, who had joined the club as a net boy, was taken on as a groundsman at the wage of £7 per week. The club sent him on an £80 course for masseurs with the proviso that he stayed with the club for at least three years. In fact, he was to spend the next decade with Dunfermline, half of the time as manager.

Any hopes of the club making a return journey to Hampden that season in the Scottish Cup came to nothing. After early victories over Forfar (5–3) at home and Albion Rovers (2–1) away, Dunfermline came unstuck, not for the first time, against Stenhousemuir (4–1) at home. This left the club to concentrate on the league where they were unfortunate in competing against Morton and Airdrie who were in splendid form. These two clubs duly won promotion with Dunfermline a poor third, eight points behind. In the last away game of the season, Dunfermline lost by the remarkable score of 7–6 against Stenhousemuir.

At the end of the season, correspondence from the Burgh Sanitary Engineer illustrated how primitive the ground was in these post-war years. He sent a letter to the club "intimating that existing sanitary accommodation at East End Park is inadequate for the use of the public and seeking that suitable and adequate sanitary accommodation be provided". This was but the first of much correspondence on this pressing theme.

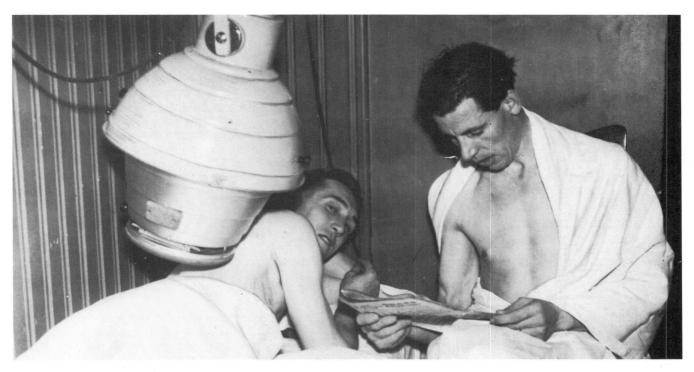

Above: *George Henderson (left) and skipper George Johnstone, receiving the "magic lamp" treatment in preparation for the League Cup Final. Johnstone won a League Cup medal with Aberdeen in 1946.*

Below: *Two rare collectors' items – the programme of the 1949 League Cup Final and of a friendly game in England.*

The Fifties

It would have been pleasing to have called this chapter, "The Fabulous Fifties", but that would have been patently untrue, though the decade did have its moments to savour. "Frantic" or "fitful" might have been more appropriate epithets. The new decade was not to usher in success in any of the three domestic trophies. In the League Cup there was no chance of history repeating itself as Ayr United came out on top of the section containing Dunfermline, Kilmarnock and Dumbarton. At the start of the league campaign the Board agreed to leave team selection to the manager and his new player-coach, Willie Finnegan, formerly of Hibs. This was not to make a great deal of difference because very indifferent form from Dunfermline meant that they finished an undistinguished programme in 10th position. In the Scottish Cup, a first-round home defeat by Clyde (3–0) added to the gloom. In March 1951, an 18-year-old joiner from Auchterarder, Ron Mailer, joined the club as an inside forward, the start of a long and distinguished association with the club which saw him play in almost every position.

By way of excuses the manager could claim that National Service often made players unavailable and good players had occasionally to be transferred to balance the books. Jackie Stewart, for example, an outside right who had recently been signed from Royal Albert, was sold to East Fife for £5,300.

The end of a disappointing season and a loss of £2,061 precipitated the club's biggest ever boardroom shake-up. One year earlier, chairman Tom Gibson had resigned, claiming that he did not carry the confidence of his colleagues and that the policy of the board was negative. At

the beginning of May 1951, Spears and Jamieson resigned. At the AGM in July, former chairmen and directors of long standing, Robert Wylie and Martin Porter, failed to be re-elected. Within the week fellow directors, D. Birrell, C. Morris and chairman Robb had tendered their resignations. The new Board which emerged comprised local farmer Hugh McMillan (chairman), John Spears (vice-chairman), Tom Younger and Andrew N. Watson. In August, Webber Lees was asked to resign and the Board once again ran the team. To cope with the ever-increasing administrative work, a secretary was appointed, George L. Brown being the first incumbent on a wage of £4 per week. Another backroom change occurred when Eddie Dowie stepped down after more than 30 years as trainer though he still continued to help the club by assisting with the reserve side. Andy Dickson took over as trainer and attended a SFA course in coaching. Jimmy Cannon was sold to St Johnstone for £1,000 while defenders W. Laird and E. Baikie joined the club on free transfers.

The shake-up seems to have done some good in so far as

Below: *The team which defeated Rangers in the 1st leg of the League Cup. Back: Kirk, John Spears, Whyte, Clarkson, Moodie, Baikie, McSeveney, Willie Finnegan, Andrew Watson. Front: McGairy, Macaulay, Mays, Wright, Smith.* (Dunfermline Press)

Right: *Eric Baikie jumping over the back of Tommy Wright.*

at the start of the new season the Pars battled their way through their League Cup section of Alloa, Hamilton and Queen's Park to top the group. In the quarter-finals, Dunfermline were drawn against Rangers, managed by the legendary Bill Struth. In the first leg, the first all-ticket game at East End Park, a record crowd of 20,000 witnessed a thrilling game. The home goalkeeper, John Moodie, signed on a free transfer from Cowdenbeath, was in excellent form as he pulled off one miraculous save after another. At the other end, Mays scored the only goal of the game to send the home fans away delighted. Afterwards the Board decided to erect crush barriers to deal with large exuberant crowds in the future. Four days later, the second leg at Ibrox was no less exciting. After 13 minutes Findlay of Rangers levelled the tie and the same player shot Rangers ahead. The Pars stormed back and despite ferocious tackling from Rangers, equalised through Wright. Clarkson missed a penalty and Mays had what looked like a legitimate goal chalked off. Driven on by the huge crowd of 44,000, Dunfermline's biggest audience so far, Rangers snatched a controversial winning goal about which even the home fans were dubious. Moodie could not hold a typical floating cross from winger Willie Waddell but he threw himself backwards to smother the ball on the goal-line. When Moodie heard the whistle sound he assumed it was for a foul for the extreme bruising inflicted on his ribs and was flabbergasted when the referee pointed to the centre spot. Pandemonium broke out but to no avail – Dunfermline were out of the cup.

Encouraged by their run in the League Cup the Athletic made a positive start to the league campaign. In the opening

games, Forfar were beaten 7–2 and Cowdenbeath disposed of by 3 goals to nil. The Board put up £400 "talent" money for promotion and wages were increased to £6 per week. The club felt confident enough to reject a £5,500 bid for McSeveney from Middlesbrough. Falkirk were also doing well (and were to be promoted) and Dunfermline's visit to Brockville at the end of September was of vital importance. Thirty buses left for Falkirk, but the huge visiting support could do nothing to prevent their side crashing by 5 goals to 1. Thereafter, the Athletic's form slumped despite new signings Corbett, a war-time Scottish cap, and Watters, a £1,200 purchase from Motherwell. By January, they were out of the promotion race and sixth position was the best they could muster. Half back Andy Whyte was transferred to East Fife for £3,250. To keep talented defender Bobby Kirk at East End Park, the club bought a house at Rose Crescent and gave him tenancy of it.

Some compensation came in the Scottish Cup. After a first-round bye, Dunfermline disposed of Clyde at Shawfield by the narrow margin of 4–3, a hat-trick from winger Jimmy Smith helping the visitors to victory. The third round produced a real cracker when 'A' Division Motherwell were beckoned to East End Park. A new record crowd of 22,295 turned up (though the ground could easily have taken more) to witness a 1–1 draw, thanks to an equalising goal from McGairy. In the replay the Pars, backed by a strong support, did well to hold their hosts to a goalless draw at half-time, but during the second half they collapsed and lost four goals to the team that went on to win the trophy.

In April, the authorities experimented with a Supplementary League Cup which was not a success. After beating Arbroath (away) 3–0, the Pars lost 4–0 to St Johnstone at home. A charity game against Rochdale in

Above: *Manager Bobby Ancell.*

Below: *G. Mays in action in the Scottish Cup against Motherwell at East End Park. Paton and Johnston are the Fir Park players.* (M. Allan)

Yorkshire, which was lost 4–2, completed a season which at times had promised so much.

The end of the season saw one of the club's biggest ever shake-outs of players – no fewer than 18 were given free transfers, including Mays, top scorer with 29 goals who went on to score more than 150 goals for Kilmarnock. It was left to the newly appointed manager, Bobby Ancell, to build a new team. As a player, Ancell was a renowned full back with St Mirren, Newcastle, Aberdeen and Dundee, gaining three caps in the process. He was a first-rate coach and had been manager of Berwick Rangers for two years. In his address in the programme to the supporters he asked of them – "I would like you all to be connoisseurs in the game of football – looking for the finer points of the play and refusing to be carried away with this 'we must win' attitude which has invaded the football scene in the recent years".

One of his first signings was the 17-year-old apprentice plumber, Jimmy Millar, from Merchiston Thistle and destined for a glorious career in Scottish football. Cost? £10 to his club and a £30 signing on fee! Another capture was inside forward George O'Brien, also 17, signed from that fertile area of talent, Blairhall Colliery, and one of the few Dunfermline-born players to play for the Pars. A new goal-keeper, Benson, quickly established himself in the first team. Jimmy Muir was signed from Arbroath and ended the season as top scorer. At the same time, three new directors were appointed: Messrs David Thomson, James Anderson and James McConville. Thomson later described his new surroundings in graphic fashion: "I was so proud at being a director of this grand old club that I was almost willing to overlook the lack of amenities there. On the cold evenings we used to sit shivering round the table with our overcoats on." A new secretary, Robert Torrie, completed the backroom changes.

Despite these changes, or perhaps because of them, the new season of 1952-53 was a most undistinguished one. In

Above: *Jimmy Millar, aged 17.*

Below: *Ancell coaching (l to r): Mackie, Clarkson, McKinlay, Baikie and Millar.*
(Evening Dispatch)

this coronation year there was to be no crowning glory for Dunfermline. The Pars failed to make any impact in their League Cup section containing Arbroath, Alloa and Kilmarnock with the last mentioned going through to the final itself. Poor league form meant one of their worst placings for years – 11th position. It was easier for Hillary and Tensing to scale Mount Everest than it was for Dunfermline to string a few victories together. Nor was compensation to come in the Scottish Cup – a first-round away defeat by Morton (3–1) saw to that. During the season the Pars played their first game under floodlights against Leith Athletic at Meadowbank on 10 February.

Despite the poor performances on the field it was decided to proceed with a wooden extension to the stand to provide an extra 1,000 seats which would pull in more gate revenue. The east side was extended by 110 feet and the west side by 73 feet. The club's overdraft stood at £2,750 and the Board decided that "any expenditure over £1 was to be first sanctioned by one of the directors." The collapse of Leith Athletic during the summer illustrated just how fragile football finances were. The transfer of Kirk to Raith Rovers for £750 helped ease the financial burden. Interest in the Supporters' Club visit to Wembley was never greater, £3 12s being required to join a special party. To ensure a fair distribution of the club's ticket allocation, a public draw had to be held with a *Press* reporter acting as a witness.

For the new season, the club signed a reliable centre half in George Duthie (25), a school teacher from Edinburgh

Team of December, 1953. Standing: Forsyth, Mackie, Benson, Clarkson, Millar, Baikie. Seated: Currie, McSeveney, Henderson, O'Brien, Mailer. (Dundee Courier)

who had failed to establish himself at Easter Road. Other newcomers included full backs Sinclair Mackie and Alec Laird (from Hibs), Colin McKinlay (26) from St Johnstone, George Samuel (24) from Aberdeen, goal-keeper Joe Mackin from Luton, Jim Chalmers (23) from Queen's Park and John Allan, a centre forward from Comrie. Old favourite, George Henderson, re-signed for his former club and, despite leaving again the following February to join Albion Rovers, went on to be the side's top scorer with 22 goals.

The club's finances received a significant boost with a better run in the 1953-54 League Cup. Crowds of around 4,000 saw Arbroath and Dumbarton fall by the wayside, leaving Dunfermline and Forfar to fight for the honours. By the last game, both sides were level on points and due to play each other. By winning 3–0 the Pars marched into the quarter-finals where old rivals, East Fife, a full-time club, awaited. The Methil side had little difficulty in disposing of Dunfermline, winning both legs comfortably: 6–2 and 3–2. Inside right 'Legs' Fleming, who used to be coached by Sandy Terris at East End Park, was the star with eight goals and he scored again in the final to help win the Cup for East Fife yet again.

The Board then turned their attention to the north terracing where the old shelter was dismantled and replaced by an all steel structure 50 yards in length at a cost of £2,000. The directors' confidence in the future was reflected in the team making an excellent start to their league campaign. Promotion fever hit the town when the team reached second top position by the end of October. By mid-November they were the only undefeated club in Britain though that record was soon to be shattered by a defeat at Coatbridge on 28 November. This was to spark off a bad run which saw their position in the league slump while their main rival, Motherwell, continued to do well.

In the first round of the Scottish Cup Dunfermline recorded a fine 4–1 win at Stranraer, Willie Candlish scoring two goals on his debut. Their joy was short-lived as Motherwell, trailing by a goal at half-time, knocked them out 5–2 in the next round at Fir Park. In March, Mailer was temporarily transferred to Darlington until his National Service at Catterick was finished and the driving force of 'Marathon Man' was missed. At the same time the club secured an excellent buy in 20-year-old outside left Felix Reilly, signed from Shotts Bon Accord for £200.

Dunfermline were unable to recapture their early promise and while Motherwell and Kilmarnock were pro-moted the Pars could only manage eighth position. At the end of April the Board sent a telegram to Wembley wishing

Above: *Inside right, George O'Brien, aged 17.*

Right: *Felix Reilly, a miner from Lanarkshire.*

three former players good luck in the forthcoming FA Cup final. The trio were Willie Cunningham, Jimmy Baxter and Willie Forbes who had emerged from the obscurity of war-time football in Fife to appear for their club, Preston North End, for one of the game's glittering prizes. (West Brom won 3–2.)

As the season ended, Mr James McConville was appointed honorary secretary, a position he still holds today. It then cost £325 per week to run the club. The transfers of McSeveney to Motherwell for £1,000 and Allan to Aberdeen for £1,750 brought in valuable revenue. At the club's AGM, Ancell called for better support for the team and deplored those local fans who left the town in droves each Saturday to follow the large city teams. In the close season, work costing £500 was carried out on the field's drainage system to avoid the heavy quagmires which a wet winter invariably produced. With no spare cash available the club concentrated on developing young players like Cuthbertson, Duncan, Cameron, Addison, Anderson and, best investment of all, John Sweeney (19), from Edina Hearts. "Talent" money of £500, however, was reserved for the team if promotion was secured.

The new season's League Cup linked Dunfermline with Brechin, Dundee United and Ayr. But for a defeat at Ayr in the last game, the Pars would have qualified for the later stages. Left to concentrate on league business the Athletic made a hesitant start, defeating St Johnstone 4–3 at home but then losing at Cowdenbeath. Inconsistent form followed and four successive defeats saw the club placed 11th

in November. After beating Albion Rovers 7–0 at home a revival followed which lifted them to fourth top position by the turn of the year. The New Year saw Dunfermline maintain their challenge despite the transfer in January of Millar, the club's top scorer that season with 20 goals, to Rangers for £5,500, a sum which wiped out the club's debts. A more than adequate replacement was found in a young centre forward called Charlie Dickson (20), an electrician to trade, who was signed from Penicuik Athletic. On his debut at Ochilview on 29 January he scored two of his club's three goals to gain two valuable points.

In the Scottish Cup, redesigned to exclude Senior clubs until round five, Dunfermline met Partick Thistle before a crowd of 11,500 at East End Park. After trailing 2–0 at half-time the Pars stormed back and levelled the score through Reilly and McKinlay with 10 minutes to go. Two late penalties, both converted by Duthie, completed a memorable fight back by Dunfermline. Excitement was high when the Athletic had to travel to Broomfield to meet Airdrie, the 'B' division leaders, in the sixth round. Sixty-three buses were specially chartered but the fans were to be disappointed when, for the first time that season, Dunfermline failed to score while Airdrie, brilliantly organised by Ian McMillan on an icebound pitch, scored seven.

However, the Pars' league fortunes continued to rise until they reached third top in April, one point behind Hamilton. In a crucial match the two challengers clashed at Douglas Park in a promotion decider which had all the hallmarks of a cup-tie. By winning 1–0, Dunfermline moved into second place, held on to it by beating Forfar 5–1 and gained promotion as runners-up to Airdrie.

At the AGM the club looked back with some satisfaction at the ground improvements they had made over the last three seasons – an enclosure erected; the centre stand and pavilion re-roofed; gas fires in the dressing-rooms; a new hot water system; extra toilets; tiled baths; crush barriers; an improved car park and the stand extended and fitted out with 3,000 seats from the defunct ice-rink. John Spears was elected chairman with David Thomson taking over as vice-chairman. When asked by the Scottish League for their opinion of TV cameras being allowed into grounds, Dunfermline voted against the idea.

Above: *Team of January 1955, who helped Dunfermline to promotion. Standing: Laird, Samuel, Duthie, Mackin, Chalmers, Mackie. Seated: McKinlay, O'Brien, Dickson, Reilly, Anderson. (Photographed at Ochilview.)*

Below: *The first of the two penalty goals scored by skipper Duthie against Partick in the Cup. (M. Allan)*

No sooner had Ancell accepted a new contract worth £15 per week than he left at the end of July to take up the manager's job at Motherwell where he was to produce his 'Ancell Babes' including Ian St John, Pat Quinn and Bert McCann. Andy Dickson, the club's trainer and physiotherapist, was chosen out of 12 applicants to succeed his old boss. As a young man, Dickson had fought with the Black Watch at Dunkirk and Normandy. Stern struggles also awaited him at East End Park over the next five years. One of his first signings was Falkirk reject, George Peebles (19), a clever ball player, bought from Dunipace Juniors for £100. Other early signings included 17-year-old forward, John Millar, purchased from Cowdenbeath for £1,500 and Gerry McWilliam, signed on a free transfer from Airdrie, who swelled the squad to 36 players.

Below: *Chairman John Spears.* (M. Allan)

Bottom: *Manager Andy Dickson.* (M. Allan)

Right: *George Peebles.*

In the League Cup, Dunfermline were drawn against Clyde, Hibs and Aberdeen, all formidable teams. The Pars created a sensation by beating Clyde, the Scottish Cup holders, by 4 goals to 2 at East End Park. Dunfermline were unable to maintain this form and eventually Aberdeen, the league champions, qualified and indeed went on to beat St Mirren in the final.

Dunfermline made an equally promising start in the league and after four successive victories found themselves second top by October. On the 17th of that month the talented left half, Billy Hume (19), was signed from Whitburn Juniors for £100 although he, like the ever-improving Charlie Dickson, often found himself unavailable because of National Service commitments. A new goalkeeper, Bill Beaton, was called up from Thornton Hibs to keep Mackin on his toes.

Though still near the top in November, the Pars' fortunes began to flag and by the end of December they had slipped half way down the table. The New Year brought a dramatic slump. The team lost their opening Scottish Cup match at Shawfield (5–0) and by February relegation loomed large. Following heavy defeats by Airdrie (7–3) and Hibs (7–1) the manager saw the necessity of buying a commanding centre half. Harry Colville, formerly of Raith Rovers, was signed from Falkirk for £1,200, and remained a full-time player. He helped steady the defence and took over as captain from Duthie. A 4–1 victory on 7 April over Clyde, also relegation candidates, and a midweek draw with Partick Thistle eased the situation, although not until a home victory (3–2) over Raith Rovers was secured on April 18 could the club breathe safely. A 1–0 victory over league champions, Rangers, in the last home game was an added bonus and drew a record crowd for a midweek game at East End – 13,500.

The AGM reported that the crowds certainly liked 'A' Division football in so far as gates went up threefold; wages and expenses also rose, leaving the club with only a small profit. The manager blamed injuries and the heavy pitch for the club's near disastrous run of defeats. A treatment room was set up in a bid to have players back to fitness in a shorter time. Robert Torrie was appointed to the Board in place of Hugh McMillan who retired. For the new season red jerseys and white pants were ordered though, as a result of arguments, the strip was used only as a second choice outfit.

The opening of the 1956-57 season saw the Pars do battle against Kilmarnock, Queen of the South and St Mirren in the League Cup. By beating the 'Buddies' in the last game, Dunfermline qualified for the first time as a First Division side for the quarter-finals against Celtic. In the first leg at Parkhead before 22,000 fans Dunfermline were hammered 6–0 but in the return game they restored some of their pride by winning 3–0. Celtic went on to win the trophy.

For the forthcoming season the call of National Service continued to deprive Dunfermline of key players like O'Brien and Peebles. For the first time the Scottish League allowed the second half of the games to be floodlit, provided both clubs agreed. This development avoided the

Billy Hume (left) and Jimmy Watson. (Dunfermline Press)

need for early starts during the winter and was hailed as a great innovation.

The lights, however, failed to shine on Dunfermline. Their form in the league, now re-named Division One, was very disappointing, causing attendances to drop alarmingly to a mere 7,000. By the end of the year the team lay fifth from the bottom and with fewer points than at the corresponding stage the previous season. Their Scottish Cup foray did not prove to be any more exciting for the fans. In February they beat Morton 3–0 at home only to lose 1–0 at Love Street in a very close game. In March, top scorer George O'Brien was sold to Leeds for £6,000. He later went to Southampton where he had a most successful career.

The spring brought yet another relegation struggle. The manager blamed poor refereeing and the fact that a dozen games had been lost by the odd goal. The only consolation for Dunfermline was that fellow strugglers East Fife and Queen of the South were also losing vital games. Not for the first (or the last) time the Pars' fate hinged on the last game of the season, when the visitors were none other than the mighty Rangers seeking only one point to pip Hearts for the League Championship.

Dunfermline were level on points with Queen of the South but as the Palmerston side had a worse goal average and faced a tough match at Parkhead, the Pars hoped that even one point might be enough to save them. On Monday 29 April the crowds packed into East End Park to witness what promised to be an epic struggle. After the regulation 90 minutes the match was tied at 3–3, enough to give Rangers the championship and to throw Dunfermline a lifeline. Then tragedy struck. As the crowd whistled for full-time Rangers' South African forward, Johnny Hubbard, sent a ball right across the goalmouth; Scott returned it and there was Simpson to slot the ball in the net. To compound Dunfermline's misery, word then came through from Parkhead that a goalless draw had saved Queen of the South. So near and yet so far!

Goalkeeper Bill Beaton (left) and Ron Mailer. (Dunfermline Press)

Goalkeeper Eddie Connachan.

Though disappointed, the Pars were determined to regain their First Division status at the first attempt. "Back in one season" became the new catch phrase. A new chairman, Mr David Thomson, took over the running of the club with Mr Tom Younger as vice-chairman. During the close season a new 150-feet covered enclosure was erected over the north terracing, the old structure being used as a cover for the West End. The new structure cost almost £7,500 and gave cover for 10,000 fans. A new goalkeeper, a 22-year-old miner by the name of Eddie Connachan, quietly signed on from Dalkeith Thistle. Mackin was subsequently transferred to Ayr for £300 and Felix Reilly was sold to Dundee for a welcome £3,250. Former Scottish cap, Jimmy Watson, a player with fine ball control, was bought from Huddersfield Town for £1,250 and proved a useful addition as did another new arrival later in the season, half back Ian Bain, bought from Raith for £600.

The new season, 1957-58, started in customary fashion with the League Cup. Cowdenbeath, Ayr and Brechin provided the opposition for Dunfermline with the Angus club going forward to the quarter-finals. Greater promise was shown in the league. The Pars won their first game against St Johnstone by the encouraging scoreline of 7–1 and after 10 games they stood in fourth top position. With gates of between 5,000 and 6,000, Dunfermline were regarded as one of the "rich men" of their division, easily outstripping their rivals in drawing power. By November, after 13 games, the club stood in second position with 19 points. During that month Charles Napier from Bonnybridge Juniors and John Sweeney, two promising youngsters, made their league debuts.

At the same time an interesting editorial appeared in the match programme on the question of floodlighting: "As Dunfermline was off the beaten track the club would find lucrative games difficult, if not impossible, to arrange. The future may, of course, hold higher hopes but meantime caution should be the guiding light." Little did the author realise how dramatically the picture would change in just four years' time.

In a bid to strengthen team morale and sharpen fitness, manager Dickson took his players away from 16-23 December for a week of full-time training at a cost of £100. A 4–0 thrashing of Cowdenbeath at first suggested that the money had been a good investment but then three successive defeats, two at home, saw promotion hopes flag. In the next game, however, the team beat Ayr and never lost another league game. The sale of Hume to Birmingham City in February for £5,000 failed to upset the rhythm of the team. An excellent replacement for him was quickly found in one of the club's best buys ever – a young Dockyard apprentice, Alec Smith (17), signed from Dunbar United for £80. Smith, whose father had also played for Dunfermline, had already turned down the chance to join Sunderland.

In the Scottish Cup, the Pars overcame Alloa 2–0 at Recreation Park. Another away fixture in the second round saw them record a handsome 4–1 victory over St Mirren, thanks to a hat-trick from Dickson; indeed, there was a double celebration that day when the reserves, now playing in the East of Scotland League, set a record by trouncing Gala Fairydean 16–1 at East End Park. The next round on 1 March gave Dunfermline a plum home draw against Rangers. The teams were:

Dunfermline: Beaton; Duthie, Sweeney; Bain, Colville, Mailer; Peebles, McWilliam, Dickson, Watson, Napier.

Rangers: Ritchie; Shearer, Caldow; McColl, Telfer, Baird; Scott, Simpson, Murray, Brand, Hubbard.

A huge crowd of 24,377, an all-time record for a Scottish Cup-tie at East End Park, saw Rangers tested to the full. A strong claim for a penalty by Dunfermline for handling by the Rangers centre half was turned down. However, after thirteen minutes McWilliam scored first for Dunfermline. The Light Blues, true to tradition, fought back with determination and an equaliser by Murray after 31 minutes followed by a goal from Brand eight minutes later put the Ibrox side ahead, a lead which they held to the end.

The Cup did not detract from Dunfermline's main goal, the league, in which they had slipped to fourth position

Going for promotion, February 1958. Standing: Duthie, Sweeney, Beaton, Bain, Colville, Mailer. Seated: Peebles, McWilliam, Dickson, Watson, Napier. (Dundee Courier)

behind Stirling, Arbroath and Dumbarton. A good run in April, including a 9–1 win over Stranraer, took them into second spot. A simple 1–0 victory over Forfar finally secured promotion as runners-up to Stirling. Overall the club set a record for themselves by scoring 120 league goals in 36 matches. Regrettably this was 22 goals short of Raith's record of 142 in 36 games in 1937-38. In all matches played the team found the back of the net on 155 occasions. The Pars owed much of their success to top scorer, Charlie Dickson, who bagged 40 goals including four hat-tricks; McWilliam scored 29, Watson 26 and Duthie, the penalty king, recorded 14. Centre half Colville never missed a game. The reserves also won the East of Scotland League. The manager received a £100 bonus and his salary was raised to £18 per week.

Despite losing £12,000 in gate money as a result of relegation, the Board were determined to build for the future and to establish the club firmly in the top division. To that end it was decided that a full-time set of players was necessary. Eight players initially signed full-time contracts with 18 players remaining part-time; manager Dickson went to Birmingham for a week to study the training methods of Aston Villa. A decision was also taken to erect floodlighting which would not only allow midweek games in the winter, but would also allow for more effective evening training. The only Fife club to have lights was East Fife. In an important move behind the scenes the Board finally tightened their control over the club and ended the squabbles which had bedevilled the club's affairs since the war. The directors forced through a motion at a specially convened meeting to the effect that future decisions would not be taken on a count of heads (which would have given individual shareholders a great deal of power), but would be based on the number of shares a person held. This meant that the directors, who had bought up most of the shares, were relatively immune from sudden dismissal and could now devote their attention to the area where it mattered most – the football field.

On the personnel front another bargain was snatched up when Harry Melrose was signed on a free transfer from Rangers. His brother, Robin, had been signed the previous year from Dalkeith but had failed to make the grade. Another newcomer was the £1,000 buy from Kilmarnock, Willie Harvey. Two well-known players, Samuel and McKinlay, left the club. Liverpool FC showed an interest

63

in Peebles but received no encouragement from Dunfermline. Club doctor, Dr J. Black, retired after 30 years' service and a new trainer, Mr Jimmy Stevenson, was employed at £14 per week. As an incentive to the players the club agreed to organise a close season tour to Switzerland in 1959 if Division One status were maintained.

Dunfermline awaited the new season with relish. Success came in the opening stages of the League Cup when they overcame Stirling, East Fife and Brechin to enter the quarter-finals. The Pars were once again to realise that the jump from Second to First Division opposition was indeed a great one when First Division stalwarts, Kilmarnock, beat them 4–1 at Rugby Park in the first leg. Although Dunfermline managed a 3–3 draw in the return leg their interest in the cup was over.

In the league, the Athletic found themselves struggling yet again. Out of the first six games only three points were gained and 24 goals were conceded. In one of their fixtures, against Raith on 6 September, referee 'Tiny' Wharton had to abandon the match after 31 minutes because of torrential rain and lightning, one of the few times this has happened at East End Park. To bolster a shaky defence, Dickson signed a new goalkeeper, Jim Herriot (18), from Douglasdale Water for £80 and established 'keeper Beaton was transferred to Aston Villa for £4,500. Connachan took over as first team choice.

At the same time, the Development Club was started to raise money for the club to finance new projects and soon had almost 10,000 members. It was becoming all too obvious to Dunfermline, and other provincial clubs, that a club could never survive, let alone expand, solely on the money that was handed over the turnstiles on a match day. Over the years, this new Club was to give thousands of pounds to keep the Athletic in the top division.

Although the team was playing badly, George Peebles caught the eye of the SFA selectors and he was chosen as an

Jackie Williamson (left) and Alec Smith. (Dunfermline Press)

Under-23 reserve for the national team against Wales. The media also took an interest in the club and history was made when BBC television cameras made their first recording at East End Park on 13 December against Dundee. They appeared again on the screen during the Ibrox game on 24 January 1959 and during the next decade were to make countless appearances. Initially, the TV cameras filmed from a structure perilously suspended from the north enclosure roof.

In the New Year, the Pars had their best run in the Scottish Cup since 1936. In the first round 10,206 paid £110 to see Dunfermline draw 2–2 with Cowdenbeath at Central Park; in the replay, the Athletic went through 4–1. This victory was followed by two more – against Montrose (away) by 1 goal to nil and against Ayr at home, 2–0. In a sternly contested fourth-round match, Dunfermline were just pipped 2–1 at Love Street by St Mirren, the eventual winners of the trophy.

Their relative success in the Cup could not make up for their slump in the league. By February, they had fallen to fourth bottom place with only 20 points from 25 games. Defender Jackie Williamson was bought from Raith in March to strengthen the defence and the £1,500 purchase proved to be a good investment. However, a 7–1 thrashing by Third Lanark at Cathkin Park left Dunfermline as firm relegation candidates. Once more the fates decided that Dunfermline's future would hang on the last game of the season on 18 April. Queen of the South were already doomed, but who would join them? Dunfermline and Falkirk were tied on 26 points though the latter had a better goal average and were due to play Raith at Brockville. Aberdeen had one point more, but had to play title-chasing Rangers at Ibrox. The Dons astonished everyone by beating Rangers 2–1 (who still took the title thanks to Celtic beating second placed Hearts). John White missed a penalty for Falkirk who only managed a 2–2 draw.

Dunfermline, however, did not require favours from anyone. Of their opponents, Partick Thistle, the match

Melrose scoring against Stirling Albion. (Dunfermline Press)

Above: *The reward for staying in Division One – officials and players and their wives in Switzerland, the club's first trip of many to the Continent.*

programme commented: "Our visitors have a reputation of lacking in consistency; on their game, they can rise to great heights and again can fade into obscurity". A dramatic 10–1 victory for Dunfermline guaranteed that this would be one game that would never slip into obscurity. Rangers' reject, Melrose, was the hero, scoring six goals (a record for a winger in a game); Peebles (2), Smith and Dickson were the other scorers. The Jags' centre half was none other than Jimmy Davidson, a Scottish internationalist with eight caps. Partick sportingly clapped the victors off the field. The heroes were: Connachan; Bain, Sweeney; Rattray, Colville, Mailer; Peebles, Smith, Dickson, Watson, Melrose.

During the close season, while the team were enjoying their promised holiday in Switzerland, a storm broke behind the scenes. While the recently formed Development Club had contributed £6,800 over 10 months, the longer established Supporters' Club had donated £7,270 over 10 years though their labour was often considerable. A rift broke out between the directors and the Supporters' Club which resulted in the latter being obliged to vacate their premises at East End Park. Eventually they found new premises in St Margaret's Street where, in the following January, they opened their very successful club at Jubilee House.

Three interesting signings for the new season were the young defender George Miller, from Royal Albert (£150) who was destined to be a future captain and manager; John 'Cammy' Fraser, another promising defender, from Gairdoch, Falkirk (£20); and David Thomson (19), a centre for-

Jim Stevenson (left) and Cammy Fraser. (Dunfermline Press)

ward from Bo'ness (£200). George Duthie left after six years of loyal service. Jimmy Watson ceased playing and was appointed coach; in October he resigned and Bain became player-coach. Later Jim Stevenson, a half back, joined the club on a free transfer from Dundee.

In the new season, 1959-60, Dunfermline disappointingly failed to make any progress in their League Cup section comprising St Mirren, Third Lanark and Clyde. Manager Dickson squashed any signs of panic with the statement: "I am in full charge. We trust there will be no talk of relegation as the season progresses." There were certainly no thoughts of doom in the club's mind as they prepared for their gala night on 26 October against Sheffield

United who had kindly agreed to a challenge match to inaugurate the new £12,000 floodlighting system which did something to remove the gloom from East End Park. In front of 9,000 spectators and the town band on a wet, miserable night, Provost Frederick performed the honours which opened up yet another chapter in Dunfermline's history. Dunfermline lost the game 4–3 although they had better fortune in the next two challenge games – a 2–2 draw against Inverness Caledonian and a 5–2 victory over Birmingham.

After 10 games in the league, the team had picked up only eight points. There was little consolation for fans to read in the press that one of their former players, Jimmy Millar, had now been capped by Scotland. The arrival of Hearts record goal-scorer, Jimmy Wardhaugh, for £2,000, could not prevent the Pars slipping to third bottom place in November; in that month Harry Colville's remarkable run of 178 consecutive matches came to an end. A more depressing statistic was the failure of the team to win an away league game in 1959. Clearly, the club faced an uphill struggle if they were to avoid relegation.

In the Scottish Cup, the team also struggled, only managing a 1–1 draw against St Johnstone in front of a 10,500 crowd at East End Park. Any hope that was raised by the splendid 4–1 victory in the replay was quickly dashed by a 5–0 home drubbing by Rangers in the league in front of 20,000 fans. Though January brought Dunfermline little success on the playing field, the turnstiles clicked away merrily with a 12,000 crowd for the Raith Rovers derby and 15,000 for the Hearts game in addition to the gates

Players and officials at the start of season 1959-60. Back row: Ferguson, Davidson, Wilson, McWilliam, Reid, Drennan, Fraser, Logan. Middle: J. Watson (coach), J. Stevenson (trainer), Brett, Miller, Rattray, Peebles, Herriot, Connachan, Sweeney, Rowan, Smith, Melrose, Thomson, R. Bell (groundsman), E. Dowie (asst trainer). Front: Dickson, Colville, R. Torrie, A. N. Watson, A. Dickson (manager), D. Thomson (chairman), J. Anderson, Bain, Williamson. (Dundee Courier)

from the St Johnstone and Rangers ties. Some of the cash was used to buy Jim Kerray from Raith for £3,600 to freshen up the attack.

The final straw for a perplexed manager came in February when his team suffered a humiliating 3–2 home defeat in the Cup to Second Division Stenhousemuir, managed by former player, George Samuel. With his club out of the Cup (where a lucrative tie against Rangers would have awaited them) and lying second bottom in the league with only four wins, Dickson resigned on the 22nd of the month. (Though guaranteed a job with the club as trainer, Dickson left at the end of the season to join the backroom staff of Dundee FC.) The vacant post was advertised in the national press with the successful applicant guaranteed full control of the playing staff, scouting and coaching. But who would want to take over a struggling, inconsistent club seemingly destined to bob up and down between the two divisions like a yo-yo?

One man was delighted to jump at the offer, an unknown quantity called John Stein, aged 37, from Hamilton, who did not apply for the job but had been invited along by the Board. On 14 March, the Board "welcomed Mr Stein, the new manager, and wished him every success". If the former miner had been run over there and then by the proverbial bus he would have merited, at best, a footnote in the annals of football history. Signed from Blantyre Victoria in 1942 he spent seven fairly unimpressive seasons as centre half with Albion Rovers shoring up their weak defence. Indeed, on one of his rare visits to East End Park as a player on 1 October 1949, Stein was powerless to prevent George Henderson scoring three goals in a 4–1 victory. In 1949 he drifted out of the Scottish game and into seeming oblivion when he joined the Welsh non-League side, Llanelly Town.

In a surprise move in December 1951 he was signed by Celtic and within a year, because of team injuries, had been appointed captain. Though not possessing the natural flair

Vital relegation game against Kilmarnock, 4 April 1960, before a crowd of 20,000.

and guile of team-mates like Tully and Collins, Stein used his talents to the full and operated as a solid, dependable centre half. Under his captaincy, Celtic won the Coronation Cup in 1953 and the League and Cup double the following season which earned him a cap against the English League in 1954. Although a niggling ankle injury forced him to retire from playing in 1956, he remained at Parkhead coaching the youngsters and bringing on such raw recruits as Billy McNeill and Pat Crerand. When the Dunfermline invitation arrived on his doorstep he had already rejected an offer from Partick Thistle to be their new manager. Stein could not have chosen a tougher baptism at East End Park where his new charges lay second bottom in the league with only 17 points from 28 games; they were two points and two games adrift of fellow strugglers, Aberdeen. Stein was realistic, announcing on his arrival: "The team is in a precarious situation. I have no magic wand."

The manager worked something near a miracle on the dispirited and apparently doomed Athletic team. He was later to confess that "we had a lot of luck, we got the breaks", but clearly there was evidence of a great tactician at work. He immediately realised that a defence which had lost 74 goals in 28 games needed to be tightened up. "I knew that if we did not lose goals we could not lose

games," he later stated. "I was not interested in forming a Real Madrid. I just wanted a team which would win points. I don't mean we decided to concentrate on defence, but you can go somewhere from a tight defence."

His first game in charge could not have been more daunting – against his old club, Celtic. A goal from Dickson in the first 10 seconds (probably a record at East End Park) calmed the home side and a further two goals in two minutes from Melrose gave Stein his first victory (3–2) which also gave the club their first win since 21 November 1959. A fine 2–0 victory at Love Street (Dickson scoring after 40 seconds) saw the Pars record their first away win since 1 November 1958, enough to raise them to third bottom spot. While Stein quickly discovered he had some fine players under him he also found that, collectively, his team had weaknesses. It soon became his habit to clear the dressing room at 2.40 pm and talk to the team about the opposition, stressing the strengths and weaknesses of individuals and indicating how he wanted the game played. As a result his side quickly began to play as one unit instead of 11 individuals.

Stein's success continued in a rearranged fixture against Cup finalists, Kilmarnock, who were also chasing Hearts for the championship. A brilliant 40-yard shot from Mailer was enough to give Dunfermline victory (1–0) and lift them to fourth bottom position while at the same time ending the Ayrshire club's run of 21 games without defeat. To give his players a chance to savour the big occasion, Stein took his players to Hampden on Saturday 9 April to see Scotland draw 1–1 with England. In their last home game Dunfermline beat Airdrie 1–0 and went three points clear of the relegation zone. On the same day, the other relegation candidates, Aberdeen and Stirling, fought out a bitter battle with the latter falling into deeper trouble.

When the Pars continued their winning run by defeating Clyde 3–1 at Shawfield, the town went wild. Dunfermline were safe from relegation; Jock Stein had pulled the club back from the very jaws of disaster. The team went on to finish in style, beating the doomed Stirling Albion 4–1 at Annfield and achieving in the process their best ever run in the First Division: six victories on the trot. A defence which had leaked like a sieve throughout the season conceded only four goals in six matches. Stein's plan had been vindicated Harry Colville, the lynch-pin of the defence and the club's most senior player, decided to hang up his boots and become the manager of Cowdenbeath. In May, Leonard Jack, the club's legal adviser and the man who had been instrumental in bringing Stein to Dunfermline, strengthened his links with the club by joining the Board in the place of James Anderson who had earlier resigned.

While the club were congratulating themselves in staying in the First Division, 1,586 fans were lucky enough to draw the club's allocation of tickets to the epic European Cup Final at Hampden between Real Madrid and Eintracht. Little did that small group of privileged fans, and the thousands who watched with wonder at their TV screens, realise that European football was soon to come to East End Park.

Rapt attention from the Dunfermline bench: Eddie Dowie, Ian Bain, Jock Stein and Jimmy Stevenson.

THE GOLDEN YEARS
The 1960s

Jock Stein (1960–64)

Jock Stein, as a Celtic player, in 1953. He was born in Bellshill in 1922 and worked full-time as a miner until the age of 27. (Glasgow Herald)

If the 'fifties had been the decade of "blood, sweat and tears" for the club then it could be said of the 'sixties that "this was their finest hour". Sweeping aside relegation worries as if forever the team were to challenge for the game's top honours not just at home but even in Europe. In the process, East End Park was transformed from a mediocre Second Division ground into one of the finest stadiums in Scotland. Many of the players and the managers were to become well-known throughout the land.

To find information now on the club's exploits the historian has not just to read the local newspapers but to turn to the national and international press for a balanced view. For almost a decade the Pars were to show that a provincial club of humble background and limited resources could vigorously challenge the richer, well-established city clubs, and give a good account of themselves. A passport, a foreign phrase book, an airline ticket, a continental map and a visa became as essential to the Pars' fan of the 'sixties as the *Wee Red Book* and a bus timetable had been to his father and grandfather. The Burt Bacharach hit of the swinging 'sixties, *Trains and Boats and Planes*, was never more appropriate than to Dunfermline Athletic Football Club.

Jock Stein, fresh from a coaching school at Leicester addressed by the trainer of the Hungarian FA, and his squad of 11 full-timers and 14 part-timers were not even to dream of this when the new season of 1960–61 began. Stein's aim was simple – "I am not aiming for the League or the Cup, but to establish Dunfermline as a First Division club."

No progress was made in their League Cup section of Airdrie, Hibs and Kilmarnock. Killie, runners-up in the League and Scottish Cup, were enjoying a purple spell in their history and easily topped the group on their way to the final. Dunfermline made a better start to the league, recording their first ever league victory at Pittodrie in the opening weeks. National recognition was given to one of the team's promising youngsters when 20-year-old Alec Smith was chosen for the Scottish League to play at Belfast. Offers and approaches for him from Leicester, Hearts, Aston Villa and Arsenal were firmly rejected. A £6,000 offer from Huddersfield, however, for Jim Kerray was accepted.

Stein added depth to his squad with several shrewd signings, a talent with which the manager was generously blessed – Jackie Sinclair signed from Blairhall Colliery for £100; Willie Callaghan was acquired from Crossgates Primrose for even less; 28-year-old Tommy McDonald, formerly of Hibs and Wolves, was purchased for £2,600 from Leicester City who also released Willie Cunningham, the former St Mirren and Irish internationalist, for £1,850. As part of the deal, Leicester travelled north to play a friendly under the lights and, despite the skilful Gordon Banks in goal, lost 3–2.

The bubble burst, however, when Motherwell inflicted a 6–1 defeat on Dunfermline at East End Park on 24 September, the club's first league defeat since Stein took over.

The start of the season 1960-61. Back row: McDonald, Rattray, McKechnie, Logan, Herriot, Thomson, Duncan, Stewart, Callaghan. Middle: Stevenson, Bain, Sinclair, Benvie, Williamson, Wardhaugh, Sweeney, Connachan, Miller, Clark, Fraser, Kerray, E. Downie, R. Bell. Front: Dickson, Peebles, Melrose, L. Jack, A. Watson, T. Younger, D. Thomson, J. Stein, R. Torrie, J. McConville, Mailer, Smith, Stevenson. (Dundee Courier)

Not long afterwards the young Jim Herriot made his first-team debut in goal. Dan McLindon was bought from Bellshill Athletic for £200 and proved to be another excellent acquisition by Stein. The team even made it, albeit temporarily, to fourth top position in the league. Despite the loss of Jim Stevenson from a leg-break on 3 December at Easter Road, the club were sitting comfortably with 17 points from 17 games by the end of the year. Humbug Park at Crossgates was bought for £500 by the club to give players every opportunity for proper match practice. Further victories in the New Year against Hearts (their first at Tynecastle for seven years) and against Motherwell allowed the club to consolidate its league position and to take a more relaxed attitude towards the Scottish Cup.

The first round drew the Pars and Berwick Rangers out of the hat, the game to be played at the English ground on 28 January. A special train of 300 fans and numerous cars and buses made the trip to swell the crowd to 4,150 (receipts £525). Another wasted journey looked on the cards when the home side struck first. However, goals from Dickson, McLindon (2) and Smith saw the Athletic safely through to the second round. Further national honours came to Dunfermline players when Dickson was chosen as a reserve for the Scottish League team while Miller was included in the Under-23 squad to play the Army at Motherwell.

With relegation worries easing, the Pars made the long trip to Stranraer for their second round match on 11 February before a crowd of 2,750 (receipts £280). By way of planning, the meticulous Stein had organised training on small pitches to prepare his team for the tight confines of Stair Park. In a tough encounter, Melrose had the ball in the net no less than four times before his fifth attempt was allowed to stand and then Dickson added a second goal. A goal from Beaton put the home side back in contention before McDonald made victory secure.

Dunfermline's hopes of progressing further in the Cup received a setback when the next round handed them yet another long distance away draw, to Aberdeen, the 1959 beaten finalists. A crowd of 15,455 (receipts £1,780) packed into Pittodrie to witness a right ding-dong battle. After 11 minutes Brownlee put Aberdeen in the lead; counter-blows from Smith, Dickson and McDonald seemed to put the game beyond the Dons when Brownlee scored his second goal to put the tie wide open. Dunfermline put their heads down and two more goals, from Melrose and Peebles, decided the tie. Coutts and Miller added further goals for their clubs to make the final score 6–3 in Dunfermline's favour.

Fortune finally favoured the Pars with a home draw, against Alloa. On 11 March, exactly a year since Stein joined the club, a crowd of 10,790 (receipts £1,131) saw goals from Peebles (2), McDonald and Melrose which put Dunfermline 4–0 up after only 23 minutes. No further goals were scored, but these were enough to put Dunfermline into the semi-finals for the first time ever.

Amidst great excitement and anticipation Dunfermline met their old cup rivals, St Mirren, at Tynecastle on 1 April. Amongst the 31,930 crowd were 10,000 Pars' fans who witnessed a 0–0 draw, perhaps a moral victory for the Fife club who played for the last 35 minutes with only 10 men after Dickson had to retire injured following a clash with Clunie. In the replay before 16,741 a Melrose drive in 67 minutes was deflected off defender Stewart into the net to produce the only goal of the game. Dunfermline were ecstatic and fans booked their tickets for Hampden. The Northern Ireland FA acknowledged Cunningham's sterling defensive qualities by giving him his 31st cap against Wales and selecting him for the forthcoming World Cup series. Once again the Athletic had internationalists on their books!

Stein was the first to appreciate that though reaching the final for the first time was most commendable, winning the trophy would require even greater endeavour, especially when the opposition would be Celtic, proud winners on 17 previous occasions. It was Stein's task to ensure that his players were mentally attuned for the heady atmosphere of a big game. He bought his players new outfits of blazers and flannels to give them a sense of identity and to raise their morale. Seamill Hydro at West Kilbride was booked

Above: *Stein and Stevenson talk to their players a few days before the final (l to r): McLindon, Peebles, Fraser, Cunningham, Thomson, Miller and McDonald (seated).* (Dundee Courier)

Right: *Referee Hugh Phillips watches the two captains shake hands: Duncan McKay and Ron Mailer.*

as a retreat where players and staff could unwind and plan the downfall of Celtic. Stein later commented: "The most difficult thing with a provincial club is to instill in them the idea that they are as good as the big city clubs. If you treat players in a small time fashion you get a small return. Treat them big and the return is big." Throughout his first season, Stein had done all he could to promote this confidence and enthusiasm: players were driven in style to see big midweek matches; the club took out membership at Pitreavie Golf Course and lunch vouchers were issued for a local restaurant.

A 6–0 defeat in the league by Clyde on 12 April certainly brought the club down to earth again. Nothing, however, could dampen the enthusiasm and fever that gripped the town as the big day approached – Saturday 22 April, Hampden Park, kick-off at 3.00 pm. Thirty thousand Dunfermline fans made the pilgrimage to Scotland's national stadium to boost the crowd to 113,228, the largest crowd the Pars had ever played before (and ever would, for that matter). The teams lined up as follows:

Dunfermline: Connachan; Fraser, Cunningham; Mailer, Williamson, Miller; Peebles, Smith, Dickson, McLindon, Melrose.

Celtic: Haffey; McKay, Kennedy; Crerand, McNeill, Clark; Gallacher, Fernie, Hughes, Chalmers, Byrne.

Dunfermline winger, Tommy McDonald, should have been in the line-up but was forced to withdraw on the eve of the match because of appendicitis.

Roared on by the crowd, two and a half times the population of Dunfermline, the Pars kicked off. Right from the start the game was played at a tremendous pace. Though Dunfermline were often out-shouted they were never out-played, giving as good as they received. The game was hard, but never dirty. In the seventh minute, McLindon, brought in for the indisposed McDonald, should have scored from a Melrose free-kick. Despite the lack of scoring, the game was full of excitement. The Athletic defence did well to contain a lively Celtic forward line which had previously beaten them at Parkhead in the league. Undoubtedly, the inspired goalkeeping of Eddie Connachan helped drive the Pars on as he thwarted the Celtic attack on several occasions. Dunfermline were handicapped when centre half Williamson was injured and had to leave the field before the end of the first half. He returned in the second half, only to go off again and finally reappear on the wing for the last five minutes. In the last few minutes of the game a move from Melrose and Peebles almost produced the winning goal for Dunfermline. Stein felt his team had done enough to win the game.

On Wednesday 26th, the replay went ahead at Hampden before a crowd of 87,660. Since floodlighting had not yet been installed in the stadium the match kicked off at 6.15 pm. Celtic were forced to make one change when full back Kennedy also took appendicitis and had to withdraw in favour of the young O'Neill who, without any league games under his belt, was choosing a fine night to make his first-team debut. With the injured Williamson being unable to play, Stein was forced to make several changes: Sweeney was brought in as left half, allowing Miller to take over as centre half, while up front Thomson replaced McLindon. Final tactics were worked out at a secret training session in the afternoon at Douglas Park, Hamilton.

The replay was as exciting and as evenly contested as the first game. In the first half, both sides had excellent chances to open the scoring; indeed, Hughes had the ball in the back of the net only to have it ruled offside. In the second half, Celtic stepped up the pressure and would have scored on several occasions but for a series of brilliant saves from Connachan who was having the game of his life which reduced the Celtic attack to absolute despair. Just as the Fifers seemed to be on their knees they dramatically took the lead in 68 minutes. Thomson passed to Peebles and raced in on the winger's return cross. On the way, the ball came off a Celtic defender to allow Thomson, bending low, to nod the ball well out of Haffey's reach.

The tempo increased as Celtic threw everything into attack for the equaliser while Dunfermline resolutely defended. As the minutes ticked away, Alec Smith chipped forward a lob which Haffey first clutched, then dropped in front of the on-rushing Dickson. The forward could hardly believe his luck as he poked the ball into the net. The Cup was on its way to the Auld Grey Toun for the first time ever! In their 76th year, Dunfermline had won the 76th Cup Final.

The triumphant journey home gave the team an idea of what to expect in Dunfermline as the villages of Cumbernauld, Dennyloanhead, Bonnybridge, Larbert, and Kincardine turned out in their thousands to cheer on the cup-winners. In Dunfermline, thousands thronged the streets to make the scene something like Hogmanay, the Gala Day and VE Day all rolled into one. Assembling at the public park at 10.30 pm in the traditional, open-topped double decker, the exuberant party set off through packed and delirious crowds to the civic reception in the City Chambers. A deafening cheer went up when Ron Mailer held up the coveted trophy from the balcony.

Inspired goalkeeping from Connachan as he deflects a raging shot from Hughes.

Above: *Goal number one – a diving header from Thomson beats Haffey*. (Dunfermline Press)

Below: *Ron Mailer held aloft with the Cup*. (Daily Record)

Chairman David Thomson caught the mood of the moment when he remarked at the reception: "It has been an uphill fight to put the Athletic on the map. No longer are we regarded as a fourth rate combination: we are in the top class division. We intend to remain at the top. We are now on a par with the greatest clubs in the world and we are going to make sure we have the facilities to meet teams like Real Madrid and Barcelona in Dunfermline."

Once the cup excitement had died down, Stein signed a new contract on 1 May tying him to the club for another five years. The Board decided to plough their cup profits into a new stand, to be built the following year at a cost of £60,000. A special stand appeal inviting patrons to take out 10-year loans at 5% interest was instituted by director Leonard Jack. This fund would mean that players would not have to be sold to finance it. As Stein put it: "If we had accepted offers for players we could have built two new stands. Eight players could have been transferred for considerable sums but we have no intention of considering them now. We want a top class stand for our supporters to watch a first class team."

During this most eventful period in the club's history, one appointment went completely unnoticed – a 15-year-old schoolboy left his local secondary school at Rosyth and was employed as an assistant to the groundsman. The youth was Alec Edwards who was to help the club to even greater triumphs.

Above: *Climbing the steps of the City Chambers are: Peebles, Melrose, Fraser, Miller, Dickson, Mailer and Connachan.*

Below: *A jubilant Dunfermline team on the open-decked bus.*

Above: *The team acknowledges the acclaim of the crowd from the balcony of the City Chambers.* (Daily Record)

Below: *The triumphant party slowly winds its way down the High Street to make it a most memorable night in the town's long history.* (M. Allan)

Top left: *Spare a thought for one of the most unlucky men in Dunfermline – injured centre half, Jackie Williamson.*

Above: *Captain Ron Mailer with the two goalscorers – Dickson (left) and Thomson. (Dundee Courier)*

Below: *The successful team display their trophies of 1960-61 – the Fife Cup, the Scottish Cup and the Penman Cup. Back row: Fraser, Mailer, Connachan, Herriot, Miller, Sweeney, Cunningham. Middle: McLindon, Peebles, Smith, Thomson, Dickson, Melrose, McDonald, Williamson. Front: Stevenson, Jack, Torrie, Thomson, Watson, McConville, Stein. (Dunfermline Press)*

SEASON 1961-62

The pre-season trial matches which had been a long standing feature at East End Park were discontinued. Instead, the Pars undertook a new venture, a pre-season trip from 4-6 August to Northern Ireland where they played Coleraine. The club enjoyed warm hospitality and had the extra bonus of winning their game 2–1. Despite this extra preparation and the advantage of a squad which now had 18 full-timers in it, Dunfermline were unable to make any headway in the League Cup. In a group consisting of the Athletic, Motherwell, Dundee United and Aberdeen it was the Lanarkshire side which won through to the quarter-finals.

International honour was given to Dunfermline goalkeeper, Eddie Connachan, who was selected to play against the Irish League. Another hero of the cup final replay, goalscorer David Thomson, was transferred to Leicester for £8,000. The abolition of the maximum wage in England that year was increasingly to attract talent from East End Park as it was to do from all over Scotland. A more than adequate replacement was signed in the person of John Lunn (17), originally signed as an outside left from Blairhall Colliery but later converted by his new manager to a solid defender. Also added to the squad were two players who were to give outstanding service over the next decade: half back Jim Thomson, foolishly given away on a free transfer by St Mirren, and forward Bert Paton, acquired from Leeds United.

The Pars might have been forgiven for not being too excited about their League Cup campaign as the glamour of European competition now beckoned them. Dunfermline were only the fourth Scottish club to enter Europe, thus beating Celtic, Aberdeen and Dundee United to foreign shores. As Cup winners their name went into the hat for the draw of the European Cup Winners' Cup where they were paired with St Patrick's of Dublin in a preliminary round.

In the first leg at East End Park on 12 September 1961, 10,000 fans saw their team make a successful European debut by winning 4–1, the goals coming from Melrose, McDonald, Peebles and Dickson. The team was: Connachan; Fraser, Cunningham; Mailer, Miller, Duffy; McDonald, Smith, Dickson, Peebles, Melrose. The return leg two weeks later was the formality that it promised to be with the visitors notching another four goals through Peebles (2) and Dickson (2) without any conceded.

Safely into the next round, Dunfermline were to come face to face with the troubles and headaches that went hand in hand with the enchantment of Continental football. No one relished the gruelling trip behind the Iron Curtain to face the new opponents, Vardar from Skopje in Yugoslavia. In the early days of European football, no dates were set for playing matches and a great number of phone calls had to be made before the Yugoslavs finally arrived in Dunfermline on 25 October for the first leg. The home side easily won 5–0 in front of 12,000 fans, aided by the dismissal of a Yugoslav in the second half; Smith, Dickson (2), Melrose and Peebles were the scorers. Although Dunfermline lost the ferocious return leg 2–0, with no help from a fastidious referee who punished the visitors for almost every tackle, they had done enough to enter the quarter-finals and to keep their interest in Europe alive till the New Year.

In the more mundane world of league football, their bread and butter, Dunfermline made a poor start by winning only two games by the end of October. Their narrow win at Annfield on 4 November was their first away victory in the league since 10 April. Connachan continued to give inspired performances between the posts and was rewarded with a cap for the Scotland side which lost 4–2 after extra-time in the World Cup Qualifying Play-Off

Below: *European action at East End Park – Melrose scores goal number four against Vardar.* (Dunfermline Press)

match against Czechoslovakia in Brussels on 29 November. He thus became the first Dunfermline Athletic player since Andy Wilson to win a full cap for Scotland. Cammy Fraser was also selected for the Under-23 side against Wales. Stein was offered the vacant manager's job at Easter Road, but the Board refused to entertain the idea.

At the AGM in November, the chairman looked back with pride on a very successful year. He cautioned that while income during the year had doubled, expenditure had gone up threefold and that without the Development Club the football club would be in serious financial trouble. Stein hoped for a prosperous future – "I am sure that no club in Scotland has so many potential young players as our club and I am confident that in a year or two they will emulate anything we have done in the past season. The supporters need to bury their Second Division complex." With the club in so many different competitions and the bonus system becoming more complicated the club passed the payment of wages over to their accountants, J. Condie and Co, further evidence that the "big time" had truly arrived.

After their victory against Stirling Albion in November, Dunfermline made excellent progress in the league and enjoyed a run of 12 games without defeat, disposing of St Mirren 7–0 in the process. In that game, Dickson scored six goals and put his team fifth top at the turn of the year.

When the European competitions resumed, Dunfermline found themselves playing the crack Hungarian side, Ujpest Dozsa, conquerors of Ajax, in front of an 18,000 crowd in Budapest on 13 February. After only eight minutes, Dunfermline went into a shock 2–0 lead after goals from Smith (40 seconds) and McDonald. The home side rallied and two goals on the half hour mark brought them back into the game. Now that they had found their scoring touch the

Above: The Dunfermline party is entertained in the mayor's parlour in Skopje, later to be devastated by an earthquake.

Below: All great players must start somewhere – Alec Edwards as boot boy. (M. Allan)

Czechs scored another two while McDonald pulled one back to give the Fifers a tremendous chance of qualifying for the semi-finals at the first attempt.

East End Park was packed with 24,049 fans the following week to see if their team could overcome a one goal deficit. The fact that the final was to be played at Hampden gave added spice to the game. Despite much of the pressure the Pars could not break down a tightly drilled defence in which the goalkeeper and centre half were magnificent. In fact, it was the visitors who scored – a header from the brilliant young Bene early in the second half which killed off Dunfermline's hopes. This was to be the only home defeat which the Pars were to experience in 20 European ties. Stein, however, was pleased with his side's baptism in Europe and regarded the extra games and experience as a bonus for his developing protégés.

Meanwhile, Dunfermline had begun their defence of the Scottish Cup with emphatic home wins over Forfar (5–1) and the rabbits of the tournament, Wigtown and Bladnoch (9–0). Another home draw against Stenhousemuir seemed an easy passport, but the Pars were surprisingly held to a goalless draw by the "Warriors" though they coasted home comfortably in the replay, 3–0. In the quarter-finals, Dunfermline were paired once again with St Mirren at Love Street. This time the Paisley side scraped through by the only goal of the game to knock the holders out of the cup.

Although their interest in the cups was now over, the Pars continued to enjoy their best ever season in the league, reaching third position by March. On the 19th of that month, Alec Edwards, aged only 16 years, 5 days, made his

Above: *Dunfermline players doing a spot of sightseeing in Budapest.*

Below: *C. Dickson having his leg pulled by trainer Stevenson. Watching them are Stein, Edwards, W. Callaghan, Sinclair and Cunningham.* (M. Allan)

Above: *A training session at East End Park, March 1962.* (Dundee Courier)

Below: *The Dunfermline party pictured at Prestwick returning from their successful tour of Norway, May 1962.* (Dundee Courier)

senior debut for the club in their home match against Hibs, which was won 4–0. After their last home match against Kilmarnock on 24 March, the workmen moved in to dismantle the old stand in preparation for work to begin on the new structure over the close season. In the crucial league game on April 7, Dunfermline faced fellow championship contenders, Rangers, at Ibrox where Dunfermline had yet to achieve a victory. The Ibrox record remained intact with the 'Gers winning 1–0 to dash any lingering hopes the Pars still had of winning the title. The final table saw Dunfermline sit proudly on fourth position, their highest placing ever and good enough to challenge for a place in the Fairs Cup for the following season; it certainly made a pleasant contrast from relegation worries. Their tally of conceding only 15 league goals at home was a record unequalled throughout Britain. Well might the club feel satisfied as they set off on 6 May for a 13-day tour of Norway. When not admiring the scenery they played three games and convincingly won each – Hangar (8–0); Kristiansund FC (4–0); and Rosenborg Trondheim (3–1). The tour games allowed Edwards the chance to settle into the team pattern.

SEASON 1962–63

The squad showed few changes from the past season. Stout defender Jim McLean, signed towards the end of the pre-

The architect's impression of the new stand, Halbeath Road. (Dundee Courier)

vious season from Ayr for £1,500, quickly established himself in the side as a pillar of strength. Another notable newcomer was the darting winger, Tommy Callaghan, signed from Lochore Welfare for £20; once again the club had a set of brothers on their books and what a formidable pair they turned out to be. Andy Matthew and John Sweeney were released on free transfers.

In the League Cup, Dunfermline were paired with Kilmarnock, Airdrie and Raith Rovers. In their first game, which coincided with the opening of the new stand, the Pars encountered Kilmarnock who, ironically, were the last club to play in front of the old stand. Despite being 2–0 up at half-time Dunfermline failed to give the 7,400 crowd a victory, a 3–3 draw being the outcome. In the return game at Rugby Park, Killie beat Dunfermline, went on to the quarter-finals and only lost in the final to Hearts.

On 12 September, Dunfermline received the unexpected but welcome piece of news that they had just been accepted into the draw for the Inter-Cities Fairs Cup. Originally, Hearts, who had finished lower in the league than Dunfermline, were to be Scotland's representatives (along with Celtic) since the rules of the competition demanded that only major cities and not provincial towns like Dunfermline could compete. When a Greek club withdrew at the last minute the Athletic gratefuly accepted the vacant place. However, the football press did not give the Pars much of a chance when they were paired against Everton, nicknamed the "Bank of England" team because of the vast

Above: *The old stand being demolished, April 1962.* (M. Allan)

Below: *The proposed stand from inside the ground. The TV room near the roof was never built.* (Dundee Courier)

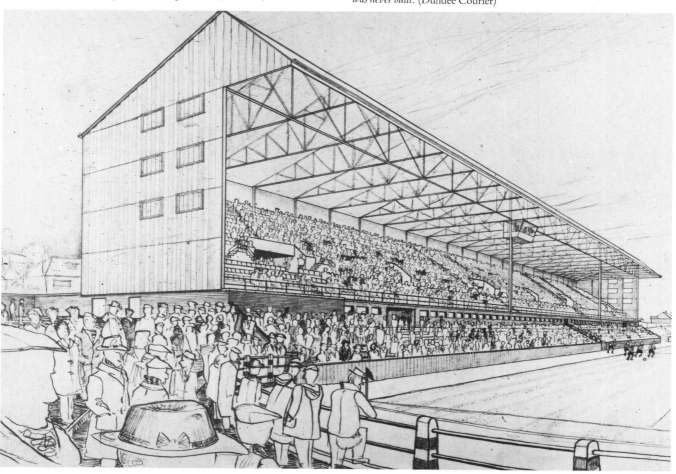

The new stand being well patronised during this floodlit match against Everton, October 1962.

sum of money which the club had spent on enticing players like Jimmy Gabriel (from Dundee), Alec Young (Hearts) and Billy Bingham (the future Ireland manager) to Goodison Park. The Merseyside team, managed by Harry Catterick, were considered clear favourites against the Scottish side which, by contrast, had cost very little to assemble. In fact, only two weeks before the first match, the Pars seemingly put themselves at a further disadvantage by transferring Cammy Fraser to Aston Villa for £23,500, a record for Dunfermline and also for a full back in Scotland. Stein later quipped that the stand should have been named after the defender, so welcome was his transfer fee.

Few gave the Athletic much of a chance as they lined up at Goodison Park for the first leg on 24 October in front of a crowd of 40,240. The teams were:

Dunfermline: Herriot;   Callaghan,   Cunningham;   Thomson, McLean, Miller; McLindon, Smith, Dickson, Melrose, Peebles.

Everton: West;   Parker,   Thomson;   Gabriel, Labone, Harris; Bingham, Stevens, Young, Vernon, Morrissey.

In a very hard match in which method was abandoned for muscle, Dunfermline's tight defensive wall was only breached once. After 25 minutes defender Cunningham had the misfortune to head a dangerous ball against the crossbar in an Everton attack. Despite protestations from the Dunfermline defence, the Irish referee judged that the ball had in fact crossed the line and awarded a goal to Everton. There was little constructive football in the second half and the visitors left the ground content that only one goal had been conceded and relieved that no one had been

seriously injured or attacked by the hostile crowd as they left the field.

A crowd of almost 23,000 crammed into East End Park the following week to see if their team, showing no changes in line-up, could pull off a shock victory. They did not have to wait long because after only five minutes, Miller crashed a 20-yard shot into the net. The game was played at a cracking pace with no quarter given by either side though it never degenerated into the foul play of the first leg. Both sides had their chances to clinch the tie, but it was Melrose, released by top defender Cunningham, who became the hero when with only three minutes to go he slotted the winner past the goalkeeper. The Pars' victory not only put them into the next round, it fixed them on the footballing map of Europe as a team worthy of respect.

The second round of the cup brought equally tough opponents in the form of Valencia, holders of the Fairs Cup and conquerors of Celtic in the previous round. On 12 December on a cold night in the Mastalla Stadium in Spain the team took the field in front of a crowd of 25,000. Right from the kick-off, Dunfermline were in trouble. Herriot dropped the ball from a free kick after only two minutes and the Spaniards were one up. Two more goals before the interval and one after it in the 52nd minute made it a dismal night for Scotland's representatives. As the 46-strong party returned to Turnhouse in the chartered Viscount, the *Press* noted that "only the most fanatical of Dunfermline supporters can now hope that the Athletic will qualify to meet Hibs in the third round".

Despite the apparently hopeless task that faced the team about 15,000 "fanatical" supporters did turn up on the

Stein and his players inspect the Stadium of Light in Lisbon before their vital play-off against Valencia. Only 3,000 spectators were to turn up.

frosty night of 19 December to find if Santa Claus was going to visit them this year. Jackie Sinclair and Alec Edwards replaced Dickson and McLindon from the first leg. The crowd tasted a sample of what was to come when Peebles almost scored after five minutes. Six minutes later, Dunfermline did score when the same player headed an Edwards' cross into the net. This was to spark off a goal rush which enthralled the home crowd. Two goals from Sinclair in the 16th and 18th minutes rattled the Spaniards and put the Pars only one goal behind. A goal from the Spaniards in the 22nd minute, however, showed they were far from dejected. Before the interval, Dunfermline struck back and two goals, from centre half McLean and Smith, put the Athletic ahead 5–1 and level on aggregate.

Disaster struck the home side early in the second half when McLean, the hero of the first half, scored again – this time, unfortunately, heading past his own 'keeper to put the Spaniards out in front once again. Not to be denied, the Pars battled on and justice was done six minutes later when a second goal by Smith once again levelled the tie. Although both sides had more chances to net the winner, no more goals were scored. Dunfermline had pulled off a remarkable come-back by winning 6–2 on the night and levelling the tie at six goals each, thus forcing a play-off on a neutral ground. (The current rule of away goals counting double did not apply then.)

Lisbon was eventually chosen where both sides lined up on 6 February in front of less than 3,000 fans in a ground which could hold 50,000. Because of the severe winter in Britain this was Dunfermline's first competitive game since Boxing Day although the lack of match practice was not evident in their play. Despite having much of the pressure in the first half, Dunfermline could not score and were to regret their missed chances when full back Mestre scored the only goal of the game after 61 minutes against the run of play. Valencia went on to win the trophy while the Pars were left with little financial profit to show – the final game yielded £310s in gate money to meet a travelling bill of £2,000.

Against this background of exciting European adventures, Dunfermline made another bid to win the League Championship for the first time ever. They started in fine form beating Dundee United 4–0 at Tannadice and followed it up with a 6–0 win over Raith Rovers during which Edwards scored the first of his many league goals. A further six victories before Christmas plus a draw against Rangers, their first league point at Ibrox, put them near the top of the league. After Christmas their form slumped, beginning with a defeat at Parkhead on Boxing Day. One of the worst freeze-ups this century ensued and it was 6 March before the Pars played another league game, dropping a valuable point at Easter Road. In fact, they were to win only one away game during the remainder of the

season, at Stark's Park against relegated Raith Rovers. This was not championship form and the Athletic ended the season in a disappointing eighth position.

The Scottish Cup gave the fans little over which to enthuse. After a bye in the first round they were drawn to play against Cowdenbeath at Central Park. After two postponements because of the icy conditions and with no sign of a let-up the game was eventually switched to Stark's Park where Dunfermline won 3–2. When the fourth round dictated that the Pars had to travel to Aberdeen, the fans took this as a good omen, remembering that they had previously triumphed there in 1961 on their way to winning the cup. History was not to repeat itself. After 10 minutes, Herriot had to retire with a broken thumb, leaving the Pars to fight on with 10 men. In fact, Dunfermline finished the game with only nine men after McLindon was sent off on the hour mark after a clash with Cooke. Miller took over in goals and was powerless to stop Aberdeen score four goals, two of them from the penalty spot.

As a consolation prize, the Athletic won the Fife Cup, beating Burntisland Shipyard 13–1 on their way to the final. There they beat East Fife 4–1 to give them one prize in a season which, up till Christmas, had promised so much but eventually yielded little. Stein still saw great hopes for the future. At the AGM he prophesied: "In spite of the successes over the past two seasons I can promise the supporters the best is still to come." Stein's ability did not go unnoticed throughout Britain. After Alf Ramsay left Ipswich Town to become England's successful team manager the English club approached Stein, only to be given a polite refusal. Raith' were also looking for a manager and turned, in vain, to skipper Willie Cunningham, and then assistant trainer, Ian Bain. In April, Cunningham was appointed coach and promised a benefit game. The club was looking to the future.

Top left: *Monument to the Fishermen, Lisbon.*

Above: *John Lunn.* (Dunfermline Press)

Below: *Any club in Britain would have been proud of this forward line. Standing: Melrose, Dickson, Sinclair. Kneeling: Edwards and Peebles.* (Dundee Courier)

SEASON 1963–64

Several changes were made to the team for the new season. In defence, Cunningham and Williamson retired as a result of recurring injuries, Stevenson was given a free transfer and Connachan, no longer first choice in goals, accepted a £5,500 transfer to Middlesbrough (though he later returned to Scotland to play for Falkirk and thwart many a Dunfermline attack). Joining the squad were two provisional signings, Pat Wilson (17) from Blairhall Juniors and Jim Fraser (17) from St Andrew's United, and Jim Kerray who re-signed for his old club from Newcastle for £3,000. Stein offered his resignation after arousing controversy over a newspaper article, but the Board wisely let the matter drop.

After another short trip to Ireland, beating Coleraine 2–1, Dunfermline failed for the fifth successive year to make any progress in the League Cup. Dundee came out top of their group which also contained Airdrie and Third Lanark.

Without any European distractions the club could give all their concentration and energy towards doing well in the league. The team made an excellent start by winning five of their first seven games and drawing the other two. BBC cameras covered two of Dunfermline's games in successive weeks and by the end of the season the club were to receive over £1,000 for TV coverage. Their first defeat came at the end of October at Dens Park where a skilful Dundee side, led by the superb Alan Gilzean, narrowly won 2–1. In the following month, the Board granted Stein and his trainer permission to go to Milan at the expense of *The Daily Express* to study the training methods of Helenio Herrera, the great coaching maestro. The Board also decided to erect lights around Humbug Park to allow training during the winter evenings.

The club's first defeat at home did not come until the end of November when in front of a crowd of 21,000, Rangers ran out winners by four goals to one. A welcome break from the gruelling routine of trying to capture league points came on 9 December when 10,000 enthusiastic fans turned up on a cold winter's night to pay tribute to Willie Cunningham and Jackie Williamson in their testimonial

match. Former stars Connachan (Middlesbrough) and Fraser (Aston Villa) along with Colrain (Ipswich) guested for the Pars against an impressive Newcastle side with Gordon Marshall and Bobby Moncur in their line-up. Dunfermline recorded a pleasing win of 2–0, Kerray and T. Callaghan the marksmen.

At the AGM, chairman Thomson looked back on another year and congratulated Jim Herriot for his selection in the Scottish League side which won 4–1 at Windsor Park, and Alec Edwards who was chosen for the GB Youth side. He stated that only four major transfers had occurred in the last four years and these had not disturbed the rhythm of the team. Thomson, one of the club's ablest and most successful chairman, decided to stand down after six and a half years to let the honours go round. Mr Andrew Watson, an amateur footballer and cricketer in his younger days, took over with Mr Bob Torrie as vice-chairman.

Before the end of the year, Stein acquired a new goalkeeper as extra cover – Eric Martin, signed from Blairhall Colliery for £80. Stein could feel satisfied with his team's achievements, their good league performance having taken them to third in the table. The New Year, however, brought disappointment. A goalless draw at home with Queen of the South was followed by two defeats at the hands of Hearts and Kilmarnock. The defeat of Killie was especially galling as not only were they too chasing the title but had recovered from two goals down to win 3–2.

In January, the league programme was interrupted as usual by the Scottish Cup. After a bye in the first round, Dunfermline trounced Fraserburgh 7–0 in the second round. Dickson scored five goals and John Lunn and Tommy Callaghan chose a good occasion on which to make their cup debuts. Before the next round the Pars received a tremendous boost to their morale by beating Celtic 1–0 at home, Billy McNeill obliging with an own goal. To build up team spirit and make further preparations, Stein followed the now familiar pattern of taking his players away for a few days, on this occasion to Largs. In the third round, an equally convincing victory of 6–1 was run up against East Stirling away from home to put Dun-

Jim Kerray scoring against Dundee, 31 August 1963. Note the structure for the TV cameras in the background. (Dunfermline Press)

Above: *Training for the new season, August 1963.*

Below: *Eddie Connachan in action.*

fermline into the quarter-finals with a good home draw against Ayr to follow. Pleasing though this achievement was, it was followed by the news that supporters had been dreading to hear – Stein had asked to be released at the end of the season from his contract (which still had several years to run) and the Board had agreed to do so. After four years of performing near miracles with a provincial club, Stein had decided that the time was ripe to seek greater challenges. He felt that even in a good season, Dunfermline could never attain the same drawing power or glamour of one of the bigger, well-established city clubs. Though greatly disheartened, the team did not allow the news to affect their performance in the quarter-finals where, with the aid of a Dickson hat-trick, they overwhelmed Ayr 7–0. In the following week, the Board appointed former captain and coach, Willie Cunningham, as Stein's successor. Capped more than 30 times for his country, Cunningham was the natural choice given his knowledge of the game generally and his familiarity with the players and set-up at East End Park in particular.

Before Stein departed he had one last challenge – to steer Dunfermline to victory in the Cup over a very competent Rangers side. In the long history of the Cup this was only the second time the two sides had clashed. On the Saturday before the semi-final, Rangers gained a psychological advantage by beating the Pars in a league game at Ibrox though the narrowness of the defeat (2–1) did not dishearten the Athletic as they travelled to Dunblane Hydro to prepare.

The semi-final itself, played at Hampden Park on 28 March in front of 68,000 fans, was a sad swan-song for Stein. Handicapped by the absence of pivot McLean through injury, the rearranged side never fired on all cylinders. The teams were:

Dunfermline: Herriot; Callaghan, Lunn; Thomson, Miller, T. Callaghan; Kerray, Peebles, Dickson, Smith, Sinclair.

Rangers: Ritchie; Shearer, Provan; Greig, McKinnon, Baxter; Brand, McMillan, Millar, McLean, Wilson.

Despite having the wind in their favour in the first half, the Pars found the going tough against a determined defence. One minute before half-time, Davie Wilson, Rangers' outside left, scored what turned out to be the only goal of the game. The rhythm of the game in the second half was constantly destroyed as a series of fouls and bookings made good football a rarity.

A few days later, when it was confirmed that Stein had been offered the manager's job with Hibs following Galbraith's departure, the Board released Stein and announced that Cunningham would take over immediately. Shortly afterwards, Jimmy Stevenson, trainer for nine years, followed his old boss to Easter Road and was later replaced by Andy Stevenson (no relation), assistant trainer at Cathkin Park. Although Cunningham guided his new charges to a run of four games without defeat in the league, the side could only manage fifth position in the table. With 45 points gained this was the Athletic's highest number of points so far; the winning of the Fife Cup was small consolation. Of importance for the future was the fine performance of the reserve side in finishing third in their league.

Cunningham was given a further chance to experiment in the new competition which was set up at the end of the season – the Summer Cup, organised along lines not dissimilar to the League Cup. Dunfermline were purposely drawn with three other clubs from the East – Hearts, Hibs and Falkirk – to cut down on travelling. After six games Hearts topped the section, but a prior commitment in America meant they had to withdraw. Hibs and Dunfermline were tied in all respects in second place and a play-off was arranged at Tynecastle. Hibs, under Jock Stein, of course, won 3–1 and went on to win the cup.

Above: *Keeping the ball up with Edwards (right) is Pat Wilson.*

Below: *The team of mid-August 1963. Standing: W. Callaghan, Lunn, Herriot, Mailer, McLean, Miller. Front: Edwards, Peebles, Dickson, Sinclair, Melrose.* (Dundee Courier)

Willie Cunningham (1964–67)

SEASON 1964–65

The side which the new manager took for the now familiar pre-season trip to Ireland contained a few changes. Ron Mailer, who had been out of the first team for some time, finally decided to hang up his boots after 13 years with the club. Jim Kerray, the club's top scorer with 21 goals the previous season, was transferred to St Johnstone for £6,250. In their place, Cunningham signed three forwards – John McLaughlin from Millwall (£2,500), John Kilgannon from Ayr and, shrewdest acquisitionn of all, the former Queen's Park player, Alec Ferguson, from St Johnston, in a straight exchange for Dan McLindon. The new side clicked well together and recorded two fine wins over Linfield and Coleraine.

Before the new season was underway, the Board received an interesting letter from the SFA "regarding the many excessive displays of exuberance by players on the scoring of a goal and requesting Directors to instil into players an appropriate sense of discipline". In the opening games of the League Cup there were ample opportunities for the Dunfermline players to conform to the new guidelines. Victories of 4–1 over Airdrie (away), 2–0 over Hibs (home) and 3–1 over Third Lanark (home) set Dunfermline up to qualify for the quarter-finals for the first time in six years.

Their opponents were to be Rangers with whom they had already fought out a goalless draw at Ibrox in the opening league game of the season. The Pars looked forward with confidence to the first leg on Monday 14 September at East End Park and the players relished the chance to avenge their Scottish Cup defeat in the previous season. A large crowd of 20,000 failed to see Dunfermline play at their best and a 3–0 defeat killed off interest in the second leg which was played two days later. Dunfermline were unable to provide a miracle and although they led 2–1 at one stage they had to settle for a 2–2 draw which eliminated them from the competition.

Willie Cunningham with A. Edwards (left) and J. Sinclair. (M. Allan)

In parallel with success in Europe went an equally good run in the league, beginning with a goalless draw at Ibrox. After his team had demolished Falkirk 5–1 at East End Park in September, the manager presented Melrose with the ball as a memento for scoring all five goals. Another notable victory was the 7–2 defeat of Clyde which saw Ferguson score his first hat-trick for his new club which put Dunfermline well up the table.

Despite success on the field, grumblings were to be heard from the dressing-room. Alec Smith's wish to be put on a monthly contract was turned down and a bid of £15,000 from Rangers was rejected. George Miller, who had recently been capped against the League of Ireland, had expressed a wish to leave for some time, and in October he was transferred to Wolves for £28,500. His brother-in-law, Jim Herriot, also desired to go, but found no encouragement from the Board.

They did, however, allow Charlie Dickson to depart to Queen of the South for £2,150. Dickson must rank as one of the all-time greats at East End Park. In the decade that he served his club he scored almost 240 goals in around 500 appearances: 29 were scored in the League Cup, 154 in the League, 19 in the Scottish Cup, 5 in Europe plus a miscellany in other minor games. His double hat-trick (all goals being scored successively) against St Mirren in 1961 was a record for a centre forward at East End Park. By scoring 25 First Division goals in 1959-60 he surpasssed the previous record set by Bobby Skinner (24 goals) in 1926-27. Strangely enough he had no hard shot to offer and he was anything but tricky on the ball. However, his qualities more than compensated for these apparent deficiencies – he was enthusiastic, had the heart of a lion, was fast on his feet and was deadly with his long legs in goalmouth skirmishes. 'Mr Inspiration' would certainly be missed.

Manager Cunningham complained through the press of the fall in gates at East End Park. He felt, with much justifi-

Top left: Kilgannon leading out Ferguson, Edwards, Peebles, Smith and Melrose. (Dundee Courier)

Below: McLaughlin scoring the first goal against Orgryte in the Fairs Cup. (Dunfermline Press)

As the door on one cup shut another one opened. Former chairman, David Thomson, had been elected to the executive of the Fairs Cup and partly through his influence the number of participating clubs was increased by 16 to 48, thus allowing Dunfermline, as well as Celtic and Kilmarnock, to go forward. Dunfermline were drawn against the Swedish club, Orgryte, and played the first leg at East End Park on 13 October. After a year out of Europe the fans were keen to see the return of top class football to Dunfermline though the 8,000 crowd did not expect their team to go one goal behind after 19 minutes and then 2–1 behind after 25 minutes despite McLaughlin's equaliser. Both Swedish goals were scored by the talented Simonsson. Sinclair managed to equalise with a header before the interval and after half-time two further goals from McLaughlin and Sinclair saw the Pars eventually win 4–2. The team was: Herriot; Thomson, Callaghan; Smith, McLean, Miller; Peebles, Kilgannon, McLaughlin, Melrose, Sinclair.

In the second leg in the Ullevi Stadium in Gothenberg one week later the Dunfermline defence, with centre half Miller outstanding, held out to force a goalless draw in front of a crowd of not much more than a thousand. Absent from the team were Peebles and Kilgannon who were replaced by Lunn and Ferguson. Little did Alec Ferguson then realise that two decades later he would leave the same stadium as manager of a triumphant European Cup Winners' Cup side.

Charlie Dickson. Twenty years on, the cry can still be heard today – "Bring on Charlie Dickson".

cation, that his team's success deserved gates of at least 10,000 while anything less meant loss of revenue, atmosphere and encouragement.

European action returned to East End Park on 17 November when the Athletic lined up against the strong German side, VFB Stuttgart, in the first leg of the second round tie. Not for the first time Dunfermline enjoyed most of the play, but were unable to convert their superiority into goals against a side which contained three internationalists. The 15,000 home fans must have thought their home team was never going to score when a Peebles' penalty kick was saved by the visiting 'keeper. Some justice was eventually done when Tom Callaghan drove home a superb 20-yard shot to give his team a single goal lead for the away leg.

Two weeks later it was Herriot's turn to save a penalty. In what seemed a fair tackle, Tom Callaghan dispossessed a German forward as he raced in on goal. When a penalty was awarded – with only seven minutes left – pandemonium broke out as the victim of the tackle struck Herriot to the

ground. After five minutes of bedlam, during which it seemed the goalkeeper might have to be carried off, the centre forward strode up to take the penalty kick. Acting on a hunch, Herriot dived the correct way to bring off the save of his life. Despite a series of vicious fouls from the Germans, the Fifers hung on to enter the third round on a 1–0 aggregate.

Dunfermline's joy was completed in 1964 when in the last league game of the year, two goals from Sinclair and Ferguson gave them victory over Celtic for the first time ever at Parkhead. Their good fortune continued into the New Year with four league wins out of five in January, form which was acknowledged when three players, Herriot, Lunn and Sinclair, were chosen to play for the Scottish League on 20 January. (Sadly the game was put off because of bad weather.) Nor was the comfort of the fans neglected. Two 50-feet extensions at a cost of £3,595 were to be added to the north enclosure.

Round three of the Fairs Cup brought another trip to Spain for the Pars, this time to Bilbao. The team that took the field on 27 January was: Herriot; Callaghan, Lunn; Thomson, McLean, T. Callaghan; Edwards, Paton, McLaughlin, Ferguson, Sinclair. The manager had decided that the best means to defend was to attack. These tactics would have brought the Pars a goal but for the fine goalkeeping from Iribar. Dunfermline often looked the more dangerous side and the inability of Bilbao to break down a strong defence brought them the jeers of the home fans. However, with only three minutes to go, tragedy struck for Dunfermline. Herriot punched the ball out only for it to strike Thomson on the head and drop perfectly for Yosu, the outside left. His shot was not seen by Herriot and the ball slipped past him into the goal to give the Spaniards a one-goal lead for the return leg.

The Pars did not see this as a great setback, especially as they had successfully pulled back a four-goal deficit inflicted during their last visit to Spain against Valencia. Before they could play the return leg in March the Athletic now had to turn their attention to the domestic scene and the Scottish Cup. The first round sent them to Dumfries to tackle Queen of the South. Despite the efforts of Dickson to score against his old mates, Dunfermline won 2–0 in front of 6,700 fans. Dickson did not remain long at Palmerston Park and later in the year he emigrated to Australia.

The second round proved much more troublesome to Dunfermline. On paper, their opponents, Third Lanark, struggling at the foot of the First Division, should have presented few problems. Certainly the bookies thought so by giving odds of 7 to 1 for Dunfermline to win the Cup. The Pars looked to be going through when Ferguson put them one up, but the game turned dramatically when Herriot was sent off for a foul on Murray. From the resultant penalty, stand-in keeper Thomson was unable to prevent the Cathkin side from equalising. In the replay at East End Park, Third Lanark shocked the home side by forcing yet another draw (2–2) which extra time was unable to alter. In the second replay, at Tynecastle on 1 March, the Pars fought back twice from being a goal behind to win 4–2 finally.

The fixtures were beginning to pile up and sap the energy of the team. When Dunfermline welcomed Bilbao

Above: *Boarding the plane for the first game against Bilbao. This was a familiar scene in the 1960s.* (Dundee Courier)

Below: *Alec Smith (right) scores Dunfermline's only goal at home against Bilbao.* (Courier)

Above: *Herriot comes out of the Turnhouse customs with the rest of the team after he had returned home to get his passport.* (Daily Record)

to East End Park on 3 March, this was the Pars' fifth match in 11 days. A crowd of 16,500 turned up on a frosty night to see if the team could progress further in the Cup. A goal by Smith after 20 minutes suggested that it was only a matter of time and pressure before the Spaniards wilted. However, with almost every Spaniard back in defence and with the keeper again in splendid form, the Pars could not pierce the iron defence for a second time. After the game, luck deserted captain Jim McLean when he lost the toss which decided that Dunfermline would have to travel to Bilbao once more for the play-off.

Without too much time to reflect on what might have been, Dunfermline had to pick themselves up for their third round Scottish Cup-tie against Stirling Albion at home. Two goals in each half gave the Athletic a fairly straightforward passage into the semi-finals.

At this moment, manager Cunningham must have felt he had the whole world at his feet. He had just signed a new contract which tied him for five seasons to the club. In his first season he has steered his club into the quarter-finals of the League Cup and into the semi-finals of the Scottish Cup. In the league, his team were mounting their strongest challenge yet to winning the elusive title. In one of the most

open contests for years it seemed possible that any one of five clubs – Rangers, Hearts, Hibs, Kilmarnock or Dunfermline – could clinch it. Further good results like a 6–0 defeat of Morton and a 2–2 draw at Pittodrie (with the Dons equalising 2½ minutes into injury time) had put the Pars into second top position, two points behind Hearts but with two games in hand. In Europe, the manager still had confidence that his team could go further in the Fairs Cup. There was even talk in the dressing-room of Dunfermline doing the "treble", an achievement never seriously considered by any Scottish club.

Sadly, the Pars could not keep the momentum going for the final five vital weeks. The first disappointment came in the decider at Bilbao on 16 March. In a thrilling game, the Pars went down 2–1 but only after a terrific struggle. The turning point in the game came when the Swiss referee (who had also officiated at the Stuttgart game) awarded the home side a soft penalty to give them a first-half lead. Dunfermline stormed back in the second half through a splendid header from Smith and were unlucky not to take the lead on several occasions. With only five minutes to go Bilbao scored a magnificent goal to put the Fifers out of Europe, consoled only by a standing ovation for their brave performance.

In the league, Dunfermline continued to pile on the pressure with wins over Stirling and Partick. Against Dundee on 13 March the Athletic suffered a setback by dropping their first home point of the season in a 3–3 draw. The following week the other Dundee team visited Dunfermline and inflicted on them their only home defeat of the season (1–0). The Pars picked themselves up and a convincing victory over Third Lanark of 8–0 put them back in contention only to lose more ground at Easter Road in a 1–0 defeat. Dunfermline pressed on and three successive victories against St Mirren, Third Lanark and, most important of all, Rangers, made for an intriguing grandstand finish.

	P	W	D	L	F	A	Pts
Hearts	32	21	6	5	87	47	48
Dunfermline	32	21	4	7	77	34	46
Kilmarnock	32	20	6	6	57	33	46

If Dunfermline could win their last two matches Hearts would have to gain more than two points or else an inferior goal average would send the title to Fife. The Pars' chances were enhanced by the fact that Hearts and Kilmarnock played each other on the last game of the season.

It was with great anticipation that the fans turned up at East End Park on 17 April to see if their team could maintain their winning run against St Johnstone. The home crowd were shocked to see Dunfermline go a goal behind after 24 minutes and, although Ferguson equalised 11 minutes later, a disjointed Athletic attack chose that crucial occasion to have an off-day. No more goals resulted, giving Dunfermline only one point while Hearts were gaining two precious points by beating Aberdeen at Pittodrie. In one afternoon, Dunfermline had seen their championship hopes wilt away although to be realistic, equally vital points, especially against the Tayside clubs, had been dropped throughout the season.

The season, however, might still have rewarded Dunfermline with a prize. While the exacting league programme was drawing to a climax the Pars met Hibs at

Melrose watches Thomson leap over Ferguson while Edwards jumps over Smith.

Tynecastle on 27 March before a crowd of 33,306 for a place in the Scottish Cup final. Hibs, under new manager Bob Shankly, were never allowed to settle by a Dunfermline attack thirsty for goals. A goal in each half by Melrose (17 minutes) and Smith (52 minutes) demoralised a disappointing Hibs side.

Once again not just the club but the whole team and surrounding district looked forward with great expectation and interest at Dunfermline's second appearance in the Scottish Cup final in only four years; once again their opponents were Celtic who had just appointed none other than Jock Stein as their new manager in place of Jimmy McGrory. An intriguing contest between teacher and former pupil awaited 100,000 fans at Hampden Park on 24 April. The teams were:

Celtic: Fallon; Young, Gemmell; Murdoch, McNeill, Clark; Chalmers, Gallagher, Hughes, Lennox, Auld.

Dunfermline: Herriot; Callaghan, Lunn; Thomson, McLean, T. Callaghan; Edwards, Smith, McLaughlin, Melrose, Sinclair.

Interestingly, two brothers, the Callaghans, were appearing in the final, a rare feat. There was no place in the Pars' line-up for their eventual top scorer of the season with 21 goals, Alec Ferguson.

In 1961, Dunfermline had been the underdogs; in 1965, proudly perched above Celtic in the league, they could look back on a most successful season and could more than match Celtic, who had not won the cup for 11 years, in experience and skill. In the opening stages of the contest, Dunfermline shocked the large Celtic support by scoring through Melrose after 15 minutes. Auld equalised for Celtic after half an hour only for the Pars' lead to be restored before half-time when a thunderbolt from McLean almost burst the net. After the interval, no doubt encouraged by a pep talk from Stein, Celtic went all out for the equaliser which they duly scored in the 51st minute, again through Auld. Neither side would settle for a draw, especially Celtic who drew on all their reserves of stamina to keep the play in the Dunfermline goal area. A perfect header by Billy McNeill from a corner was enough to give Celtic victory. Though Dunfermline battled gallantly and helped to make it an exciting and enjoyable final, they discovered that there was little consolation in being runners-up. There would be no opened-decked bus for them this time though the £15,000 cheque from the final was most welcome.

As fate would have it, the finalists met at East End Park four days later in the final league game which might have

Above: *Jubilation as Melrose opens the scoring at Tynecastle against Hibs in the semi-final of the Scottish Cup.* (Dunfermline Press)

Below: *Dejection as Jock Stein's Celtic beat Dunfermline in the 1965 Final.* (Dundee Courier)

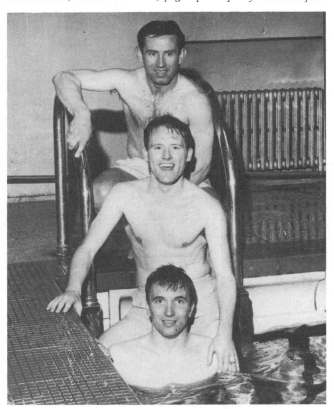

Below: *Peebles, Melrose and Smith enjoying a dip in the pool of Dunblane Hydro.*

Above: *Team photograph, April 1965. Standing: Stevenson, W. Callaghan, Lunn, Thomson, Paton, Herriot, Ferguson, McLaughlin, Smith, T. Callaghan, Cunningham. Seated: Kilgannon, Melrose, Edwards, McLean, Peebles, Fleming, Sinclair. (Dundee Courier)*

promised so much. With their league hopes already dashed, all the Pars could hope to do was to restore the pride they had lost on Saturday. This they accomplished in fine fashion by thrashing the Cup-winners 5–1 and thus completing the double over them. Kilmarnock had already pipped Hearts for the championship by the smallest of margins and Dunfermline ended up only one point behind in third place, their highest ever place in the league (and still a record today, as was their pointage: 49 points).

In contrast to the glamour of Europe and the thrill of Hampden Park, the Summer Cup seemed rather small beer to a club which had just seen a possible League and Cup double snatched out of their hands. Once again Dunfermline were drawn alongside Hibs, Hearts and Falkirk and once again the Easter Road side went on to the next stages of the cup and indeed to win it.

One fascinating statistic on which to close this remarkable season: the Pars played in front of no less than 750,000 spectators!

SEASON 1965-66

The team which did battle for most of the season showed a number of changes. Jackie Sinclair was transferred to Leicester City for £25,000 and to replace him, Cunningham bought Hugh Robertson, an experienced left winger from Dundee, for £13,000. While at Dens Park he had been, capped for Scotland in 1962 against Czechoslovakia (along with Connachan) and in the same year he helped his club to win the league championship. As well as playing in the European Cup he had also participated in the Cup Winners' Cup.

Goalkeeper Herriot was bought by Birmingham City for £18,000. An interesting footnote to this transfer was that a Yorkshire vet happened to hear Herriot's name mentioned on *Match of the Day* and decided to adopt it as his *nom de plume* for his now famous vet books. Herriot's young deputy, Eric Martin, became first choice goalkeeper. McLaughlin was transferred to Motherwell for £3,500 while Kilgannon went to St Johnstone for £2,550; Jim Fleming was bought from Partick Thistle for £4,000. Alec Totten, formerly of Liverpool, joined the club from Dundee on a free transfer. The manager was instructed to go as high as £25,000 for the young Motherwell striker, Joe McBride, but failed to beat Celtic for his signature. Maxwell, the former Celtic player, was signed from St Johnstone for £7,000. Edwards' request for a transfer was turned down by the Board. Later in the season, Harry Melrose, an East End favourite, moved to Aberdeen for £3,000. Recent media coverage had again highlighted the bewitching skills of the South Americans, and Dunfermline tried – unsuccessully as it happened – to sign two of them.

Behind the scenes, Robert Methven was appointed assistant trainer. Former chairman, David Thomson, became vice-president of the Scottish League. Club physician, Dr Robson, emigrated to Canada and was replaced by Dr John C. Yellowley whose association with the club was to progress from consulting room to boardroom.

The club continued to improve the ground on which £150,000 had been spent over the last six years. Now that the enclosure had been extended (in the spring of 1965) estimates were sought for an enclosure at the western end of the stadium. The Scottish Football Writers' Association congratulated the club on providing them with "magnificent press facilities". To accommodate the ever-increasing visits

Above: *Hugh Robertson.* (Dunfermline Press)

Bottom left: *Raising funds has always been a problem for the club.*

of the TV cameras, a new stand was built to house their equipment. Two new cafeterias were opened under the stand. In anticipation of further success the Board ordered a showcase and even sought the price of two flagpoles!

On the playing field, the team were to enjoy another successful season with another nail-biting climax. In the League Cup, the Pars had the misfortune to be drawn alongside league champions, Kilmarnock, who, like the Athletic, were enjoying one of their best spells ever. Convincing home wins against St Johnstone (5–1) and Partick Thistle (6–2) were not enough to prevent Killie heading the section by three points.

A bye in the first round of the Fairs Cup and the early dismissal from the League Cup ensured that Dunfermline could devote all their attention to the early months of the league campaign. The first half of the season saw them make good progress, beginning with a fine 3–1 defeat of Motherwell (away) followed by an even better 1–0 defeat of Kilmarnock at Rugby Park. The team's away form was excellent, demonstrated by an outstanding victory of 3–2 over Rangers at Ibrox on Christmas Day which gave the Pars their first ever victory there. For a long time afterwards fans were to remember the superb goal scored by

Above: *Relaxing at Renfrew Airport before flying out to Copenhagen are (l to r): Tom and Willie Callaghan, Lunn, Paton, Fleming and Hunter.* (Dundee Courier)

Below: *The Dunfermline party boarding the plane for Denmark.* (Dundee Courier)

Paton which left Ritchie totally helpless. In fourteen previous league encounters there, Rangers had won 12 games and run up 45 goals for the loss of only 11 goals. This victory put Dunfermline within three points of the leaders. By New Year's Day, they were undefeated away from home though at East End Park they had suffered two defeats, one of them to title-chasing Celtic.

Almost as a matter of routine now the fans turned to Europe to see if their team could be the first Scottish club to win a European trophy. The second round of the Fairs Cup had granted Dunfermline a seemingly easy task against the amateur Danish club, Boldklub 1903. For the first leg on 3 November, Cunningham fielded the following side from which W. Callaghan and A. Edwards were omitted: Martin; Thomson, Lunn; Smith, McLean, T. Callaghan; Wilson, Paton, Fleming, Ferguson, Robertson.

In front of a 14,000 crowd, the Pars, playing in their 21st European contest, breached the tall Danish defence only once in the first half, through Fleming. After the interval another four goals from Robertson, Paton (2) and T. Callaghan gave Dunfermline the chance of a holiday in Copenhagen a fortnight later. In the second leg, played before a crowd of only 1,500 on a freezing cold night, Dunfermline never looked like losing the game, far less the tie though they did go one behind through an own goal from Lunn. Goals from Edwards and Paton put the Pars into a

2–1 lead at the interval, and although Boldklub did equalise, a further two goals, from Paton and Ferguson, gave Dunfermline their passport into round three. Significantly, this was the Scottish club's first away victory on the Continent though they did win in the Republic of Ireland in 1961.

In recognition of their outstanding play, Lunn and Edwards were chosen for the squad of the Scottish League to play the Irish League at Ibrox. Benefits were paid to George Peebles, the club's longest serving player, and Willie Callaghan. On 24 November, a testimonial match was held for former captain, Ron Mailer, who had retired the previous season after 13 years of sterling service. The talented Czech team, Dukla Prague, boasting 250 caps, provided the opposition on an extremely cold night which kept the crowd at 8,000. The game resulted in a 2–2 draw with Ferguson scoring both of the home side's goals.

The next round in Europe brought another crack side to East End Park in the form of Spartak Brno. A local accountant, George Klimczak, was called in to act as interpreter. In the first leg on 26 January, Dunfermline scraped through with a 2–0 victory. The Czechs, who had just come out of winter hibernation, put up a dour struggle

In training: Bert Paton, Pat Wilson and Alec Ferguson. (Evening News)

Above: *Trainer Andy Stevenson (left) and his assistant, Bob Methven.* (Dunfermline Press)

Below: *Paton and Ferguson celebrate as Partick Thistle lose another goal in their Scottish Cup-tie.* (Dunfermline Press)

before the 12,000 crowd for an hour until a Paton goal finally broke the deadlock. A penalty from Ferguson just before the end added to Dunfermline's lead although there were many at East End Park who doubted whether such a lead would be enough in Czechoslovakia.

As expected the Athletic found the second leg a very trying affair. Cunningham was in hospital and handed reponsibility over to trainer Stevenson. A gruelling 10-hour journey did nothing to bolster the Pars' spirits. These setbacks did not adversely affect the team as they contained the Czechs to a goalless draw despite severe tackling and poor refereeing. The *Press* hailed it as "a tremendous display of tactical, defensive football" and was full of praise for the heroics of 'keeper Martin. The quarter-final draw dictated that Dunfermline would meat the winners of a play-off between Real Zaragoza and Hearts.

While campaigning in Europe, Dunfermline began their interest in the Scottish Cup in a bid to reach the final for the second year running. Round one brought Partick Thistle to East End Park on 5 February when three goals from Smith, Paton and Fleming (for only one lost) saw Dunfermline through to round two in front of a 9,500 crowd. Their next opponents, Stirling Albion, were not the push-over that many thought they would be. In front of a crowd of similar size the Pars were held to a 0–0 draw at Annfield though they made amends in the replay by winning 4–1 in front of 14,303 supporters; Ferguson and Paton scored twice.

A much stiffer test came in the quarter-finals when Kilmarnock were drawn to oppose Dunfermline. Ground advantage undoubtedly aided the Pars and the 19,363 crowd certainly saw a match to remember. For most of the first half the home side kept the visitors pinned back but, as

Above: *Edwards scores a great winning goal against Kilmarnock.*

Below: *The Spaniards were to be Dunfermline's next opponents on 16 March 1966.*

is often the case, a breakaway resulted in Killie going in at half-time, one goal up. The Pars kept battling in the second half and were relieved when Paton equalised after 67 minutes. Just when it seemed a replay would be necessary, Edwards collected a pass from Robertson and slotted the ball past the 'keeper to give Dunfermline a sensational last-minute winner, reckoned to be worth £10,000 to the club. For the third successive year, the Pars had reach the semi-final of the Scottish Cup.

Once again the season was building up to a tremendous climax for Dunfermline as they maintained a strong challenge in the League, Cup and Europe. The month of March would decide if the Pars would write their names yet again into the record books. Cunningham was obliged to re-enter hospital and sadly, in the space of three weeks, the carefully constructed pack of cards fell apart.

In the league, Dunfermline had consolidated their position near the top following their famous Christmas victory over Rangers. Throughout January and February they lost only three points – all away, at Rugby Park and Tynecastle. In March, however, a 4–3 home defeat by St Mirren, a 6–1 defeat by Clyde and a 3–2 home defeat by Aberdeen saw the Pars slip irretrievably behind Celtic in the title chase.

In the cup-ties, disaster also struck. Former winners of the Fairs Cup, Real Zaragoza, had beaten Hearts in the play-off to win the right to meet Dunfermline in the quarter-finals. One of Dunfermline's largest crowds for a European match, 20,000, turned up on Wednesday 16 March to watch the Spanish visitors who, only one month previously, had sacked their manager, Hon, for "lack of

DUNFERMLINE ATHLETIC F.C. LTD.

Inter-Cities Fairs Cup · Quarter Final · First Leg

DUNFERMLINE ATHLETIC
v. REAL ZARAGOZA / HEARTS

EAST END PARK, DUNFERMLINE
DATE TO BE ANNOUNCED
Kick-off 7.30 p.m.

WING STAND (EAST)
SEAT

№ 32   Row   7/6
         M

If match postponed this ticket is valid for the altered date
NO MONEY WILL BE REFUNDED

discipline in the team" in favour of Fernando Davcik. Certainly, the team that Dunfermline faced were a disciplined side and not without a lot of skill, especially from centre forward Marcellino. Although the Spaniards were often hemmed back in defence the Athletic attack seldom looked like scoring. With only 10 minutes to go the Pars had a strong penalty claim turned down and the fans began to make for the exits. Then, in the 87th minute, an Edwards' cross found Paton who headed home a brilliant winner. Zaragoza were down but not out and a fierce drive from Marcellino was just blocked on the line by Lunn.

Before the second leg could be played, Dunfermline had to meet Celtic in the semi-final of the Scottish Cup at Ibrox on Saturday 26 March. The teams were:

Dunfermline: Martin;   Callaghan,   Lunn;   Smith, McLean, Thomson; Fleming, Ferguson, Hunter, T. Callaghan, Robertson.

Celtic: Simpson; Young, Gemmell; Murdoch, McNeill, Clark; Johnstone, McBride, Chalmers, Lennox, Auld.

A crowd of 53,900 turned up on a rain-soaked afternoon to see a game that never lived up to its billing. Goals in either half from Auld and Chalmers sealed Dunfermline's fate. Though Dunfermline perhaps did not realise it at the time the Celtic team they had faced was beginning its greatest era ever at Parkhead.

With only four days to recover their stamina and regain their composure, Dunfermline took to the field in Spain on Wednesday 30 March in a bid to enter the semi-finals of the European trophy. Fleming, Hunter and Robertson were dropped in favour of Edwards, T. Callaghan and Peebles. Dunfermline played a defensive game and with 'keeper Martin in splendid form they still had their first-leg lead intact at half-time. Twelve minutes into the second half, Zaragoza scored to level the tie and late in the game went into the lead. In the dying seconds, Ferguson pulled a goal

back to send the tie into extra time. Zaragoza scored again only to see Ferguson score his second goal of the night. When a play-off seemed more and more likely, Villa delighted the home fans and sent the Dunfermline party home dejected by scoring in the last three minutes. Once again Dunfermline's only consolation was a cheering ovation from 40,000 appreciative Spaniards.

By losing their second cup-tie in a matter of days, the Pars had every right to feel dejected. Through their concentration on cup-ties in the spring, Dunfermline's position in the league had suffered and when they returned from Spain, the best they could hope for was a place in next season's Fairs Cup. Emphatic victories in April over Falkirk (6–1) and Partick (6–2) helped restore confidence in the dressing-room. In their home game against Dundee, an excellent equaliser from T. Callaghan gave the Pars a share of the points in a game through which they had struggled with only 10 men for 75 minutes. Defeats in the last two games of the season by Rangers and Celtic confirmed that the Old Firm would not give up lightly their stranglehold on Scottish football.

Celtic topped the league with 57 points; Dunfermline came fourth, 13 points behind. In the process, the team set a new club record of 94 First Division goals, though the number of goals conceded, 55, was also remarkably high judged by their own new high standards.

Alec Ferguson, who had scored no less than seven goals in the victories against Falkirk and Partick, ended up as the club's top scorer in only his second season at East End Park. Out of his total of 39 goals, 31 were scored in the league which smashed Dickson's previous record of 25 goals in 1959–60, and is still the club record today. Fergie, in fact, put in for a transfer but his request was refused. With an eye to the future that summer he attended a coaching course at Largs. Cunningham also asked to be released from his contract and his request was similarly rejected.

Opposite: *Paton scores the only goal of the game against Zaragosa.* (Dunfermline Press)

Above: *Planning future strategy are (l to r): J. McConville, D. Thomson, A. Watson (chairman), W. Cunningham, R. Torrie and L. Jack.* (M. Allan)

Right: *Willie Callaghan.* (Dunfermline Press)

A great deal of discussion took place at this time regarding league reconstruction. Hearts had proposed a three-tier league set-up of 16-12-12 clubs in three divisions. Dunfermline supported this suggestion but the league threw out the idea. The league also asked clubs for their views on the use of substitutes and the Athletic supported the innovation, even if the withdrawn player was not injured. This proposal was passed and became operational in the following season. Initially, only one substitute was allowed.

Originally, the Board had planned an ambitious tour of South America at the end of the season but this idea fell through and instead a tour to Switzerland and Austria was organised in May. As the club flew out to Zurich they must once again have reflected on what might have been, if only . . . So near, and yet so far.

SEASON 1966-67

Two old favourites were to leave East End Park before the new season was fully underway. George Peebles was transferred to Stirling for £4,000. Signed in 1955, 'Peebs' was the longest-serving member of the team. Alex Smith, often the subject of transfer speculation, was finally sold to Rangers for £51,000, a record between Scottish clubs. His brilliant ball control and shrewd passing would be qualities difficult to replace. Their departure marked the end of an era as they had been the only players left at East End Park who had seen the club rise from obscurity to the pinnacle of success.

Two new players joined the club and were soon to make their mark. Pat Delaney, a former Under-23 internationalist and son of the famous Celtic forward, was bought for £17,000 from Motherwell. In October, Roy Barry was purchased from Hearts for £13,000 to give greater strength to a defence which had been weakened by injuries. John McGarty was also signed, on a free transfer from Hibs.

After a summer dominated by TV coverage of the World Cup in England, it was business as usual at East End Park. The season opened with a challenge match against a talented Arsenal side containing stars like George Eastham, Ian Ure, Don Howe, Terry Neil and Frank McLintock and the Pars did well to hold the London side to a goalless draw. The season officially got underway on 13 August with the customary League Cup programme, Motherwell, Partick and Falkirk providing Dunfermline's opposition. In the first game against Motherwell, a small piece of history was made when Gus Moffat came on for the visitors and became the first substitute to score a goal. Two goals, however, from Thomson and Paton were enough to give Dunfermline victory. They lost only one game out of six and went on, for the seventh time since the competition began in 1946, to the quarter-finals where they encountered old cup rivals, Celtic, who had qualified without dropping a point.

Dunfermline were comprehensively beaten by the Glasgow side who went on in the season to win everything they entered, including the European Cup. In the first leg at Parkhead, Celtic won 6–3 and in the second leg one week later won 3–1 to enter the semi-finals with ease. At this

Above: *Ferguson scores against Zagreb.* (Dunfermline Press)

Bottom left: *Roy Barry.*

time, the Board minutes record that: "Mr Thomson agreed to take up the question of party songs being sung during matches with the secretary of the Scottish League."

In the meantime, the Pars entered their fifth year of European competition. In a preliminary round they had the good fortune to draw one of the weaker clubs, FC Frigg, from Oslo, although in the first leg, played in Norway on 24 August, Dunfermline received a fright when the Scandinavians took a shock lead. However, the Athletic gradually got on top and an equaliser from Ferguson, followed by two quick second-half goals from Fleming, put the Fife side in a commanding position. Alec Totten made his European debut, deputising for the injured Lunn. In the return leg, new signing Roy Barry moved straight into the team and saw his side record another comfortable 3–1 win, two goals coming from Delaney and the other from T. Callaghan. Only 7,000 fans turned up, Dunfermline's poorest crowd for a European match.

The second round brought much tougher opposition in the form of Dinamo Zagreb, of Yugoslavia. In the first leg at home on 26 October, the Pars got off to a wonderful start with a goal from Delaney after only seven minutes. Delight soon turned to dejection when the Yugoslavs first equalised then went into a shock 2–1 lead early in the second half. Encouraged by the 10,000 crowd and a sparkling display from Edwards, Dunfermline hauled themselves back into

A team photo from 1966-67. Standing: Hunter, W. Callaghan, Thomson, Martin, Anderson, Delaney, Lunn, T. Callaghan, McLean. Seated: Edwards, Paton, Fleming, Ferguson, Robertson. (Evening News)

the match. A penalty from Edwards and two late goals from Ferguson gave Dunfermline a 4–2 victory and hope for the second leg. The team (for both legs): Martin; W. Callaghan, Lunn; Barry, McLean, T. Callaghan; Edwards, Fleming, Delaney, Ferguson, Robertson.

In Yugoslavia one week later the Athletic attack was given little chance to add to their lead. After 30 minutes, centre forward Zambatta, who had scored in the first game, put his side back in contention with a goal converted out of half a chance. The same player signalled the lighting of bonfires and fireworks when he scored his second goal (which looked suspiciously offside) to level the tie on aggregate at 4–4. Though no further goals were scored, Zagreb went through on the basis of the new rule which counted away goals as double in the event of a tie. Though the Yugoslavs went on to win the trophy it was small consolation to the Dunfermline side who felt that they would have dismissed their unspectacular opponents but for slack defending in the first leg.

For the first time since entering Europe, Dunfermline could not look forward to seeing their name come out of the hat in the New Year. In previous seasons this would have been seen as a blessing, allowing the club to concentrate on the league, but season 1966-67 was to witness a rather poor display from the club.

The league campaign started inauspiciously with a goalless draw against Ayr, the team who had just been promoted and who were subsequently to be relegated. Their first home match saw them lose to Hibs by the incredible scoreline of 5–6! For the first hour, Hibs ran riot and led the

Athletic by 4–0. Then Hunter and Delaney pulled two back only for Alan McGraw to kill the game seemingly with a fifth goal for Hibs with only 14 minutes to go. The Pars refused to give up and in an amazing seven-minute spell further goals from Delaney, Robertson and Ferguson tied the game at five goals each. In the final minute, Hunter shot the ball past 'keeper Allan only for the referee to rule that the ball had not crossed the line. Play immediately switched to the home goalmouth and in the closing seconds of an outstanding tussle, Hibs snatched the winner. The 10,000 crowd certainly received full value for their money that September afternoon.

Dunfermline slipped further behind in the championship challenge when they lost 1–0 to the other promoted side, Airdrie, in their next game. In fact, the team had to wait until 15 October to record their first league victory when they won 5–0 at Love Street. When Celtic visited East End Park on 19 November, the crowd were to marvel at yet another scintillating game. This time it was the Pars who forged ahead, leading 2–0 after 34 minutes. Celtic pulled one back only for Dunfermline to score another. On the stroke of half-time, Celtic, striving to maintain their unbeaten record, managed to reduce the deficit to 3–2.

The second half proved to be just as entertaining. Three minutes after the interval, Ferguson seemed to put the game beyond the visitors when he made the score 4–2. This

Celtic side were made of stern stuff and two goals in two minutes from Auld and McBride levelled the score at 4–4 with 20 minutes left. After 90 minutes, everyone had settled for a draw when a controversial incident occurred. When Chalmers headed wide from an Auld free kick, referee 'Tiny' Wharton signalled for a goal kick and ran up the field. His attention was then drawn to a linesman and after consultation he awarded a penalty kick for an infringement involving Barry. McBride duly converted to give Celtic a sensational victory. How often does a team score nine goals in two home games and not win any points? In the following week, Dunfermline slumped 6–2 at Motherwell. By the end of the year they had only won five games and already the league championship had slipped beyond their grasp.

Behind the scenes a number of developments were taking place. Willie Cunningham again asked to be released from his contract and was only persuaded to remain when the club agreed to remove a lot of administrative responsibilities from him. To that end the club appointed the former Hearts' idol, Tommy Walker, as administrative assistant. At the same time, the scouting system was reorganised. Tom Callaghan broke his leg during the game against Clyde and was sidelined for three months. Edwards and Martin were chosen for the Under-23 team to play at Wrexham. Ferguson was later chosen to play against the

English League at Hampden. Bent Martin, the goalkeeper whom Celtic had brought over from Denmark, was bought for £3,500 which paved the way for the transfer of his namesake, Eric, to Southampton for £25,000, demonstrating yet again how sound Dunfermline's business practice was at this period. Jim McLean, who had recently been refused a transfer, gave up playing on medical advice. In February, Fleming was transferred to Hearts in a straight swop which brought Dom Kerrigan to East End Park. Directors Watson and Thomson received long-service badges from the SFA.

In the New Year, the team's league form showed a marked improvement with only four defeats being recorded for the rest of the season; indeed, a rare "double" was inflicted on Rangers. However, the damage had been done earlier in the season and the Athletic could only finish a disappointing eighth with 38 points.

In January, the fans looked towards the Scottish Cup as the only prize that could bring some cheer to a disappointing season. The first-round draw gave them a tricky visit to Rugby Park. By half-time the Pars seemed to be home and dry, Ferguson having put his side 2–0 up. Killie fought back in the second half and retrieved the two goals necessary to force a replay. The Cup always seemed to have more appeal than the European competitions and a crowd of 19,000 turned out to watch a hard-fought game which was settled by a single goal scored by Ferguson.

The second round brought the Pars another awkward away tie to Firhill. Partick took the lead and it took another

B. Martin (left), H. Robertson and A. Ferguson letting their manager, W. Cunningham, win at golf. (Dundee Courier)

Above: *Alec Ferguson, Dunfermline's most expensive transfer at £60,000 and the club's top goalscorer in Division One with 31 goals.* (Evening News)

Ferguson goal before half-time to level the score and force a replay. At East End Park, Dunfermline found it much easier to prize open the visitors' defence and by the end they had won 5–1. If Dunfermline were going to win the Cup they were certainly going to have to work hard because the next round gave them their third away tie, one which they did not relish - Dundee United at Tannadice. This match also looked like ending with a replay necessary until a goal-mouth scramble produced the only goal of the game to take the Taysiders through.

For the club and the supporters the season was as good as over; all hopes of qualifying for Europe had disappeared. Ferguson was again the top scorer with 29 goals and national recognition came his way when he and Willie Callaghan were selected for the Scottish team which was to go on a world tour in the summer. It was agreed that the manager would enter into talks with Rangers' manager, Scot Symon, over Ferguson's future with the possibility of Alec Smith returning to East End Park in a part-exchange deal. There was no such good fortune for Fergie's brother, Martin, also on the club's books, as he was given a free transfer.

The club's reputation abroad meant that there was never any shortage of offers for the team to go on overseas tours. At one stage, a tour of North America looked likely, but this fell through. A trip to South Africa seemed another possibility until it was pointed out that the country had been suspended by FIFA. Eventually a trip to Cairo was arranged for the end of the season. Lightweight suits (at £18

10s each) were ordered and all the necessary travel arrangements were made. The after-effects of the inoculations forced the team to withdraw from the Fife Cup. Then at the last minute the deteriorating situation between Arab and Jew in the Middle East and the ensuing Six Day War caused the whole trip to be cancelled.

When it seemed as though the club was to be resigned to a quiet summer holiday, the news broke on 22 June that Cunningham wished to break his five-year contract and that the Board had agreed to let him go. Cunningham explained to an astounded press that he was disenchanted with the game and that, with no ulterior motives, he wanted to make a break from football. (The lure of football eventually proved too great and in October 1968 he was appointed manager of Falkirk. In 1971 he was offered, but declined, the job of managing Scotland's football team.)

Ground capacity (architects' estimates), 1967:	
Stand	*3,032*
Stand enclosures	*2,718*
West terracing	*6,010*
North enclosure	*7,360*
East terracing	*8,040*
Total	*27,160*

George Farm
(1967–70)

George Farm disputes the ownership of the Scottish Cup with Celtic manager, Jock Stein, 30 April 1968. (Dundee Courier)

SEASON 1967-68

Out of 30 applicants for the vacant manager's job, George Farm, the Raith Rovers' boss, was appointed in July 1967. After the war, Farm had played in goals for Armadale before being transferred to Hibs. From Easter Road he went in 1948 to Blackpool where he played in over 500 games during which he won a FA Cup Winners' medal in 1953 (along with Stanley Matthews) and 10 Scottish caps. He returned to Scotland in 1960 to Queen of the South and later became their player-manager. After that he managed Raith Rovers and had just helped their team into Division One when the summons to manage Dunfermline proved irresistible. Cunningham's administrative assistant, Tommy Walker, moved to Kirkcaldy to take over Farm's old job.

The transfer market occupied Farm almost immediately. Pat Gardner, a prolific goal-scorer, was bought from Raith Rovers for £17,000. The man he was to replace was Alec Ferguson whose transfer to Rangers was finally concluded. Before Dunfermline had acquired Fergie on an exchange, his old club, St Johnstone, had put him on the market at £3,000 and received no offers. Rangers bought their new forward for £60,000, thus breaking the old record between two Scottish clubs when Smith had gone to Ibrox in 1966. Other new signings included goalkeeper Willie Duff (who had gained a Cup medal with Hearts in 1956) on a free transfer from Peterborough and forward Barry Mitchell from Arbroath for £13,000. A young goalkeeper, Stewart Kennedy, was also signed from Camelon Juniors. Mr James Smith became the new administrative manager.

Though the club would not be competing in Europe in the forthcoming season the fans did have a chance to view a crack continental side when Borussia Dortmund visited East End Park in a pre-season friendly. With two of their World Cup stars on show, Emmerich and Held, the Germans defeated the Pars 3–2.

The new manager's first real test came with the League Cup in August. In their section containing Kilmarnock, Partick and Airdrie, Dunfermline could only manage two victories and ended as runners-up to the Ayrshire side. This disappointing start to the new season was carried over to the league campaign itself. Despite defeating his old club at Kirkcaldy in the opening game, Farm had to wait until 4 November before his side won at home, beating Clyde 1–0 with a Robertson penalty. Before then, Hearts had their first win at East End Park for six years.

At the AGM, the manager admitted his side had started off badly, but he hoped their form would improve. The proposal from the Celtic chairman that the Fife clubs should amalgamate was greeted with derision by the shareholders. The Board affirmed that since the major ground improvements were now over they hoped to concentrate on building up the team. It was agreed to increase the number of directors from four to five and the club doctor, Dr John Yellowley (43), was co-opted on to the Board. In his younger days he had played both cricket and football; in fact, at the end of his war service in the Navy, he turned down an approach from Queen's Park. He brought in a new rule that before a player joined the club he should first be medically examined. Shortly afterwards, Mr David Thomson, the architect of earlier triumphs, died.

When the balance sheet recorded a loss of £20,000 the Board gave serious consideration to selling Humbug Park, but Farm persuaded them to retain it. The Board allowed him to set up an Under-18 and an Under-16 team which would hopefully feed through young players to the first team in years to come and prevent talent leaving the area. To execute this ambitious policy, Andy Young, the Scottish scout for Leeds United, was hired. Young, a former player with Raith Rovers, was one of the best talent-spotters in the game and in joining Dunfermline he turned down the job of part-time manager at Cowdenbeath. In due course, expensive alterations costing £20,000 were carried out to Humbug Park: a new fence was erected round the perimeter, the pitch was re-aligned, dressing-rooms were constructed, a car park was created and a bungalow was even built to house the groundsman.

This ambitious youth policy would take years to pay dividends and the management were more concerned about immediate problems. As Farm had promised, their league form did improve to enable the club to face the Scottish Cup with some confidence. When the draw sent them to Parkhead the team realised that they would need more than just courage and high hopes. In the previous season, Jock Stein's men had won the European Cup and just about everything else that glittered. The Board were cautiously optimistic and decided to authorise the printing of tickets in advance just in case the Pars could scrape a draw.

Most of the 47,000 fans who turned up at Parkhead on 27 January confidently expected high-flying Celtic to sweep Dunfermline aside. A hard-working Athletic side refused to let Celtic settle and went in at half-time greatly encouraged by the blank scoreline. In the second half, Celtic received

Above: *Pat Gardner.*

Below: *Gardner scores Dunfermline's second goal to seal Celtic's fate in the Cup at Parkhead.* (Dundee Courier)

Above: *The Dunfermline defence is caught out in the opening minutes as Wilson (left) opens the scoring for St Johnstone in the first game.*

Opposite, top: *Barry and Miller lead their teams out onto the Hampden turf.*

Opposite, bottom: *Gardner volleys home the first goal past Cruickshank.*

the fright of their lives. A goal from Robertson in the 64th minute silenced the Parkhead support and when Gardner scored another 10 minutes later as a result of a poor pass back by Cattenach, Dunfermline were home and dry.

Aberdeen provided the opposition for the next round. Dunfermline's home advantage seemed to count for little when a Jimmy Smith goal after 39 minutes put the Dons into the lead in front of a crowd of 14,668. A penalty equaliser from Robertson in the 55th minute eased the pressure on the home side and East End Park went wild when Edwards clinched the tie with a goal five minutes from time.

For the second year running Dunfermline and Partick were again paired in the Scottish Cup. The 16,000 fans who turned up expecting an easy victory over the team that Dunfermline had earlier thrashed 4–0 were quickly disappointed. The Pars made very heavy weather of the task in front of them and only a single goal 10 minutes from time by Paton separated the two teams.

For the fifth time in seven years, Dunfermline had once more reached the semi-finals of the Cup. As on the two previous occasions that Dunfermline won through to the final, the venue was Tynecastle. This time their opponents were St Johnstone, managed by Willie Ormond, and a crowd of 14,268 turned up on 30 March to see both teams do battle. It became obvious early on that the Pars had chosen the wrong day to hit rock-bottom form. After Wilson had put the Perth side ahead after four minutes, Dunfermline struggled to string their game together. Gardner saved his colleagues' blushes by equalising in the 53rd minute with a freak goal. The Saints' keeper booted a clearance straight into Paton and the rebound fell neatly to Gardner who shot into the empty net.

In the replay, again at Tynecastle, Dunfermline seemed to be on edge and allowed St Johnstone to dominate the midfield. No one was surprised when, in the 65th minute, one of the outstanding players of the tie, Alec McDonald, put St Johnstone ahead. Never despairing, the Pars battled on and received their reward when Paton scored the

equaliser. With only six minutes to go, Dunfermline had a great chance to win the game when they were awarded a penalty. Robertson failed to score from the spot and Paton's rebound was saved. In extra-time, the Athletic began to dominate the game and new signing Ian Lister, a £2,000 buy from Raith Rovers who had come on as substitute, netted the winner. The other semi-final decided that Hearts, winners of the Cup on five previous occasions and captained by George Miller, would be their opponents.

For the third time in seven years the club and the town were caught in the grip of cup fever. By the time the final came around, Dunfermline had managed to clinch fourth place in the league. Just as he had done before previous cup games, Farm took his players off to Dunblane Hydro to plan victory over Hearts who were lying 12th in the league.

On 27 April, thousands of fans left the east of Scotland to make their way towards Hampden. Though Dunfermline supporters found it difficult to hire buses since Hearts' fans had already approached the same companies, nevertheless 150 buses and countless cars made the trek from west Fife. The total crowd was a disappointingly low one (indeed, the lowest since the war) – only 56,365. This was partly because neither team came from the west of Scotland and partly because Rangers carried on with their league fixture against Aberdeen at Ibrox on the same day in the search for points to clinch the championship. Pressure from Dunfermline succeeded in giving the Final pride of place from 1969 onwards, too late for themselves. (For the record, Rangers lost and Celtic won the title.)

The main surprise in the Pars' line-up was the exclusion of Jim Fraser in favour of John McGarty, a free transfer from Hibs, for only his third senior game for his new club.

Roy Barry, who had earlier shocked colleagues by asking for a transfer to England on account of alleged persecution from referees, retained his place. Interestingly, three Scandinavians: Jensen, Martin and Möller, were appearing in a Scottish Cup Final.

Dunfermline: Martin; Callaghan, Lunn; McGarty, Barry, T. Callaghan; Lister, Paton, Gardner, Robertson, Edwards. Sub.: Thomson.

Hearts: Cruickshank; Sneddon, Mann; Anderson, Thomson, Miller; Jensen, Townsend, Ford, Irvine, Traynor. Sub.: Möller.

If the first half gave the neutral fans little to enthuse over, the second half more than compensated. Gradually a weak Hearts side allowed Dunfermline to dominate and score their first goal through a volley from Gardner after 56 minutes. Three minutes later, Paton was about to score when Cruickshank upended him. From the resulting penalty kick, Lister scored to ease the Pars' worries. An own-goal from Lunn brought Hearts back into the game in the 70th minute but not for long. In the 73rd minute, Gardner scored another goal to send the Cup back to Dunfermline for only the second time.

Although the team were forbidden to do a lap of honour because of possible crowd trouble, the rapturous welcome that awaited them in Dunfermline more than made up for it. The recent Eurovision Song Contest hit, *Congratulations*, allowed the ecstatic 15,000 crowd to say it all. The team rounded off an eventful day with a civic reception in the City Chambers, turning the clock back seven years.

Above: *Ian Lister makes it 2–0 after 59 minutes from the penalty spot*

Below: *An own-goal from Lunn (on ground) brings Hearts back into the game – but not for long.*

Above: *Gardner puts the issue beyond doubt with goal number three.* (Dundee Courier)

Below: *Celebrations in the Dunfermline dressing room.* (Dundee Courier)

Top left: *George Farm congratulates the players.*

Top right: *Alec Edwards, Roy Barry and Hugh Robertson feeling on top of the world.* (Dunfermline Press)

Below: *1961 all over again.*

The season was almost over, but not quite. The rearranged fixture list had paired Dunfermline and Celtic together at East End Park on Tuesday 30 April. There was nothing really at stake and yet a record crowd, which will stand for all time, turned up to see the unique spectacle of the Cup holders playing the League Champions in the season of their success. It is estimated that 310 buses, five trains and numerous other forms of transport brought about 19,000 Celtic fans to see if their team could amass a record number of points for a 34-game league. (Rangers' all-time record of 76 points was achieved over 42 games in 1920-21.)

The officials at the turnstiles recorded that 27,816 customers paid to gain entry but this figure does not take into account the few thousand who broke in. Walls were scaled, gates burst open and crush barriers broken down as 30,000 fans scrambled to see the play. One Glasgow man, who simply walked in through a hole created in a wall, later sent the club a P.O. for 5/- to cover his admittance. Twice the referee had to stop play when fans climbed the floodlight pylons, scaled onto roofs, and spilled onto the pitch. In one incident a 67-year-old man from Glasgow died from head injuries sustained in a fall.

Then there was the game itself. The Pars contained the highly skilled Celtic attack and went ahead after 27 minutes through a Gardner goal. After the interval, Lennox equalised and went on to score the winner from what seemed an impossible angle. Celtic thus reached 63 points and went one better than Hearts' total in 1958. By recording 16 away wins in a season, Celtic set yet another record.

Dunfermline, led by Roy Barry, parade the Cup at East End Park before their game with the League Champions, Celtic. (Evening News)

At the end of the season, the club went ahead with the most adventurous overseas tour yet – to North America where a gruelling schedule awaited them. Sixteen players, the 12 of the Cup Final team plus Fraser, Totten, Mitchell and Duff, accompanied by Farm, Stevenson, Methven, the much travelled secretary, Jim McConville, and three directors, flew out on 9 May. Because of internal problems in Bermuda the glamour part of the tour was cancelled. The tour of America and Canada was an exhausting one and not well organised by the American promoters. Despite inaccurate and sensationalist reporting the club not only gained success on the field but made many friends and received invitations to return.

To crown a memorable season, the club were presented with the Regal-Thomson Shield for being Dunfermline's "Citizen of the Year" in recognition of the honours they had brought to the Auld Grey Town.

North American Tour	
Fall River Astros, Mass.	*0–0*
(abandoned at H-T)	
Manchester City, Toronto	*1–1*
Manchester City, Connecticut	*1–1*
Greek American SC, New York	*0–2*
Kansas City Spurs	*1–1*
Manchester City, Vancouver	*0–0*
Manchester City, Los Angeles	*0–0*
St Louis Stars, California	*3–1*
Rochester Lancers, NY	*8–1*
Ukrainians, Philadelphia	*7–0*

Scorers: Paton 7, Mitchell 6, Gardner 3, Lister 3, W. Callaghan 1, T. Callaghan 1.

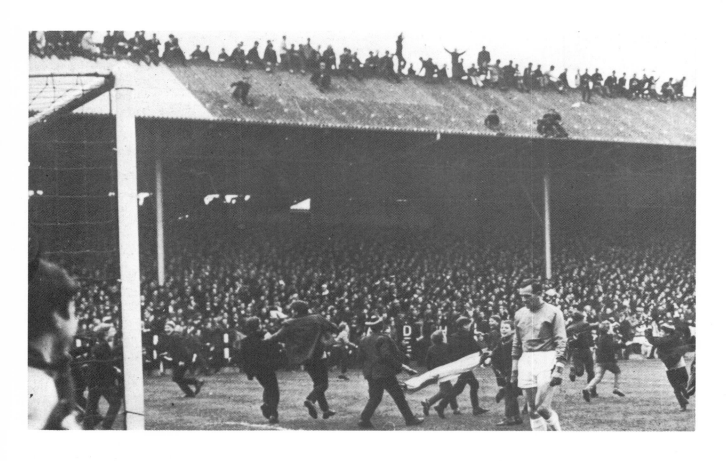

SEASON 1968-69

For the new season, George Farm strengthened his squad by signing three new players: Willie Renton from St Mirren for £7,750, Ian Cowan from Falkirk for £4,500 and George McKimmie from Dundee Violet. Barry had already withdrawn his tranfer request and decided to remain with the club. Any hopes of quickly adding to the silverware were dashed with a dismal showing in the League Cup which saw Dunfermline finish at the bottom of the section containing Clyde, Dundee United and Aberdeen and score only seven goals in the process.

It was the European Cup Winners' Cup which was to bring Dunfermline the greatest honours during the season. A first-round draw against Apoel from Nicosia in Cyprus gave the club an easy start. Up 5–0 at the interval the Pars added another five goals in the second half to set up a European record for the club of 10–1. The team which ran riot on the night of 18 September was: Martin; W. Callaghan, Lunn; McGarty, Barry, Renton; Robertson, Paton, Edwards, Gardner, Lister. (Subs.: T. Callaghan, I. Cowan. UEFA now allowed two substitutes.) Robertson and Renton, each scored two, the Callaghan brothers scored three goals while Barry, Gardner and Edwards completed the rout.

The return leg in the Mediterranean two weeks later

Opposite, top: A dispirited Ronnie Simpson after Gardner opens the scoring for Dunfermline. There was a record crowd in the ground and hundreds more were perched perilously on the roof of the enclosure and up the floodlight pylons. (Dunfermline Press)

Opposite, bottom: Roy Barry and Billy McNeill lead out their teams for an unforgettable match, 30 April 1968.

gave the Athletic a chance to enjoy the sunshine and scenery. In between, they notched up a more modest victory of 2–0 (Gardner and W. Callaghan scoring) to progress into the next round where another eastern Mediterranean club provided the opposition – Olympia of Greece, a competent side containing six internationalists. When Farm and trainer Stevenson went on a spying mission to Athens they saw a team which tackled strongly and which would command their full respect; subsequent meetings fully justified their first impressions.

In the first game at East End Park on 13 November, the 7,000 crowd saw Dunfermline apply incessant pressure in the first half without anything to show for it. The Greeks defended in depth and were not slow to use brute force when skill had failed. Four minutes into the second half, the Pars got the breakthrough they so desperately needed when Barry Mitchell, making his European debut, opened the scoring. In the 57th minute, Edwards scored a second goal and went on later to score his side's third. A late goal from Fraser sent the crowd home contented but wondering what kind of reception their team would receive in Athens.

Two weeks later their worst fears were to be realised when it looked as though Dunfermline were going to be kicked off the park in the second leg. The Greeks made a perfect start by scoring three goals in the first half hour and threatening to pound Dunfermline into the ground. The failure of the weak Czech referee to punish vicious fouls from the home team encouraged them to even greater

Below: Cup-winning side, 1968. Standing: J. Stevenson, P. Gardner, T. Callaghan, J. McGarty, B. Martin, B. Paton, R. Barry, J. Thomson, J. Lunn, G. Farm. Seated: J. Yellowley, R. Torrie, I. Lister, W. Callaghan, A. Watson, H. Robertson, A. Edwards, L. Jack, J. McConville.

DUNFERMLINE ATHLETIC FOOTBALL CLUB, SCOTTISH CUP WINNERS 1968

Above: *R. Barry, A. Watson, G. Farm, J. McConville, A. Cameron and others meet Archbishop Makarios in Cyprus.*

Below: *The Dunfermline defence are unable to prevent Olympia scoring their first goal.*

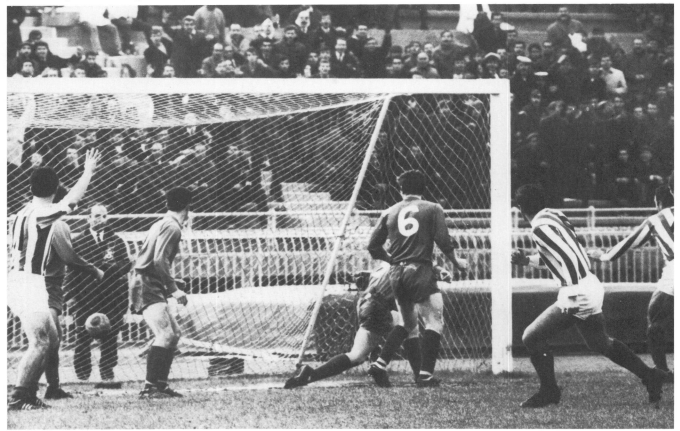

Above: *Willie Renton.* (Dunfermline Press)

Bottom right: *High winds shatter one of the giant TV screens being erected at East End Park to relay the West Bromwich game live from England.* (M. Allan)

excesses, especially in the second half as the Greeks desperately sought the equaliser. At one stage, the two captains were warned that the game would be abandoned unless tempers cooled. Ten minutes later, Mitchell was sent off and had to be physically dragged off the field by his manager. However, the 10 men hung on to record a 4–3 victory on aggregate.

Hopes of an all-British final were dashed when the third round draw brought West Bromwich to East End Park. A capacity crowd of 25,000, a record for a European game, turned up on 15 January hoping to see their team repeat their handsome victory over their previous English opponents, Everton.

Dunfermline: Duff; Callaghan, Lunn; Fraser, Barry, Thomson; Robertson, Paton, Edwards, Renton, Gardner.

West Bromwich: Osborne; Fraser, Wilson; Brown, Talbut, Kaye; Martin, Lovett, Astle, Collard, Hartford. (Manager A. Ashman.)

Though no goals were scored, the crowd witnessed an exciting game of football, full of end-to-end action. The match was hard and stoutly contested but never dirty. Several times, the Athletic looked as though they might have scored, but the team which had scored so prolifically in the earlier rounds found itself unable to put the ball in the back of the net.

Refusing to believe that their team had missed their chance, 2,000 fans travelled to the Midlands for the return leg on 19 February, while another 12,000 braved howling gales at East End Park on the same night to view the game on giant screens which had been erected to show the game live via close-circuit TV. Weather conditions were little

better down south but that did not stop a crowd of 32,000 turning up at The Hawthorns. On a bone-hard pitch, Dunfermline had the perfect start in scoring a goal through Gardner after only two minutes. Thereafter, a valiant rear-guard action, brilliantly organised by Barry, kept the talented English forward line at bay. After 90 minutes that single goal was enough to send the Pars into the semi-final of a European trophy for the first time in their history and to end West Bromwich's three-year unbroken home record. Seldom has a Scottish club twice put English opposition out of a European competition.

When the semi-final draw was made only one club separated Dunfermline from a place in the final at Basle – Slovan Bratislava. Disappointingly, only 16,559 fans turned up on 9 April for one of the club's most important games. The Board and management always maintained that European football was never a money-spinner and it is not difficult to see what they meant. The game followed the all too familiar pattern of the home side attacking relentlessly while the visitors coolly soaked up the pressure although the Czechs gave ample warning that they could be dangerous on the attack. With the interval approaching and nothing to show for all-out attack the Pars opened the scoring through Fraser on the stroke of half-time.

After the break, Dunfermline should have gone further ahead when Gardner narrowly missed after the Czech keeper had struck his goal-kick straight at the Athletic forward. The Czechs always thought they could snatch an equaliser and their confidence was cruelly rewarded when, with only seven minutes left, Duff failed to catch a lob which allowed the Czechs back on to level terms. No

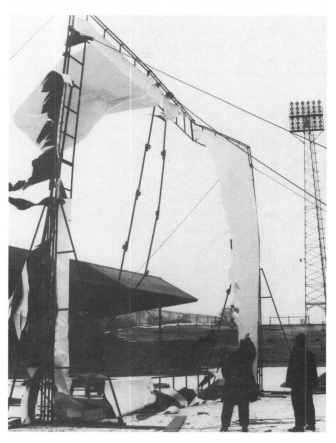

A happy Dunfermline party arriving back at Waverley station after defeating West Bromwich 1–0. (Dundee Courier)

further scoring resulted and, as in the previous round, there were few supporters who failed to appreciate the enormity of the task which faced their team in the return leg.

On 23 April, in Bratislava, Dunfermline's fine early play suggested that they would be difficult to dislodge from the tournament. A mistake in the 24th minute, however, allowed Capkovic, the scorer in the first leg, to open the scoring. After that the Czechs, determined not to surrender their lead, brutally broke up any promising moves from the visitors. A more positive and authoritarian referee than the Yugoslav on duty would quickly and effectively have brought the offending Czechs to order. Fierce tackling and numerous off-the-ball incidents killed the game as a football spectacle and allowed the home side to hang on to their slender lead. Five players were booked and with just over half an hour to go Gardner was sent off to complete a miserable evening for the Athletic. It was small consolation for Dunfermline when their conquerors beat Barcelona in the final.

Pride of place has rightly been given to Dunfermline's European exploits but their league programme was not without thrills and missed opportunities. The team's opening game against Raith Rovers at home produced a fine 3–2 win but this was immediately cancelled by a 1–0 defeat at Tynecastle. A creditable 1–1 home draw against Celtic before a crowd of 23,000 was followed up by three victories which put them joint top of the league with Celtic by mid-October. However, they suffered a setback in the next game by losing 3–0 to Rangers, their first defeat at Ibrox since March 1964.

During the following month, the Athletic lost a valuable player and faithful servant when Tommy Callaghan was transferred to Celtic for £30,000, a record for the Glasgow club. His brother's request for a transfer was turned down. Both had earlier been selected to play against the Irish League at Dublin. The team was further unsettled when Barry renewed his transfer request, hoping to go to an English club to make a fresh start. As cover in the defence, the tall centre half, Doug Baillie, was signed from Falkirk, having had previous experience with Airdrie, Rangers and Third Lanark. Ominously for the future, the Board applied to the Bank for overdraft facilities of up to £20,000.

A defeat at Easter Road before Christmas followed by away defeats at Parkhead (before 43,000 fans) and at Perth after the New Year blunted Dunfermline's title challenge. Thereafter, a run of 11 games produced only one defeat, away to Clyde, which was sufficient to guarantee them third position in the table and a place again in Europe. Assisting in this charge to the end of the season was new signing George McLean, the former St Mirren and Rangers striker bought from Dundee for £22,000, which was the highest fee the club had ever paid for a player. McLean got a chance to play against one of his old clubs when Rangers visited East End Park for the last game of the season. Though no places in the league were at stake, 11,700 fans turned up to see the Light Blues win 3–0 and end the Pars' unbeaten home record for the season.

In the Scottish Cup, supporters had great expectations that their team might retain the coveted trophy and so become the first club outside the Old Firm to accomplish this feat since the Great War. The defence of the trophy got off to a good start when they easily beat Raith 2–0 at Kirkcaldy on 25 January, Gardner and Paton the scorers.

Fans took the pairing of Aberdeen and Dunfermline in the second round as a good omen since the Pittodrie club was overcome in each of the previous cup-winning campaigns. Though originally scheduled for Saturday 8 February, the game was postponed because of inclement weather and other commitments until Tuesday 25th. When the Pars found themselves 2–0 down early in the second half it looked like the end of their cup hopes. A goal by Fraser in the 58th minute gave the Athletic a lifeline and just two minutes from the end Renton levelled the tie at 2–2. The replay was held the following night at East End Park, the Pars' fourth game in eight days and not long after their epic struggle against West Brom. When Aberdeen went a goal up after 10 minutes, Dunfermline found they had a real fight on their hands. Summoning up every ounce of energy they desperately strove for the equaliser, but McGarr was in excellent form in goal and thwarted Dunfermline on several occasions. Throwing everything into attack, Dunfermline left themselves open at the back for Robb to score the vital second, and killer, goal to give the Dons victory. This was the club's first defeat at home in the Scottish Cup since they ignominiously lost to Stenhousemuir in February 1960.

Right: Centre half Doug Baillie. (Dunfermline Press)

Below: Relief for Dunfermline as Fraser opens the scoring against Slovan Bratislava on the stroke of half-time. (Dundee Courier)

Above: *An unusual training stint for the players at McKane Park before leaving the next day for their tour of Norway.* (Daily Record)

Left: *Goalkeeper Willie Duff.* (Dunfermline Press)

Opposite: *Walking out to board the plane at Turnhouse for the flight to Bordeaux are: G. McKimmie (left), George McLean, Barry Mitchell and John McGarty.* (Daily Record)

A short tour of Norway completed another eventful season for the club. Solid performances in the league had assured the team yet again of a high position in the table; fewer and fewer fans could now remember what it was like to be fighting in the closing weeks of a season to avoid relegation. Though their run in the Scottish Cup was short, their progress in the Cup Winners' Cup reminded Europe that the Pars were still one of the Continent's top clubs. In the spring, Farm had signed a contract tying him to East End Park for five years. For the first time, the Board recorded in their minutes that the manager of the club would receive a £2,000 bonus if he won a European trophy, signalling that the possibility of landing such a cup was no mere pipe-dream. Despite its successes, the club never became a monolithic, uncaring structure, as many former players will testify; it still found the time to bestow wedding gifts on players taking the plunge, to give interest-free loans to staff and to offer friendly advice to troubled minds.

SEASON 1969-70

As the "swinging sixties" drew to a close, Dunfermline's ever-growing reputation meant that invitations from English clubs to play in friendlies were always forthcoming and two such challenges were taken up before the start of the season. In their game at Birmingham against Aston Villa, managed by Tommy Docherty, the Pars lost 3–2 and later at Blackpool they again lost by the odd goal of the game, 2–1 on that occasion. These relatively poor results were repeated in the League Cup. Despite all the glory that the club had throughout the sixties in the Scottish Cup, the League and in Europe, their poorest form was always reserved for this competition. During the decade, it will be recalled that the club only qualified on two occasions for the quarter-finals and each time they were comprehensively beaten. Their latest cup venture proved to be no better. For the second year running, they came bottom of their section, allowing Aberdeen to go forward.

In the opening game at Pittodrie, the team lost the services of a key player when defender Jim Fraser was carried off for the second time in his career with a broken leg. There were further problems for the defence when 'keeper Martin asked for a transfer. Earlier, the Board had enquired whether Southampton would be prepared to swap their unsettled 'keeper, Eric Martin, for his Danish namesake, but had met with a negative response. Farm, himself a former 'keeper, was clearly unhappy about this crucial position and had already given one of his reserve custodians, Stewart Kennedy, a free transfer. Kennedy went on to have a chequered career with Rangers and the Scottish international team. Also released on a free transfer was full back Alec Totten who had the misfortune to be understudy

to two of the best defenders in the business, Willie Callaghan and John Lunn, who were to play their 300th game together later in the season. Being groomed in the reserves was one of the best prospects seen at East End Park in recent years – Dave McNicoll, a young defender signed from Butterburn Youth Club.

Once again it was European involvement which brought the Pars to the headlines. For the first time, Dunfermline drew French opposition in the form of Girondins from Bordeaux, in the first round of the Fairs Cup. The French representatives were known to be a very competent side, but what surprised the crowd of 11,363 in the first leg at East End Park on 16 September was the dirty play served up by the visitors. As a result of constant pressure, Dunfermline went ahead through Paton after 27 minutes. Ten minutes later the team would have gone two up had McLean not hit the post with a penalty kick. In the second half, Bordeaux made it easy for the home side when two of their players were sent off for crude tackles. Further goals against the depleted team from Mitchell, Paton and Gardner gave Dunfermline a comfortable four-goal lead to take to France. The team on duty was: Duff; Callaghan, Lunn; McGarty, Baillie, Renton; Mitchell, Paton, Edwards, Gardner, McLean.

The return leg two weeks later turned out to be the nightmare that many had feared. Abysmally weak refereeing yet again allowed the home side to set football and skill aside and to concentrate on crippling the opposition. Egged on by a seething crowd of 20,000, the French tried in vain to reduce the Pars to their level of butchery. Although the visitors lost a goal after 18 minutes they never looked like losing the tie and a late goal near the end gave the French a 2–0 victory on the night. Dunfermline's problems were far

The Dunfermline party waiting to board the bus which will take them on the first part of their journey to Poland: From left: Gardner, McGarty, Martin, Renton, Farm, Mitchell, Duff, Robertson, Paton, Edwards, McNicoll, Lunn, Thomson, Cowan and Callaghar (Dundee Courier)

from over. The team was chased off the field into the dressing-room where they locked themselves in for over an hour. With the help of the police and guard dogs, the team was eventually escorted safely back to their hotel.

Their opponents in round two, Gwardia of Poland, were to provide a total contrast. The Polish Army side contained four internationalists and were known to be a fast team proficient at passing the ball accurately. The first leg at East End Park on 5 November failed to produce the fireworks of the earlier round. The game was certainly not a classic though it did contain plenty of honest endeavour. After McLean put his side into an early lead, Dunfermline failed to capitalise on a number of chances and allowed the Poles to come back into the game in the 63rd minute when a defensive error put the visitors level. The winner from Gardner 17 minutes from time sent the 11,000 crowd home with some hope of progress into the next round.

In Poland, two weeks later, Renton took the pressure off his colleagues by scoring a fine goal after only three minutes. Thereafter, a sound Athletic defence, ably marshalled by Baillie, was able to frustrate anything which the Poles threw at them. No more goals were scored and Dunfermline held on to record their first ever victory behind the Iron Curtain and to enter the third round on a 3–1 aggregate. The Board thanked the Poles for their excellent hospitality and recorded that "the match, without doubt, was the fairest the club had undertaken in a Euro-

pean competition away from home".

Dunfermline were under no illusions as to the quality of their third-round opponents, the Royal Sporting Club of Anderlecht, an experienced and well-organised Belgian side although it was noted that they had never yet put a British side out of a European competition. In the first leg in Brussels on 17 December, Dunfermline did well to finish the game behind by the only goal of the game which the Belgians scored on the stroke of half-time.

The return leg on 14 January turned out to be full of excitement and drama. After nine minutes, George McLean received a tremendous ovation for the great solo goal he scored to level the tie on aggregate. Seven minutes later, Edwards had a great chance to kill off the visitors when his side were awarded a penalty kick. Edwards missed, the ball striking the post then rebounding off the 'keeper's face before it was cleared. The second half was only seconds old when Mitchell brought out another great cheer from the 11,700 crowd with a well-taken goal to put the Pars ahead on aggregate. As the minutes ticked away it seemed as though Dunfermline were about to record another famous victory. Then disaster struck in the last 17 minutes. The Belgians broke out of defence and snatched a goal to level the tie at two goals each. As Dunfermline would have gone out on the away goals rule everyone surged forward to seize the vital goal. Sadly, it came at the other end where Anderlecht scored their second goal of the night to bring despair to the home support. The Pars battled on and though another McLean goal gave Dunfermline a deserved victory on the night, the 3–3 aggregate score was enough to put the home side out of Europe.

"Ah well, that's it over for another year," one fan might

Above: *G. McLean, third from left, opens the scoring against Gwardia at East End Park.* (Dundee Courier)

Below: *G. McLean, P. Gardner, A. Edwards, B. Paton, B. Mitchell.* (Dundee Courier)

have remarked to his friend on the way home, as though he was putting away the Christmas decorations in the attic until the next time. What the fans could not have appreciated that night as they wearily trudged home was that they had just witnessed the end of an era which had begun almost 10 years earlier.

Meanwhile, in the league campaign, Dunfermline had got off to the sort of start which suggested to the fans that perhaps they might yet manage to win this elusive honour. Their programme began with a fine away win over St Mirren which gave McLean his first hat-trick for his new club in their 3–1 win. Though they contrived to drop a point at home to newly-promoted Ayr, they made amends the following week by defeating Celtic 2–1 at East End Park in front of almost 23,000 fans. Form like that put them second top in the league by October. The eventual transfer of Barry to Coventry City for £45,000 and the departure of Lister for £3,000 to St Mirren seemed to have little adverse effect on the team's fortunes. In early November, a 2–1 victory over Aberdeen put them in top position and un-defeated at home. Rumours that Farm might take over White's job at Ibrox brought a firm denial from the manager.

With victory on the way against Gwardia Warsaw in mid-November, the Pars looked to be on the crest of a wave when everything began to go wrong. On the last Saturday of November, Dunfermline lost an important away game to one of their main rivals, Hibs, followed two weeks later by their first home defeat at the hands of Dun-dee United. In this game Paton broke his leg and was to be sidelined for several months.

To try to solve his goalkeeping problem, Farm signed John Arrol from Dundee for £3,000, paving the way for Bent Martin to be later released on a free transfer. To give added fire to a forward line which had failed to score a goal in six of their last eight games in 1969, Peter Millar was signed from Arbroath for £10,000 and Jim Gillespie was acquired on a free transfer from Raith Rovers. Gillespie cer-tainly made an impression in the first game of the New Year by scoring two goals against his old club to give the Pars a 3–0 victory. Away from home, Dunfermline had a disastrous run losing six games on the trot to kill off any hopes of qualifying for Europe, far less winning the title. By the end of the season, Dunfermline could only tie with Morton in ninth place, 22 points behind the champions; in the process they scored only 45 goals in 34 games, easily one of their worst performances of the decade, though sufficiently meritorious to gain entry to a new competition involving the top six clubs from either side of the border, the British Cup sponsored by Texaco.

Their sojourn in the Scottish Cup is easily written. In a repeat of the draw two seasons ago, when Dunfermline won the Cup, the draw sent them to Parkhead to meet the cup-holders. Dave McNicoll (18) led his team out as the club's youngest captain ever. Undaunted by the 50,000 crowd, the Pars looked like repeating their success when they opened the scoring through Gillespie. Even when Hughes equalised, it looked like Dunfermline had weathered the Celtic pressure and would take the game to a replay. A last-minute goal from Hood decided that Dunfermline would make an early exit from the Cup which, coupled

The squad photographed during a break in training at Dunblane. (Dundee Courier)

Above: *George Farm being encouraged to play it cool by several willing helpers.* (Daily Record)

Below: *No comment required.* (Daily Mail)

with their dismissal from the Fairs Cup ten days earlier, and their indifferent league form, left the fans with little to cheer about for the rest of the season.

For the future, the supporters were pleased to note that Dave McNicoll and Jim Brown had been selected for a trial for the Scottish Youth Professional Select, while old campaigner, Willie Callaghan, became only the third Athletic player to win a full Scottish cap when he played against Wales at Hampden on 22 April; one month earlier he had played against the English League at Coventry. McLean was top scorer with 19 goals.

The defeat by Anderlecht certainly marked a turning point in the club's history. Never again in the first century of their existence would Dunfermline ever compete seriously in European competition. On the outbreak of war in 1914 the British Foreign Secretary remarked: "The lamps are going out all over Europe; we shall not see them lit again in our lifetime." Fitting words perhaps on which to draw the curtain on the Glorious Sixties. The passports lapsed, the vaccinations were no longer required, the telephone lines to European consulates were disconnected and the airline schedules were thrown away; an Alexanders' bus timetable would once again suffice.

The end of the season was not without its humour. On 25 May, the Board minutes recorded that "assistant groundsman R. Parker had broken his false teeth while attempting to start the mower. Claim sent to the Guardian Assurance Company". History, alas, has not recorded the outcome.

FALL FROM GRACE

Decline in the Seventies

SEASON 1970-71

The first full season of the new decade began inauspiciously amidst acrimony. On the first day of training, Alec Edwards and Barry Mitchell failed to turn up for training and were disciplined. Renton also stayed away from training and was given a free transfer. Fraser, Callaghan and Gardner put in for transfers but later withdrew them. Indeed, Fraser, now fully recovered from his broken leg, went on to captain the side. Paton was still recuperating from his leg break and was unable to play. Doug Baillie had already left to become a sports journalist. Four new young players made up the squad of 23 full-time players – Jim Wallace (16), an inside forward from Sauchie; Jim Scott (16) from Leven Royal Colts; Andy Tracey (19) from Lochore Welfare and Bonar Mercer (17), a former schoolboy internationalist.

The opening game of the season, a friendly match against Hearts, gave the fans a foretaste of what was to become all too commonplace in the next few months – defeat, on this occasion by 4–2. The League Cup fixtures saw Dunfermline lose five games on the trot, including a 6–0 defeat from Rangers in front of 18,000 fans. Overall, the team could only muster four goals and one point to finish well behind Rangers, Morton and Motherwell. Despite this poor showing, the team actually received an increase in wages to entice the two rebels back to the fold. Mitchell soon made his peace, but the club was deprived of Edwards' valuable services until November.

Nor was there any improvement in their league form. In the opening game, at Somerset Park, lowly Ayr trounced

P. Gardner, A. Edwards, B. Mitchell, J. McBride and H. Robertson on the putting green at Largs.

the Pars 4–1. In that game another promising youngster, Kenny Thomson, made what was to be the first of several hundred appearances for the team. Thomson, a half back, had been signed from Dunfermline United and initially remained a part-timer. His grandfather, Mr Jim Thomson, had been a member of the successful Qualifying Cup team of 1911. In the following game, the Pars had a chance to halt their slide against newly-promoted Cowdenbeath, now managed by Andy Matthew, a former Athletic player. This was the first time the two sides had met each other in the First Division since 1927-28. Though Dunfermline had then gained three points from their neighbours, on this occasion they were beaten 2–1 in front of their own fans. The manager was also reprimanded by the Board for suggesting in the programme that an amalgamation of the four Fife clubs might possibly be the best way for the county to challenge the Old Firm seriously.

With eight games gone without a victory pressure began to build up on the manager, forcing him to issue a statement entitled, "I won't resign". The timely intervention of the first leg of the Texaco Cup on 16 September should have given the manager time to re-group his beleaguered troops, but the match at White Hart Lane against a talented Spurs side destroyed what little confidence the team still had. The English side, containing names like Mullery, Peters, Gilzean, Perryman, England and Chivers, won easily by 4–0. Two further league defeats by Hearts (whose reserves won 10–1) and Falkirk (managed by Willie Cunningham and fielding A. Totten, A. Ferguson and G. Miller) added to the gloom at East End Park. To bolster up a shaky defence, experienced defender John Cushley (27) was bought from West Ham for £5,000. Everyone heaved a sigh of relief when a 1–1 draw at Love Street on 26 September brought the Pars their first league point although it

The Dunfermline team at Tannadice in October 1970. Standing: Callaghan, Cushley, Fraser, Arrol, McNicoll, Lunn, McKimmie (sub). Front: Gardner, Robertson, Mitchell, Walsh, McLean. (Dundee Courier)

did nothing to alter their place at the foot of the table. For the first time in a decade the word "relegation" was being whispered across the terracing. The final straw for the club came on Tuesday 29 September when Spurs further humiliated Dunfermline 3–0 in the return leg. A special meeting of the Board was convened the next day at which Mr Andrew Watson (65) resigned as chairman for health and business reasons, though he remained on the Board. Local lawyer Leonard Jack stepped up to become chairman with Dr Yellowley taking over as vice-chairman. The first action of the new Board was to sack George Farm as manager.

On 22nd October, 39-year-old Alec Wright beat off 38 applicants to become the new manager. He had begun his playing career as a half back with Partick Thistle before moving to East Fife. After coaching positions with Clyde and Partick he was appointed the full-time manager of St Mirren, a part-time side. During his four years at Love Street, he had helped steer the 'Buddies' to promotion in 1968. The club he had just joined was in a precarious position. After Farm's departure, the team had lost each of their three games to anchor them firmly at the foot of the table In Wright's first nine matches only four points were secured from four draws. Fortunately for the club, fellow strugglers like Ayr and Cowdenbeath were doing little better. On 19 December, the club received the best possible Christmas present when it recorded its first victory of the season – a 4–1 victory over Airdrie at East End Park to end a dismal run of seven draws and 17 defeats. Two more precious points were gained on Boxing Day when Ayr were defeated 5–0.

The changeover of managers brought the inevitable shuffles behind the scenes. Wright brought in Willie McLean from his old club to be trainer, with the former incumbent, Andy Stevenson, becoming physiotherapist. Assistant trainer Bob Methven left the club. George McLean was sold to Ayr for £10,000 and to replace him, former Celtic striker, Joe McBride, was bought from Hibs for £3,000. International goalkeeper Ernie McGarr was signed from Aberdeen for £5,500 to tighten up the defence and he went straight into the first team. Mr James Watters was persuaded to sever his connection with East Fife and to join the Board at East End Park. A native of Buckhaven and an architectural draughtsman by profession, Watters had played in goals for Hearts (1944–56) and then for East Fife and was now a successful businessman in Dunfermline.

In an otherwise gloomy situation, the club could take some pride from the inclusion of five of their 'S' signings in the Scottish Under-18 Schoolboy side, with a sixth chosen as a reserve. The products of the youth policy were Jim Paterson, Jim Leishman, Gordon Pate, Peter Brown, David Stobie and Robert Marshall.

The big talking-point in football in Dunfermline at the start of 1971 was not so much the club's defeat again by Cowdenbeath, as the Ibrox disaster which claimed the lives of 66 spectators. The calamity was to have repercussions throughout football, not least in the eventual demand through the resultant Wheatley Report that grounds throughout Scotland be made safe for the public. Thanks to the far-sighted policies of the Board in the sixties, Dunfermline possessed a ground which required few modifications to comply with the new stringent safety requirements.

In January, the Scottish Cup provided a welcome break from the nerve-racking ordeal of gaining league points. Under the new format for the Cup, the major clubs were exempt until round three by which time the weaker teams would have reduced themselves in number in earlier rounds. Fortune favoured the Pars by giving them their first home draw since 1968 and against relatively easy opposition at that, Arbroath. For 77 minutes, however, it

seemed as though Dunfermline, trailing 1–0, might make an inglorious exit until three late goals from Millar, Gardner and McBride saw them safely through. The fourth round sent the Athletic to Parkhead to tackle Celtic who had already beaten Dunfermline twice in the league. In front of a 37,000 crowd, Wallace put Celtic ahead only for former clubmate, McBride, to slot home the equaliser. Local hopes of a spectacular upset in the replay were dashed when a goal from Harry Hood settled the issue. It was small consolation for Dunfermline to claim later that they had been put out by the eventual winners of the trophy.

The cup defeat meant that their total concentration could now be given to retrieving an apparently hopeless situation in the league. Hopes were raised by a good victory over Dundee United in February, their first victory over the Tannadice side at East End Park for seven years. Thereafter, the Pars were to win only one other league match, against Morton, although five were to be drawn. By the last game of the season, Cowdenbeath were already doomed despite completing the double over their neighbours; the second bottom berth would go to either Dunfermline or St Mirren who were level on points. Both lost their last games against Airdrie and Celtic respectively and superior goal difference, used for the first time instead of goal average, kept Dunfermline up by the smallest of decimal places to complete an escape act that would have done Houdini proud. Significantly, the club's top scorers for the season, Gardner and McBride, could muster only 10 goals each; throughout the season not a single away victory was recorded.

During the summer, a financial crisis developed which threatened to destroy the club; in simple terms the club was on the point of bankruptcy. Throughout the sixties, the club had been very successful, ploughing its profits into ground improvements and only selling players as a last resort; skilled players were often found from local junior teams or picked up at bargain prices from senior clubs. In order to compete with the Old Firm the club paid high wages and bonuses, but even at the pinnacle of their suc-

Opposite: *The Scottish Schoolboys U-18 side which met England at Broomfield contained five Dunfermline players. Back row, to right of keeper: Marshall and Leishman. Front (middle three): Brown, Paterson and Pate (capt).*

Above: *Wallace of Celtic beating Cushley to put his club ahead in the Cup.* (Dundee Courier)

Below: *Centre half Dave McNicoll.* (Dunfermline Press)

cesses the team never received on a regular basis the massive crowds which Rangers and Celtic took for granted. The attendance at top European games, for example, was often struggling to pass the 10,000 mark while awkward foreign trips yielded little financial return. Latterly the club had begun to splash out considerable amounts of money in buying new players, sometimes with little to show for their investment but an ever-increasing overdraft. Keeping up with the Joneses was not in Dunfermline's tradition or capabilities. In the year ending July 1970, the club lost £13,015; one year later the loss had risen to £58,338 (and would have been much greater but for donations) with no large outgoing transfers to ameliorate the situation. A poor season with no challenge for any of the major honours either at home or abroad was enough to ring the panic buttons at the Bank. Leonard Jack, convalescing from illness in the Cotswolds, was summoned back from his holiday to mastermind a recovery.

In July, a public appeal was launched to avert the kind of shutdown which had previously befallen Third Lanark. The Town Council, businesses and private individuals were feverishly urged by the chairman to invest in Patrons' Loans to raise the necessary cash. While the club floundered, two unsuccessful take-over bids were mounted by Edinburgh councillor, John Kidd, and Glasgow businessman, Jim Murphy, which would have taken control of the club out of the town.

Sufficient money did come into the club to keep it solvent, but once again the club found itself in the harsh position of having to cut its coat according to its cloth. The days of air travel and continental hotels seemed to be fast slipping away as an era of austerity, soon to be aggravated by soaring inflation and declining gates, returned. To strengthen the Board, two new members were appointed – Mr William M. Rennie, a successful local building contractor, and Mr William Jamieson, the director of a painting firm.

SEASON 1971-72

The key to this season can be summed up in one word – youth. Few of the old guard who had won the Cup in 1968 and taken the club into Europe were left or were fit to play. Two loyal servants, Jim Thomson and Hugh Robertson, were freed. As a result of the deteriorating financial position there was no money to splash out on new players. Instead, the club turned to its youth policy and hoped that the promising youngsters on their books would mature quickly enough to give the team the vital blood transfusion it so desperately required. Despite belt-tightening, the club was able to retain 24 full-time players with another four signed on a part-time basis. The average age of the squad was only 22 years and exactly half were under 21 years. Joe McBride, at the grand old age of 32, was the only player over thirty. No fewer than 19 of the squad had been with the club for less than two years.

Overshadowing these statistics was the sudden death on 29 August of Leonard Jack, chairman for less than a year. As a director of the club for the past 11 years, he had striven to keep Dunfermline amongst the top clubs, not just in Scotland, but in Europe. His legal training, his administrative talents, his untiring energy, his business acumen and his sound judgment had skilfully guided the club through many crises, none less than the most recent one which helped precipitate his death. His son, Mr Douglas Jack, was co-opted on to the Board. Dr John Yellowley stepped up to become chairman with Mr Jimmy Watters becoming vice-chairman. To encourage young fans to follow "their team", a Junior Supporters' Club was started by Martin Sisman, and in the stand complex a new Patrons' Room was opened to cater for those who had helped bail the club out over the summer.

Team of 1971-72. Back row: Lunn, Pate, Gardner, Wallace, Paton, Graham, McBride, Mercer, Watchman. Middle: McLean, Gillespie, Mitchell, Leishman, McGarr, Fraser, Arrol, Cushley, McNicoll, Miller, A. Stevenson. Front: P. Brown, Paterson, Brown, Scott, Wright, Thomson, Callaghan, O'Neill, Edwards. (Dundee Courier)

The manager had a good chance to experiment with his young players during a pre-season tour of Ireland. One game was played in the Republic against Finn Harps (0–0) while the other two, against Coleraine (0–0) and Newtonards (1–1), took place in the North. The disappointments of the tour were carried over to the Challenge Match arranged against West Ham at East End Park on 9 August. The Hammers, managed by Ron Greenwood, contained a galaxy of stars – Clyde Best, Billy Bonds, Trevor Brooking, Bobby Ferguson, Geoff Hurst, 'Pop' Robson, plus England captain, Bobby Moore. A goal from Gardner knocked the English club off their stride but a hat-trick from Hurst eventually gave them a 3–1 victory.

With Paton back in the side after a long lay-off, Dunfermline, playing in a new all-white strip, made a promising start in the League Cup. Victories over Airdrie and Hearts and an away draw at Perth saw the Pars top their section at the half-way stage. Even more pleasing for the management was the way that teenagers like Mercer and Brown were fitting into the team. Sadly, John Lunn had a recurrence of the illness which had sidelined him for several months in 1967 and he was unable to play any part this season. Defeats in the next three games sent the Pars to the bottom of their section for the fourth year in succession.

The League also started with optimism when newly-promoted East Fife were defeated 1–0 at Bayview, the goal coming from young 'Pud' Paterson who was making his first team debut in the league. This marked the club's first away league win for 18 months. In the same month, another of the youngsters, Jim Leishman, also broke into the first team. In mid-October, the ubiquitous Joe McBride was on the move again, this time to Clyde for £1,000. Following him out was Alec Edwards, still only 25, one of the club's most talented players of all time. Edwards, the winner of

five youth caps, an amateur international cap and an Under-23 cap, had clearly been unsettled for some time and Hibs snatched him up for a mere £13,000.

The departure of these experienced players and the blooding of raw youngsters was soon reflected in dismal results in the league. However, their narrow 2–1 home defeat by a Celtic team that contained Hay, Gemmell, McNeill, Connolly, Macari and Dalglish, showed that the young team was not without ability and determination. Off the field, the club gained their only trophy of the season when John Cushley, Alec Wright and Jim Fraser beat Leicester City in the final of the popular BBC show, *Quiz Ball*.

Their victory over Airdrie on 30 October was only the second win of the season. In the following week, not only did the team lose narrowly at Easter Road, but Bert Paton was carried off for the second time with a broken leg. Four successive defeats in December put them firmly at the bottom of the league with relegation once again a distinct possibility. In his New Year's message, the new chairman recorded that "as we take our first steps into 1972 my most earnest wish is that former glory will eventually be restored to East End Park and that the nightmare of 1971 will be soon erased from all our minds". The nightmare was to continue. It took a victory against Aberdeen on 22 January to give the club their first victory in 13 games. Another two youngsters were added to the squad in the hope that the right blend could be found. One was Ken Mackie, a 16-year-old schoolboy from Kirkcaldy, and the other, Graham Shaw (20), provisionally signed from Musselburgh. Gardner was transferred to Dundee United for £5,000.

Hopes that a good run in the Cup might make amends were quickly dashed at the first hurdle when the team was drawn to play Raith Rovers at Stark's Park. Raith were now managed by George Farm and trained by Bob Methven, former staff, of course, at East End Park. Without putting up too much of a fight, Dunfermline were beaten 2–0. This humiliation, coupled with another defeat from Celtic, was enough to convince the Board on 21 February that the manager and his coach had to go. The Board turned to

Top left: *The 1971* Quiz Ball *Champions: J. Cushley, A. Wright and J. Fraser.*

Above: *Graham Shaw.* (Dunfermline Press)

former player and captain, George Miller, now with Falkirk by way of Wolves and Hearts, to rescue the club from the abyss into which it had plunged. As he walked through the doors of the stadium his mind must have wandered back to the spring of 1960 when he, as a young player, had watched a new, untried manager appear to rally a team which had lost its confidence.

In only his second game, Miller appeared to have made a breakthrough when youngsters Paterson and Mackie (making his debut) gave Dunfermline á 2–1 victory over Hibs which was followed up by an away draw at Rugby Park and victory at Perth. Despite a defeat at Dens Park, where Graham Shaw made his debut, a victory over Morton gave the Pars a life-line which was promptly thrown away by a 2–2 home draw versus Clyde. A marvellous and unexpected 4–3 win over Rangers at Ibrox, with Leishman netting the winner, still gave the Athletic a chance to avoid the drop. For the last game of the season, Dundee United, under new manager Jim McLean, were the visitors. Hindsight has shown that a victory would have given the Pars the two points they needed to overtake Clyde and tie with East Fife whose inferior goal difference would have relegated them. History has recorded that Dunfermline lost 1–0 before a crowd of 8,500 and were relegated, despite winning the same number of points as last year, to the Second Division, a berth they had not occupied since 1958.

Barry Mitchell, the club's top scorer with eight goals, was transferred to Aberdeen for a welcome cheque of £25,000. After 16 years on the Board, Mr Bob Torrie resigned. To build up team morale a post-season trip to Spain was arranged from 29 May to 12 June. This tour produced a 1–1 draw against Tarragona and a 1–0 defeat against Tortosa. A third game should have been played in Barcelona but, because of an administrative error which had advertised Dunfermline to play as Charlton Athletic, the match was cancelled.

SEASON 1972-73

Although the policy of the Board was to regain First Division status at the first attempt, economies had to be made. Andy Young, who had been enlisted to nurture young talent, left the club and the Under-18 team was scrapped. The playing squad was cut to 16 full-time players. Humbug Park, on which so much money had recently been spent, was sold in the course of the season to a building company. John Cushley, who had missed much of the previous season through injury, was given a free transfer and joined up with his former boss Alec Wright, now manager of St Mirren. Bert Paton, despite a tempting offer from Rangers, retired from the game. Early in the season, Willie Callaghan received a free transfer and signed for Berwick Rangers, managed by none other than Harry Melrose. Jim Fraser also left the club and joined Airdrie. Recurring illness finally forced another stalwart, John Lunn, to give up playing after 11 magnificent years with the club. Ian Bain, another loyal servant, retired from the training staff. All links with the Stein era were now virtually severed and a new tradition and ethos would have to be fashioned.

Jim Thomson, after a year away from the club with Raith, returned to East End Park to coach the reserves and train the dozen part-timers on the club's books. Former sprinter Jock Thomson, father of wing half Kenny, was brought in to assist with training in the gym. With no money to spend, Miller had to turn to the free transfer market to boost his playing staff. Best of the bargains was the signing from Dundee of Alex Kinninmonth (30) who quickly established himself as captain of the side. Other signings included Nelson from Hibs, Billy Mitchell from Celtic and Kenny Watson, still a schoolboy. McGarr was transferred to East Fife with centre forward Joe Hughes

Top left: *Former player, captain and now manager, George Miller.*

Below: *Skipper Alex Kinninmonth.* (Dunfermline Press)

1972-73 Squad. Back row: Paterson, Beresford, McLardy, Marshall, Mercer, Pate. Middle: Miller, Mackie, Wallace, Tempany, McGarr, Fraser, Arrol, McNicoll, Leishman, Gillespie, A. Stevenson. Front: Brine, Edmonds, Thomson, Kinninmonth, Callaghan, Scott, Lunn, Brown, Hamill. (Dundee Courier)

coming to East End in exchange. The team reverted to its customary black and white shirts.

The opening challenge matches against English opposition at home did little to bolster morale. Huddersfield, who had just been relegated from the top division in England, won 1–0 and Sheffield Wednesday, fielding former Pars' favourite Jackie Sinclair and ex-Ibrox star Willie Henderson, won 4–2. Manager Miller took up an invitation to examine the training methods employed by European champions, Ajax, in Holland. Though Miller found the methods of manager Stefan Kovacs very enlightening, it was obviously too late to put these ideas into practice for the League Cup which began in disastrous fashion for Dunfermline.

As an experiment, a new format was adopted for the Cup whereby two clubs from each division made up each section. Dunfermline were unlucky to be drawn against Dundee United whose new manager, Jim McLean, was beginning to do for his club what Stein had performed for the Athletic a decade earlier. To suffer two defeats by the Taysiders could be accepted, but failure to beat Second Division Stenhousemuir brought it home to the club that their anticipated elevation out of the lower division would be no formality. For the fifth year running, Dunfermline came bottom of their section.

Confirmation that a hard struggle awaited the team in the league was confirmed when the opening games against Queen of the South and Cowdenbeath brought two defeats and no goals. After stern warnings from the manager the team knuckled down to the task ahead of them and five successive wins put them into fourth position. After a disappointing home defeat by Clyde, another fine run of six successive victories (including an 8–0 thrashing of Brechin City) saw the Pars rise to third position. The visit of Berwick Rangers on 2 December brought back several old favourites to East End Park – Harry Melrose, Willie

Callaghan (who scored a goal), Ian Lister and Pat Wilson. A 2–1 defeat for Dunfermline followed by an away defeat at Montrose left the fans wondering if their team really could gain promotion.

Thereafter, however, only two defeats out of 19 league games were enough to secure promotion into Division One as runners-up to Clyde. Despite the good performances on the field, attendances at home had slumped to between 2,000 and 5,000, a level from which they were seldom to rise in subsequent seasons. The Board reckoned that ideally gates of around 12,000 were required to keep the club at the top.

The team which bore the brunt of the promotion effort was: Arrol, Leishman, Wallace, Thomson, McNicoll, Kinninmonth, Nelson, Scott, Mackie, Shaw, Hughes, Gillespie. With 95 league goals scored, the highest total in Britain, Dunfermline gained entry to the Drybrough Cup for the first time. Graham Shaw was top scorer with 27 goals. Dave McNicoll attracted the attention of Brighton and Liverpool but nothing came of these enquiries. Ken Mackie, who notched 21 goals and made numerous appearances in the Scottish professional side, was the subject of a bid from Rangers. An offer of £20,000 plus Andy Penman was rejected by the Board who wanted cash only. Later, a fee of £50,000 was agreed only for Mackie to reject the move as he preferred to gain more experience first with a provincial club.

Dunfermline's challenge for the Scottish Cup is easily recounted. In their opening match against Dundee on 3 February, the Pars, with none of their cup-winning squad left, lost 3–0 at home. In fact, since 1968 only two cup-ties had been won. A short tour of Norway with victories over Steinkler (3–2) and Aalesund (1–0) and a defeat by Rosenberg Trondheim completed a satisfactory season which at least had secured the return of top class football to the town.

Above: *Ken Mackie.* (Dunfermline Press)

Below: *Sandy Jardine watches in anguish as McCloy is beaten by a tremendous shot from Kinninmonth.* (Daily Record)

SEASON 1973-74

During the close season, several more youngsters joined the club. Twenty-year-old Gordon Forrest, formerly of Celtic, signed from Livingstone United; Ian Campbell (19) came from Lochore Welfare and local lad, Alan Evans, only 16, was called up from Dunfermline United. An old favourite returned to East End Park in the form of Jackie Sinclair, now 30. After leaving the club in 1965 he went to Leicester and then in a £65,000 deal to Newcastle with whom he won a Fairs Cup medal. After a spell with Sheffield Wednesday and a brief trip to Durban, Sinclair returned to Fife to give the team some of the experience it so desperately required. George Miller denied rumours that he was leaving the club to join Falkirk.

The season got off to an early start on 28 July with Dunfermline visiting Celtic in the first round of the Drybrough Cup before a crowd of 27,000. A 6–1 drubbing left a careless Athletic side in no doubt that only their best form would suffice in the top division. A 3–0 victory in a challenge match over Preston North End, managed by Bobby Charlton, helped to build up confidence again.

In the League Cup, two new changes were introduced. As an experiment, the offside rule was relaxed and the top two clubs would qualify for the later stages. Once again Dunfermline had to face Stenhousemuir and managed to take only one point from them; against Berwick, however, they recorded two wins. The other main contenders, St Mirren, managed by Willie Cunningham with Jim Herriot in goals, took two points off Dunfermline which gave them seven points and second top place. In the quarter-finals, a strong Dundee side won by the odd goal in nine over the two legs to eliminate Dunfermline from the competition.

In the opening game of the league campaign, it was like old times again at East End Park when Celtic, league champions for the last eight seasons, took the field before a crowd of 15,000. In a hard fought and thrilling match the Pars were unlucky to lose 3–2. During the rest of September, two draws and two victories were enough to place them in fourth top position in the table. A 3–0 defeat by

Above: *A proud moment for John Lunn as he and Jim Thomson display the Scottish Cup in 1968.*

Below: *G. Miller introduces Provost Les Wood to Norwegian 'keeper, Geir Karlsen.*

Hearts at Tynecastle on 6 October gave the Athletic their first away defeat which was followed by a crushing 4–0 defeat at home by Ayr. For the home game against Rangers, before a crowd of 17,000, Miller brought in the young Alan Evans for his first full league game. Dunfermline did well to force a 2–2 draw though, sadly for Evans, he was carried off with a break in his leg above the ankle. A 5–1 victory over Dundee at the end of the month was their finest First Division victory for seven years.

In early December, everyone at the club was saddened by the sudden death of John Lunn, struck down with the blood disease which had dogged his career for so long and which he had fought so courageously. In a tribute, the chairman referred to him as a modest, unassuming lad, liked and respected by everyone. "Athletic fans," he said, "will remember proudly his hard tackling, his goal line clearances, his speed on recovery, his attacking flair." A testimonial fund was set up for his family.

The signing of a new goalkeeper created a great deal of interest. He was Geir Karlsen, the massive Norwegian internationalist from Rosenberg, who had so impressed Celtic in the European Cup that they tried, unsuccessfully, to sign him. Since he was an amateur, no transfer fee was required. Karlsen made his debut at Easter Road against a Hibs side which had drawn twice with Leeds in the UEFA Cup. Dunfermline lost 3–2 and went on to lose their next four games to hover near the relegation zone once again. The gloom that beset the country during the power cuts

resulting from the miners' strike had spread to East End Park; a ban on floodlighting necessitated early starts once again.

Off the field, the club embarked on two new enterprises to raise more money. In October, a Sunday market was begun inside the ground and in December a new social club, the Paragon Club, was opened at a cost of £20,000. A commercial manager, Mr George Gilchrist, was appointed to oversee these ventures.

In the Scottish Cup in January, the club made history by playing their tie against Falkirk at Brockville on a Sunday. The gamed ended in a 2–2 draw with the Pars squeezing home 1–0 in the replay, thanks to a goal from Ian Campbell. Dunfermline had a great chance to go further on in the Cup when the draw brought Queen of the South, managed by ex-coach McLean, to East End Park on Sunday 17 February. Before the game, Dumfries 'keeper Ball received a presentation to mark his 500th appearance for his club although he was unable to stop the only goal of the game from Kinninmonth.

Mackie and Wallace were selected for the Under-23 squad to play against Wales and the latter also played for the Scottish League against the English League. Miller rejected a £50,000 bid for Mackie from Millwall. Mr Douglas Jack resigned from the Board because of business pressures. John Arrol was transferred to Partick for £3,000.

In the quarter-finals of the Cup, the Pars took on Dundee United and it seemed like another goal from Kinninmonth was going to be enough to take the Athletic through, until in the last minute Traynor equalised to take the game to a replay. The Tannadice side were much too strong in the second game and, after a lucky goal, ran out winners by 4–0.

The league campaign took on an increasing importance when it was announced in the spring that after a great deal of deliberation the two leagues were to be reorganised. At the end of season 1974–75, the top 10 clubs in Division One would form a new Premier Division while the remaining eight First Division clubs along with the top six clubs from Division Two would make up a revamped "First Division". The remaining clubs would constitute the "Second Division". Though the Board had often supported, and indeed initiated, league reconstruction proposals, they voted (in vain) against this particular proposal which was passed by 29 votes to eight. It was thus even more vital for Dunfermline to remain in Division One for next season to allow them a chance to compete for one of the precious top 10 places.

By 6 April, five successive defeats to Clyde, Motherwell, Dundee, Rangers and St Johnstone, had put the Pars to the bottom of the First Division thus ensuring another tense end to the season. Eventually everything once again hinged on the last day of the programme. Falkirk were already doomed. On paper, East Fife, two points ahead, had the better chance of escape as they had a relatively easy game at home against Ayr while Dunfermline were away to Dundee United who had earlier in the season beaten them. As fate would have it, East Fife surprisingly lost 1–0 while by the same scoreline the Pars overcame the Taysiders, thanks to a goal from Shaw. George Miller and his men were jubilant – Dunfermline had pulled off another miracle and could now compete next season for a place in the new Premier League. Mackie was the club's top scorer with 17 goals.

SEASON 1974-75

With a place in the coveted Premier League at stake this was to be a make or break season for Dunfermline as indeed it was to be for a host of other clubs. The chairman referred to it as "a very momentous season in the history of the game in Scotland".

Another crop of youngsters made their appearance at East End Park. The full-time squad numbered 14 in addition to 12 part-timers. Young Dave McNicoll, signed in June 1969, was the longest serving player on the club's books. Ralph Brand, the former Rangers, Manchester City and Sunderland player, joined the club as coach. Since giving up playing, he had been manager of Darlington then coach with Albion Rovers. Andy Stevenson resigned as physiotherapist after 10 years while his namesake, Jimmy, who had left the club in 1964, returned to his old haunts as the replacement.

A series of pre-season friendlies produced not unsatisfactory results. Jackie Charlton's Middlesbrough, newly promoted to Division One, were beaten 2–1 at East End Park. This game gave the home fans another chance to admire the skills of Bobby Murdoch, the club's gifted midfield player. York City were also beaten, by 3 goals to 1. Away from home the Athletic did less well, drawing 1–1 at Doncaster and losing 2–0 in the return game at York.

Hearts, Morton and Aberdeen provided stiff opposition for Dunfermline in the League Cup. Two good victories

Skipper Kinninmonth leads out his team. (Dunfermline Press)

over Hearts were the only games the Pars won which meant that their interest in this elusive trophy came to an abrupt end. In the process, the Athletic suffered a cruel blow when a badly broken leg put out solid defender Jim Leishman for the rest of the season.

Inconsistency was the hallmark of Dunfermline's league form during the autumn months. A 3–0 defeat in the opening game at Firhill was balanced by a 3–1 home victory over Arbroath followed by two draws against Dumbarton and Hearts. A crushing 6–1 home defeat by Rangers, with Parlane netting five, showed that Dunfermline's bid to gain top ten status would certainly be a difficult one. Failure to take any points from other aspiring candidates like Dundee United and St Johnstone was to cost Dunfermline dear at the end of the season. By the end of October, the Pars struck their best form to encourage even the most pessimistic that success was still possible. Alan Evans, restored to the team as a strong centre half, added solidity to the defence and won his first professional Youth cap while 'keeper Karlsen produced the splendid form which gained him further caps for his country against Northern Ireland, Sweden and Finland. A run of six games without defeat put the team in seventh position by the end of November; only a narrow 2–1 away defeat to a skilful Celtic side prevented them from further strengthening their position.

During this fine run, the Pars found the time to organise the testimonial game for the family of John Lunn. On Monday 11 November, 11,000 fans turned up to see an Athletic side, with Edwards of Hibs and Ford of Hearts as guests, take on a talented Rangers-Celtic combination which included the old maestro, Denis Law, holder of 55 caps for Scotland. The game ended in a 3–3 draw.

Above: The team on duty at Pittodrie in August 1974. Standing: Evans, Scott, Thomson, Wallace, Karlsen, McNicoll, R. Campbell, Kinninmonth. Seated: Watson, I. Campbell, Davidson, Shaw, Sinclair. (Dundee Courier)

Below: Dunfermline "crocks" on parade outside the club treatment room, "Harley Street". Jim Scott, Graham Shaw, Jackie Sinclair, Jim Leishman, Alan Evans.

Despite a poor result against Partick at home after Christmas, the Pars kept up the pressure with two good wins over Arbroath and Dumbarton to go to seventh position once again. What can only be called a disaster then struck the club. A narrow defeat at Tynecastle, their first defeat by Hearts in four meetings that season, cost them two valuable places in the table. Severe weather conditions then brought a break in the programme during which the team inexplicably lost its rhythm. On 28 January, the Athletic played their postponed third-round Scottish Cup match against Second Division Clydebank at Kilbowie Park on an icy pitch and lost 2–1 to a Bankies' goal scored two minutes from time. Four days later a priceless point was dropped against Clyde. A run of seven successive defeats in February and March effectively killed off any remaining hopes the Pars entertained of becoming the only Fife club to gain entry to the Premier League. Only three more points were to be collected till the end of the season.

At the end of April, Miller spoke of "a trying season, encouraging and full of promise early on, to be followed by bitter disappointment in our failure to reach the Top Ten. Excuses can be offered – our defensive problems with injuries to key players and the at times deplorable condition of the pitch here at East End – but basically we have not been consistent enough to justify a Premier League placing." Miller ruefully reflected that while the first 19 games had produced 19 points, the following 15 games brought only four points.

Though the Premier Division was to give Scottish football a shot in the arm, for Dunfermline it came just too late. Only a few years earlier, Dunfermline would have qualified with ease; as it was, the equivalent of relegation had befallen the club once again. The Bank Manager would note with regret the absence of Celtic, Rangers, Hibs and Hearts at East End Park – a loss of 60,000 paying customers. Ironically, Dunfermline's influence on the Scottish League in general had never been greater. Throughout the season no fewer than 10 out of the 38 clubs had managers with a close association with East End Park. The list makes interesting reading: G. Miller (Dunfermline), J. Stein (Celtic), W. Cunningham (St Mirren), G. Farm (Raith), W. McLean (Motherwell), A. Ferguson (East Stirling), H. Melrose (Berwick), A. Wright (Dumbarton), D. McLindon (Alloa) and B. Paton (Cowdenbeath), almost enough for a decent team! As the future appeared progressively bleaker at East End Park, nostalgia became all the stronger.

Right: *Alan Evans*. (Dunfermline Press)

Opposite, top: *A much younger Harry Melrose with the Scottish Cup in 1961.* (Dunfermline Press)

Opposite, bottom: *Jim Meakin.* (Dunfermline Press)

SEASON 1975–76

The close season proceedings had a depressing ring of familiarity about them. No less than 11 players, enough for a whole team, were given free transfers including, rather surprisingly, Dave McNicoll (who went to Montrose), Under-23 cap Jim Wallace and Jackie Sinclair. George Gilchrist, the commercial manager, and Ralph Brand, coach, were also relieved of their duties. Lack of money prevented the buying of any new, top-class players and the flow of talented youngsters was beginning to dry up. The squad was reduced to 18 players, only half of whom were full-time. Even skipper Kinninmonth decided that after 13 years as a full-time professional he would be better off playing in a part-time capacity.

Graham Shaw, the club's top scorer with only 12 goals, was the oldest full-time player at the tender age of 23 years. A bid of £12,000 for the striker from Hearts was turned down. Geir Karlsen decided to return to Norway and was transferred to Valvengen for £4,300. Graham Barclay (19) was hired on loan from Celtic as a temporary stop gap in goal. Talking of Celtic, the Board kindly remembered one of their former managers when they sent a *Get Well* card to Jock Stein and his wife who had been seriously injured in a road accident on the A74 in July.

During the summer, the building firm of William Rennie, on the advice of an agricultural scientist, carried out extensive work on the field to improve the playing surface to avoid the problems the club had previously experienced. The floodlighting system was also overhauled at a cost of

£7,000 to allow the increasingly popular colour television cameras to operate efficiently inside the ground. Sadly, the question now being asked was – would the TV cameras ever again be regular visitors to East End Park?

The playing season began on a note of pessimism. Two friendlies against Sunderland (home) and Albion Rovers (away) resulted in defeats of 3–0 and 5–0 respectively. Worse was to follow in the League Cup. The best Dunfermline could manage were two defeats by Hibs, two draws against Ayr and one point from Dundee. In the eight games played, the Pars had managed to score only four goals.

Hopes that Dunfermline might gain a coveted place in the Premier Division were not high. Miller's view of the First Division was to be proved only too accurate. He wrote, "While the First Division might perhaps lack the glamour and atmosphere of the Premier grade it will undoubtedly be a competitive league." In the first season, it was agreed that the fourteen clubs would play each other only twice; this meant a league of 26 games which would finish on the last day of February to be followed by a revival of the Spring Cup. Clearly, a good start was essential; there would be no time in the spring for a late surge for promotion. Relegation was never contemplated.

In the opening match of the league programme, a crowd of only 3,000 turned up to see the game against Airdrie. An uninspiring 3–3 draw was the last straw for Miller who voluntarily resigned during the following week to take up the post of manager at Brockville. Sometimes a club does particularly well when it is without a manager, but not so Dunfermline on this occasion who lost their next two games against East Fife and Hamilton, conceding nine goals

and scoring only one goal in the process. To fill the vacant manager's post, the Board turned once more to a former player in the hope of recreating former glories. The successful candidate was Harry Melrose who had been manager of Berwick Rangers for the last six years. Whether Melrose had learned anything about football management while he served under two of the finest managers in Scotland, Stein and Eddie Turnbull at Aberdeen, would soon be put to the test. The first game he watched, against Clyde at Shawfield on 20 September, ended in a 2–0 victory, the club's first win of the season and the first shut-out for 'keeper Barclay. The momentum was not maintained and the next six games ended in draws.

Fans had to wait until 15 November to see the first league win at home when Evans scored his first goal to defeat league leaders Kilmarnock by 1–0. To strengthen his squad, Melrose signed Ian Hall, the ex-Celtic and Berwick forward, from Hamilton, and Jim Meakin (23) from East Stirling. Jim Scott replaced Kinninmonth as captain. These changes did little to improve the Pars' form and the turn of the year saw them well out of the championship race in 10th position; though few wanted to admit it relegation looked a better bet than promotion. Dr Yellowley summed up the predicament well at the AGM when he referred to the situation as "Gloomsville". He wished he could offer a sign of hope but he could not; he lamented that the club was still contracted to pay top class wages even though the team had slipped from the top division. On a later occasion he drew attention to the sad decline in attendance at home matches which had diminished to two or three thousand fans.

In the New Year, the prospect that a brewing company might build a licensed restaurant on stilts at the east end of the ground helped to give some hope of better times. When Hearts raised their offer for Graham Shaw to £16,000, the club had no alternative but to part with the man whose talent

had saved the team on many occasions. As a replacement, Roddy Georgeson was bought from Berwick for £4,500.

The first four league games in January 1976 added only two points to the team's meagre tally. A third-round Scottish Cup-tie against Hibs at Easter Road on 24 January provided welcome, but only temporary, relief from the pressures of league football. Twice Hibs took the lead and twice Dunfermline gallantly fought back to equalise; a late winner from Hibs, however, gave the Pars no chance to level the score for a third time.

A draw against Airdrie at the beginning of February kept Dunfermline in second bottom position. With only three games left, all at home, hopes were still high at East End Park that relegation could be avoided. In the first of these games a resounding 5–1 victory over Clyde gave the team the boost it was needing. During that game, Jim Leishman made a successful come-back to the first team. The second last game brought Partick Thistle, managed by Bertie Auld, to East End Park. Clyde were already doomed and with the Pars, Morton and Hamilton all tying on the 20-point mark, the club desperately needed at least one point from the encounter. Thistle had already won the championship and were much more relaxed. Goalkeeper Rough was in excellent form to deny the Athletic attack on several occasions. A final score of 3–0 for the Jags put Dunfermline into deeper trouble, especially as the other two relegation candidates each gained a point.

The last day of the season did not produce the miracle that Dunfermline had been seeking. Another 3–0 defeat, to Dumbarton, on 28 February, decided that the Pars would be playing next season in the restructured "Second Division", in effect, the third division. For the third time in four years, the Athletic had been relegated. The miserable statistic of only 30 goals from 26 games told its own story. As the dejected fans trudged home, many were wondering if this

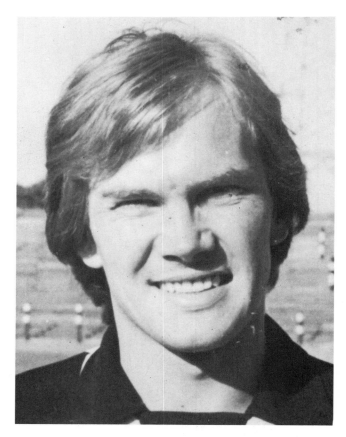

Above: *Roddy Georgeson*. (Dunfermline Press)

Below: *Jim Scott*. (Dunfermline Press)

Bottom left: *Ian Hall*. (Dunfermline Press)

was the same club which only seven seasons earlier was competing for a place in the final of the European Cup Winners' Cup. Melrose could only ruefully recall former colleagues of his playing days like Ronnie Mailer, Jim McLean and John Lunn who, although not the most skilful of players, never knew what it was like to accept defeat and whose reaction to a setback was to re-double their efforts in fighting back.

To spin out the season for the clubs of Divisions One and Two, the new Spring Cup was introduced. Organised along the lines of the League Cup and the old Summer Cup, mini-leagues of four clubs were drawn up with the top two clubs going forward to the next round. The Athletic were drawn against Queen's Park, Hamilton and Cowdenbeath, but with the league campaign over, there was little enthusiasm for this low-key affair. Three victories over the other clubs put the Pars joint top with Queen's Park (though the latter had the superior goal difference).

In the next round, played on a home-and-away basis, Dunfermline were put out by Airdrie on a 5–4 aggregate. The Cup gave the home fans a chance to see one of their old favourites in action. When goalkeeper Barclay was injured, Melrose persuaded his old comrade, Jim Herriot, to take over in goal on a temporary basis. After leaving Dunfermline to go to Birmingham City, Herriot returned to Scotland to play for Hibs, then St Mirren and finally Partick Thistle, who lent him to the Pars for a few games.

SEASON 1976–77

Demotion to the new Second Division meant that further savings had to be made. With great regret, the Board announced that all players would have to revert to part-time contracts once again. Ken Mackie, the club's top scorer last season with 11 goals, was transferred to Falkirk for a mere £6,000, a fraction of his value a few years earlier. At the beginning of the season, the club started with a pool of only 18 players which prompted coach Jock Thomson to leave the club. Two notable additions to the club were John Salton, a resolute defender from Queen of the South, and Hugh Whyte, a goalkeeper from Hibs. The six-foot 'keeper actually favoured part-time football as it allowed him time to continue with his medical studies at Edinburgh University. They were later joined by three youngsters who stepped up from the junior ranks – Jim Bowie (20) from Pumpherston, Bobby Robertson (18) from Kirkcaldy YMCA and Paul Donnelly (19) from Dalkeith Thistle.

As Dunfermline's fortunes continued to fall, so too did the calibre of the opponents they were able to attract to East End Park. Gone were the days when Dukla Prague or Arsenal would queue up for the privilege of playing the Pars. When Swindon Town and Halifax appeared in early August, Dunfermline at least had the satisfaction of winning, 2–1 on each occasion.

Any hopes that the fans might have entertained of seeing their team settle quickly were soon dashed by the performances in the League Cup. Only one victory (against Alloa) meant that the Athletic came bottom of their section with only three goals scored.

In the league, extended to 39 games to allow teams to play each other three times instead of two, the Pars found that it was easier to slip into the bottom division than it would be to climb out of it. As favourites for promotion, Dunfermline would often find themselves singled out by other sides as the team that had to be beaten; visiting clubs from inferior grounds attended by sparse crowds would

Top left: *John Salton.* (Dunfermline Press)

Below: *Goalkeeper Hugh Whyte.* (Dunfermline Press)

find the grand surroundings at East End Park, with its relatively large crowds, a great challenge which undoubtedly lifted their level of play. Dunfermline made the fatal mistake of giving their opponents a few games of a start, for after five games they had still to record a victory and lay at the very foot of Scottish League football with only two points. Eventually, on 22 September, the Pars recorded their first league victory with a fine 4–0 win at home over Clyde. Alan Evans, pushed up to the forward line, scored a hat-trick. An away draw the following week against Meadowbank, the most recent club to join the Scottish League in 1974, brought the Pars back to earth, as did an away defeat the following week against Stenhousemuir in front of a crowd of only 300 spectators. With almost one-third of the programme completed, Dunfermline lagged seven points behind the leaders, Stranraer. That Dunfermline should be seriously considered as promotion contenders by the end of the season was due to the remarkable run on which the club now embarked. Thirteen league games without defeat were to follow which raised the club to third place by the beginning of February.

During that period, Bobby Morrison, a striker, joined the club in a straight swap which took Leishman, who had never regained his fine form after his leg break, to Cowdenbeath. Director William Jamieson resigned from the Board for business reasons. In the New Year, the Scottish Cup gave home teams a chance to experience the "big time" again when Aberdeen, the League Cup holders, provided the opposition on 29 January. Under their ebullient manager, Ally McLeod, a new-look Dons side were the latest team to mount a severe challenge to break down the domination of the Old Firm. Not surprisingly, the Premier Division side were too powerful for the Athletic though only a Joe Harper goal in the 57th minute separated the two teams. A crowd of 11,899 certainly pleased the Bank.

In the league, a defeat by Queen's Park ended the club's purple patch and sent them down to sixth position; two

Above: *The Athletic line-up for 1976-77. Back row: Georgeson, McLeod, Evans, Whyte, Leishman, Salton, Hall, Melrose. Front: Hunter, Dunn, Thomson, Meakin, Markey, Cameron, Ross. On holiday: Scott, Watson and Smith.*

Below: *Jim Bowie.* (Dunfermline Press)

Above: *Paul Donnelly*. (Dunfermline Press)

Bottom right: *Bobby Robertson*. (Dunfermline Press)

decisive victories, however, restored them to third position. A forward from East Stirling, Jimmy Mullin, was signed for £3,000 in a determined bid to score more goals. One week in March was, with hindsight, to be absolutely critical. In the space of eight days, three matches were lost which effectively put an end to promotion hopes. Of particular importance was their home defeat by Alloa, now coached by Alec Totten, who went on to pip Dunfermline for promotion by one point. Despite a splendid run-in during which only three points were dropped out of 20, the damage had already been done in the opening weeks and the Pars had to settle for third place. The return to Division One would have to wait for at least another season while the club's finances continued to deteriorate, chiefly because of falling gates.

For the third successive year, Dunfermline had no option but to sell their top scorer, in this case Alan Evans, scorer of 15 goals, who had attracted the attention of Aston Villa. A fee of £21,600 was agreed upon, with more to follow should the player make the grade for the Birmingham club who had already snapped up bargains from Scotland in Alec Cropley and Andy Gray. Evans was restored to his original role as a defender and became an outstanding success, winning an English League medal, a European Cup medal plus a place in the Scottish international team. Though delighted at their former star's success, Dunfermline fans could only ruefully contemplate the job he could have done for them at East End Park in the struggles ahead. The transfer (with a further £10,800 duly forthcoming) did little to retrieve what the Chairman had referred to at the club's AGM as "the frightening decline in the club's fortunes".

SEASON 1977-78

The squad of 18 players (average age, 22 years) with which Melrose began the season showed few changes. Bonar Mercer, after a spell with Stirling and Montrose and latterly with Kilmarnock Rugby Club, rejoined his old club. Bobby Robertson and Paul Donnelly, signed provisionally the previous season, broke through into the first team. The pre-season friendlies brought two clubs of widely differing calibre to East End Park. Against Bury of the English Third Division, the Pars struggled to win 4–3. The other visitors, Celtic, fielding a strong team, reminded the home fans of the gulf that now separated the three divisions by winning 4–1. The 3,000 crowd received a special treat in witnessing Kenny Dalglish, captain for the day, play his last game for the Glasgow club before being transferred to Liverpool for whom he was to play his first game a few days later in Wembley Stadium before a crowd of 100,000 against Manchester United – a far cry from East End Park!

As an experiment, the Scottish League decided to dispense with the traditional form of the League Cup whereby four teams competed in sections of four sides. Instead, the opening game of the season saw the league programme begin immediately, with the League Cup following later in the form of a knock-out competition, played on a home-and-away basis. Dunfermline's opening game on 13 August took them across the border to Berwick where a 2–2 draw reminded players, fans and management that success in Division Two would be extremely hard to achieve. Hall, who had missed most of last season through injury, scored both goals. The chairman remarked in the next programme: "That game should at least have made it clear that we are likely to have every bit as much of a struggle as last season unless we can apply ourselves professionally for the whole 90 minutes of every game."

Above: *Ian Hall scores Dunfermline's only goal against Celtic in a pre-season friendly, 9 August 1977.* (Dunfermline Press)

Below: *Player-coach Walter Borthwick.* (Dunfermline Press)

A convincing 4–0 win over Queen's Park at home, however, had the fans believing that this would be their season. Hall went one better and scored a hat-trick for which he received a crate of whisky as part of a new league sponsorship deal to encourage goal-scoring. A 3–1 defeat in the following game at Cowdenbeath restored reality. Having received a bye in the first round of the League Cup, Dunfermline took on their second-round opponents, Clyde, over two games in the space of a week. A goalless draw at Shawfield followed by a 1–1 draw at East End Park forced the tie into extra-time which saw Dunfermline scrape through by another goal from Morrison in front of a crowd of only 1,500.

Their league form continued to suffer from the inconsistent pattern which had bedevilled the club in previous seasons and, by the time the third round of the Cup had come round, the Pars could only manage eighth position in the table. A fine 2–0 home victory over Clydebank in the first leg gave the club hope for a place in the next round. The goals were scored by Morrison, who was having a good season, and a new recruit, Walter Borthwick, signed from St Mirren to assist with coaching. When Dunfermline went two goals behind in the second leg it seemed as though the Premier Division side would overrun the visitors, but two goals from Morrison brought the Athletic back into the tie and gave them a 4–2 win on aggregate.

A quarter-final tie against Rangers at least offered the Pars a chance to sample the excitement that a big game generated and the promise of a large cheque if not victory on the field. In a note of realism, the Board set out the bonuses for the first leg at Ibrox on 9 November. After allocating substantial sums for a victory or a draw, the Board also offered a bonus for a defeat of not more than two goals. How are the mighty fallen! As it turned out the bonus was duly paid, a Jimmy Mullin goal confining the score to a respectable 3–1 defeat and encouraging a 10,000

Above: *Bonar Mercer*. (Dunfermline Press)

Top right: *Kevin Hegarty*. (Dunfermline Press)

Below: *Mike Leonard*. (Dunfermline Press)

crowd to turn up for the return leg. Dunfermline lost this match by the same score and went out 6–2 on aggregate, £6,000 better off.

From the dizzy heights of Ibrox, Dunfermline had to pick themselves up to face Stenhousemuir at Ochilview in front of 500 spectators. A disappointing 2–0 defeat kept the promotion contenders half-way down the league. After a few more games, the Pars found themselves in the ignominious position of having to play in mid-December in the qualifying rounds of the Scottish Cup, a stage which everyone thought that the club, twice winners of the trophy, had well and truly left behind forever. Clyde once again provided the opposition and a 3–0 win at Shawfield following a goalless draw, took the Athletic through to meet Brechin in round two on 7 January. A disappointing 1–0 defeat meant that since winning the Cup in 1968, the Pars had won only five cup-ties.

A harsh winter interrupted the league programme and when the weather finally relented, Dunfermline were left with a backlog of fixtures which required the team to play twice a week. Although the club was well down the table, only a handful of points separated the top clubs and by March, promotion was not totally out of the question. The signing of the former Celtic forward, Mike Leonard, a pro-lific scorer with Sligo Rovers in Eire, gave the club a welcome boost. A hat-trick in only his third game gave Dunfermline two valuable points (and another crate of whisky). In April, an away victory over Brechin brought the Pars to third top position in the league. A programme of nine games in 21 days proved to be too demanding and a number of games which were drawn instead of won allowed Clyde and Raith to secure promotion with Dunfermline coming third for the second year in succession. Bobby Morrison was top scorer with 17 goals.

SEASON 1978-79

With no new signing of any importance during the close season, the club relied largely on the same squad as last season in the hope of making it "third time lucky" in their bid to escape from the Second Division. Ian Hall, plagued by injury and illness since joining the club, finally decided to give up playing though he continued to help out with coaching at East End Park, until his sudden death at the age of 28 in the last week of September robbed the club and the game of an enthusiastic and dedicated professional.

A convincing 4–3 win over Hartlepool in a pre-season friendly started the season on a note of promise. A hat-trick from Mike Leonard gave notice that the striker was looking forward with great anticipation to his first full season with the club. A 2–0 defeat a few days later from Swansea City was not unexpected and by no means discouraging. The Welsh club, newly promoted to Division Three, had several excellent players in Alan Curtis, Robbie James and Jeremy Charles, and had recently appointed John Toshack, the former Liverpool star, as their manager. Toshack's family had come from the Dunfermline area and for 'Big Tosh' his visit was a sentimental journey to a ground in which he had often spectated as a youngster.

Before the new league programme was properly under-way, Dunfermline's plans received a setback when Melrose was rushed to hospital with a serious illness which kept him away from the club for several weeks. The Athletic's opponents, Queen's Park, also had their problems, two of their players having been killed in a road accident during a summer tour of Canada and a third player seriously injured. A 3–0 home defeat sent the fans home wondering when their club was going to get off to a good start in the league. They were not to know then that this would be the club's only home defeat for the rest of the season. An away draw with East Stirling and a fine 3–0 home win over Cowdenbeath helped restore the fans' faith.

The Board thought they had fixed up Pat Stanton to deputise for their ill manager, only to learn a few days later

Above: *Andy Rolland, player-coach.* (Dunfermline Press)

Below: *Leonard scores goal number two against Hartlepool in a pre-season friendly, 31 July 1978.* (Dunfermline Press)

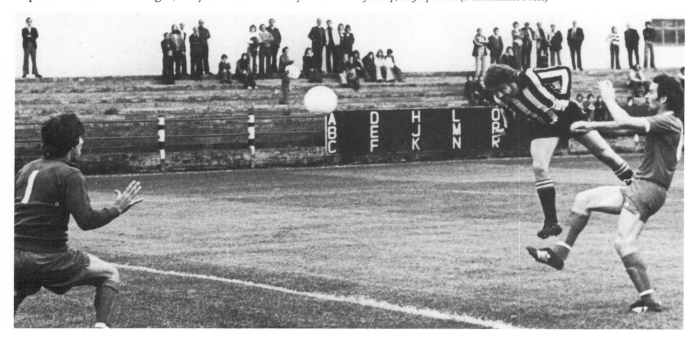

The team about to go into action in November 1978. Back row: Mercer, Rolland, Robertson, Borthwick, Whyte, Salton, Donnelly, Leonard. Front: Mullin, Thomson, Dunn, Hegarty, Dickson, Scott. (Dunfermline Press)

that the former Hibs' captain had jumped at the chance to be Alec Ferguson's deputy at Pittodrie. The Board finally got their man when they appointed Andy Rolland (35) as player-coach. The strong-tackling, attacking full back had enjoyed a very successful career with Dundee United and the chance to break into football management proved irresistible to him. Once clearance had come through from America, where he had spent the summer months, Rolland went straight into the team against Airdrie in the Pars' first-leg game in the League Cup whose format remained unchanged from last season. Rolland had an unhappy baptism, his new side losing 3–0 at Broomfield and by the same score at East End Park in the same week. At the beginning of September, Dunfermline sold Georgeson to Montrose for £2,750 and used some of the cash to bring the much travelled Kevin Hegarty (28) from Bayview. In the same mould as his more illustrious brother, Paul, Hegarty's determination and skill in the air added bite to the forward line. Meakin was transferred to Falkirk, already shaping up as promotion contenders.

Rolland's influence very quickly became apparent as the club embarked on an excellent run of 16 league games without defeat. By scoring four goals against Stranraer (in a 6–1 victory) and another four, three weeks later against East Fife (5–1), Leonard set a record for the most goals scored in one match in the new Second Division. When Melrose returned for duty at the end of October, he found his club in the healthy position of leading the division. The great run came to an end on 25 November when Falkirk beat the

Pars 4–1 at Brockville before a crowd of 4,500, their first away defeat of the season. This disappointment was followed up by another away defeat, this time to East Fife.

Severe weather conditions that winter meant that Dunfermline did not play another league game for more than two months. The Scottish Cup, however, gave the Athletic plenty of action. Again being forced to play in the preliminary stages, the Pars began their campaign on 16 December with an apparently easy home match against Albion Rovers. A 2–2 draw meant a replay which Dunfermline did well to win 3–2. The second-round draw sent them on the perilous journey to Stair Park to meet Stranraer. Another 1–1 draw forced the Wigtownshire club to make the long journey to Fife for the replay. In what was the Pars' first home game for five weeks, a Mullin goal was enough to put Dunfermline's name into the third round with the chance to draw top class opposition.

Fortune smiled on the Athletic by giving them a home tie against Hibs of the Premier Division. A crowd of over 11,000 flocked on a frosty Sunday to savour the excitement of a big Scottish Cup-tie once again at East End Park, though the hard condition of the pitch put skill at a premium. Despite losing a goal early in the second half, Dunfermline fought back and forced a draw when a fine Leonard shot left 'keeper McArthur helpless. Gate receipts of over £10,000 helped to reduce a mounting overdraft at the Bank. The strength and skill of the full-time Edinburgh side paid dividends in the replay when two second-half goals saw Hibs safely through. At least the Pars could have the consolation later of knowing they had been knocked out by the beaten finalists.

With the Cup out of the way and winter slowly relaxing its icy grip, Dunfermline turned once again to the league programme, mothballed for two months. A goalless draw at Berwick on 24 February sparked off another excellent run of 14 games without defeat which kept them near the top of the table. The signing of Ricky Sharp (23) on a free transfer from St Mirren at the end of March provided a fresh face up front and quickly paid dividends with several goals. Leonard continued to find the back of the net and received national recognition when he was voted "Player of the Year" (Second Division), by his fellow professionals, narrowly pipping team-mate John Salton for the honour. The backlog of postponed games put heavy pressure on the limited resources at East End Park and the first cracks appeared at the end of April when two successive away defeats in the space of five days to Stranraer and Albion Rovers knocked Dunfermline from top spot to third. A home draw with Forfar and another defeat, at Alloa, left the fans wondering if their team had finally run out of steam at this crucial stage in the promotion chase.

With only two games left the fans were in for another nailbiting finish. As the Pars prepared to await Dave Smith's Berwick, already assured of the Championship, the struggle for second place lay between Dunfermline and Falkirk. As the table shows both clubs had the same number of points, with Falkirk having the better goal difference over Dunfermline who had a game in hand:

	P	W	D	L	F	A	Pts
Berwick	38	22	10	6	82	43	54
Falkirk	38	19	11	8	65	36	49
Dunfermline	37	18	13	6	64	39	49

Berwick gave the 4,500 fans excellent value for money on a sunny Sunday afternoon in mid-May. In a hard-fought match, only one goal, scored by a Salton header from a well-flighted free kick from Mercer, separated the two sides.

This victory clearly put the Athletic in the driving seat for the last game of the season which was, as fate would have it, against Falkirk. The Pars, with ground advantage, required only a draw to gain promotion; a defeat would give both clubs 51 points, with Falkirk going up on a superior goal difference. A crowd of 6,000, a record for the new Second Division, turned up to see what promised to be an epic battle.

After only three minutes, Dunfermline suffered a grave setback when Salton had to be carried off with a knee injury. Falkirk spurned several chances to go ahead and both sides went in for a welcome break with no goals scored. The second half was only 10 minutes old when Perry headed home the goal which uplifted Falkirk and raised the temperature of the contest by another few degrees. Urged on by a fanatical support, Dunfermline battled on and gained a life-line when a shot from substitute Scott was handled by the Falkirk defence. Penalty! Few envied Rolland as he strode upfield to place the ball on the penalty spot. "I recall thinking," he admitted later, "that if I missed I might as well walk out of the ground and never come back." A well-struck shot gave the keeper no chance and Dunfermline were back on level terms. With just under half-an-hour to go, the fans were treated to a rip-roaring finale as each side fought for the goal that would decide its future. It never came, and the final whistle brought scenes of ecstasy not seen at East End Park for a long time. At the third attempt, the Pars were back in the First Division. Sadly, the excitement was too much for groundsman Jack Hart (73) who collapsed and died from a heart attack.

For Honorary Secretary, James McConville, promotion made a fitting present to celebrate his 25 years as an official with the club in addition to the further two years he had served as a director. During these momentous years he witnessed countless changes to the playing staff and vast alterations to the ground itself. His work took him all around Scotland, to many parts of Europe and to North America. His memories ranged from the struggles of the post-war years to the heady days of the sixties and, alas, to the disappointments of recent seasons.

Mike Leonard finished the season as top scorer with 24 goals. Kenny Thomson, who never missed any of the team's 47 games during the season, was voted "Player of the Year" by local fans.

Rolland cleanly scores the equaliser against Falkirk from the penalty spot. (Dunfermline Press)

SEASON 1979-80

No sooner had the celebrations at East End Park died down than the new season seemed to be upon the club. In the first month, no fewer than three cups awaited Dunfermline's participation. By scoring the second highest number of goals in the Second Division, the Pars qualified for the lucrative Drybrough Cup though their opponents, Dundee United, made short work of them, winning 3–0 at Tannadice.

The Anglo-Scottish Cup, played on a two-leg basis, offered the Athletic a better chance to go forward. A 1–1 draw at Firhill against Premier Division Partick Thistle, encouraged a 3,000 crowd to turn up at East End Park in the expectation of a victory. A disputed penalty for the Jags was duly converted and was enough to end Dunfermline's interest in this competition.

A draw against Second Division Stranraer in the League Cup offered the best chance of advancement, especially when the first leg resulted in a goalless draw at Stair Park. Once more the fans' hopes of victory were quickly frustrated when the visitors went into a shock two-goal lead. When the Pars fought back to take the tie to extra time no one expected Stranraer to find a second wind and run out 4–2 winners on the night.

Another game against Swansea, recently promoted to Division Two, gave the Fife fans another chance to admire the high-flying Welsh side. Augmented with ex-Liverpool favourites, Tommy Smith and Ian Callaghan, the visitors won 1–0.

With these preliminaries out of the way, the Pars could give their full concentration to retaining their hard-won place in the First Division. In a bid to secure more goals, the manager bought striker Sandy McNaughton for £6,000 from Stenhousemuir for whom he had scored 18 goals in 22 games. The 25-year-old PE teacher, who had gained amateur international caps while playing for Queen's Park,

Above: *Sandy McNaughton.* (Dunfermline Press)

Below: *McNaughton equalises against Clyde.* (Dunfermline Press)

soon proved to be a very wise investment. New signings, Graham Hutt (Inverkeithing United), David Wilcox (Airth Castle Juniors) and Jim McAloon (Queen's Park) added depth to the squad which, with 39 games in front of them including two away visits to Hearts and Motherwell, was under no illusions as to the enormity of the task ahead. In anticipation of trouble between rival groups of fans, the north enclosure was split in two by the erection of a steel fence, leaving an area of "No Man's Land" in the middle.

The opening home game of the league programme brought recent rivals, Berwick, back to East End Park. A 2–1 defeat for Dunfermline, followed by a goalless draw at Stark's Park, presented the club with an uphill struggle right from the beginning. A home win over Motherwell, managed by the irrepressible Ally McLeod, was tempered three days later by a home draw against Clyde. A run of six games without a victory firmly anchored the Athletic at the foot of the table. To inject new life and energy into the dispirited side, three new signings were made. Mark Williams, a 20-year-old PT instructor at Rosyth and the son of a former Welsh internationalist, volunteered for a trial and duly made the team as an exciting left winger with a scorching shot. John Muir (30), the former Motherwell pivot, was bought from Stranraer to shore up a defence which had been undermined by injuries to Salton and Donnelly (broken ankle). Another left winger was acquired – Colin O'Brien (24) from Bath City. Older fans remembered well his father, George, who starred for the Pars in the 1950s before moving south.

The new signings certainly paid off and a good run towards the end of the year, including a 1–0 win over league leaders Airdrie, lifted the club out of the relegation berths. In a quarrel over payments, Andy Rolland left the club. For the first time ever, East End Park staged the semi-final of the League Cup on 24 November when Dundee United beat Hamilton by 6–2 on a heavy pitch which received few compliments.

In the New Year, the weather again decimated the league programme at East End Park although the third-round home match in the Scottish Cup was eventually played. Highland League club, Buckie Thistle, never looked like causing a cup upset and went down 2–0. A large support travelled to Greenock for the fourth-round match against Premier Division Morton in the hope of witnessing a cup shock and a goalless first half suggested that might still be possible. A second half blitz, however, orchestrated by the inimitable Andy Ritchie, saw Morton through 5–0.

When league football resumed at East End Park on 23 February, after a gap of more than five weeks, a narrow victory over St Johnstone helped ease relegation worries as did three successive draws. However, by amassing only two points out of a possible 12 in the next six games, Dunfermline slumped back into trouble once again. Fortunately, their rivals were performing little better and a victory away to Clydebank, followed by a 3–3 draw against Airdrie in April, was enough to pull the Pars to safety. Dunfermline finally finished in 10th position with Arbroath and Clyde being relegated; Hearts and Airdrie were promoted.

New signing Sandy McNaughton was the club's top scorer with 19 goals. Despite returning to the First Division, the club fared badly at the turnstiles with an average home gate of around 2,600. It was left to fund-raising activities, like the new monthly lottery which donated £10,000 in its first year, to keep the club afloat. To assist with commercial activities like this, local businessman Martin Sisman (37), once a player with East Stirling, was co-opted on to the Board.

Into the Eighties

Opposite: *Season 1979-80. Standing: Rolland, Mercer, Thomson, Whyte, Borthwick, B. Robertson, A. Robertson. Front: Mullin, Dickson, McNaughton, Leonard, Hegarty, Donnelly, Sharp.* (Dunfermline Press)

Below: *Pat Stanton.* (Dunfermline Press)

SEASON 1980-81

Clubs from south of the border again provided the entertainment for the pre-season friendlies. Another once great club, Preston North End, managed by former World Cup star, Nobby Stiles, inflicted a 3–1 defeat on the Pars. Five days later, Swansea, making their third successive appearance, provided the opposition for the Ian Hall Testimonial Fund. Despite a spectacular goal from Leonard and another goal from Craig McFarlane (signed in the spring from Newcastle), the Welsh side won 3–2, and helped boost the fund to its final total of £2,000.

Dunfermline could not have chosen a more difficult opening game in the league – against relegated Dundee, now managed by new manager, Donald Mackay, who had replaced Tommy Gemmell. The visit of the Dens Park side recalled happier times in the past for both clubs. Deteriorating patterns of crowd behaviour obliged the chairman to remind home fans of the need to stamp out foul language, hooliganism and vandalism. Most of the 4,000 crowd were encouraged by the Pars' narrow victory of 1–0 over one of the favourites for promotion. Before the next game, Melrose paid out £10,000, the club's largest fee for more than a decade, to bring central defender Willie Leishman (27) from Albion Rovers. Leishman made his debut at Berwick and helped his side to a goalless draw, prompting Melrose to ponder – "Who knows, after looking at the results in the Division over the first two weeks, promotion may not be the pipe–dream that some people might think." A disappointing 2–0 home defeat by Raith brought the club back to reality.

The first round of the Bell's League Cup gave goalkeeper Whyte the first chance to play in his home town of Kilmarnock. A goalless draw in the first leg encouraged Dunfermline to think that a victory over the Premier Division side might be a strong possibility and brought out a crowd of over 3,000 for the second leg three days later. However, a revitalised Ayrshire side went through 2–1.

McNaughton's first hat-trick for the club helped restore confidence in a fine 4–0 away victory over East Stirling. Failure to follow this up with more than a draw with Dumbarton at home illustrated only too well the inconsistent form that had become the hallmark of recent Dunfermline sides. After a victory over struggling Stirling Albion everything began to go wrong for Melrose. A late penalty for Falkirk, newly promoted to Division One, started a run of five defeats for the Pars to send them into relegation trouble. The inclusion of a revitalised George Best into the visiting Hibs team drew a large crowd, but left Dunfermline with another home defeat.

McNaughton's goal-scoring skills continued to attract attention from other clubs like Airdrie, who offered £25,000, but the Board decided to hold on to their most valuable asset. At the AGM, the chairman warned that "due to the financial situation dramatic signings were unlikely in the next year or so. Because of this we must search for young talent".

A defeat by Hamilton in front of only 1,650 fans on the first Saturday of December, the team's third successive defeat and the sixth home defeat of the season, brought cries for the manager's resignation, and on 9 December, Melrose left the club. It was a sad parting of the ways for the

man who had delighted the crowds, with his skills in the late fifties and early sixties, and who had served the club faithfully and diligently during five years of financial stringency in the most thankless job of all, that of manager.

As his successor, the Board appointed Pat Stanton (36), the manager at Cowdenbeath for the last four months. As a distinguished player for Hibs for 14 years, Stanton had built up a reputation as a skilful, creative and dedicated player, worthy of more than the 16 caps he gained. A surprise transfer to Celtic brought him further honours and, when injury forced him to retire, he seized the opportunity to assist Ferguson at Pittodrie (though only after turning down a bid by Dunfermline to bring him to East End Park). After two successful years with the Dons which brought them the Premier League Championship for the first time, Stanton decided to forge his own career and succeeded Pat Wilson at Central Park. Older fans remembered the good fortune that the last manager from Cowdenbeath had brought the club when Sandy Paterson guided the Pars to promotion in 1925-26 and their only League Championship success in their 100 year history.

There were no immediate signs that the new Messiah had arrived. In the next three league games, the new manager saw his side lose by the odd goal on each occasion, to Dumbarton, promotion-seeking Raith Rovers and Stirling. Adverse weather conditions brought the postponement of many league games in January and Stanton had to rely on the Scottish Cup to give his side match practice. By a quirk

of fate, the draw took the Athletic to Stanton's old club, Hibs, for the third meeting of the clubs in five years in the Cup. The wise investment in under-soil heating by the Hibs' Board meant that the game went ahead despite the weather. A goal from Leonard after 11 minutes put the Easter Road side under some pressure until an Ally McLeod goal brought the equaliser.

The midweek replay brought a substantial crowd of almost 9,000 to East End Park; even the television cameras paid one of their rare visits to the ground. Hibs seemed to be heading for victory by a one-goal margin when a handling offence in the last minute allowed McNaughton to equalise from the penalty spot. Hibs' full-time training paid off in extra time when they went into a one-goal lead again. With only seconds left an O'Brien "goal" brought the house down, only for the referee to spot an offside infringement.

Stanton had to wait till 14 February to see his side win their first game, by 4–1 at Hamilton. A sequence of five successive defeats followed, which made relegation a distinct possibility. The crowds, which had been relatively large at the start of the season, began to dwindle to less than 2,000. With such low numbers the Police found it easy to implement the new Criminal Justice Act which came into force banning alcohol from Scottish grounds. To inject new life into his squad, Stanton called up two Junior players, both forwards: Grant Jenkins from Jeanfield Swifts and Bobby Forrest from Penicuik Athletic. Terry Wilson, nephew of the former Pars' player, was acquired from Hibs

Opposite: *Coach Walter Borthwick introduces the players to their new boss.* (Dunfermline Press)

Above: *McNaughton beats Hibs 'keeper, Jim McArthur, to send the cup-tie into extra-time.* (Dunfermline Press)

Above right: *Kenny Thomson.* (Dunfermline Press)

Below: *Bobby Forrest.* (Dunfermline Press)

for £5,000. The former Alloa player, Jimmy Thomson, joined the coaching staff from Cowdenbeath.

Everyone heaved a great sigh of relief when two goals from McNaughton brought Stanton his first home win on 1 April against Clydebank, the club's first home win for five months. Once again the momentum was not continued when they lost at Berwick, which put the club in joint second bottom place with Stirling Albion. Another tense finish to the season was promised though, with four of the remaining five games at home, Stanton felt confident his side would succeed. A valuable point from a home draw against high-flying Dundee looked even better when the results showed that fellow-strugglers, Stirling and Berwick, had also suffered reverses. A victory over Motherwell at home eased the situation, though only temporarily, as the following game against Dumbarton was lost. It took a draw with Berwick (already doomed) in the second last game, to give Dunfermline the vital point it needed to ensure that Stirling would be relegated.

For the second year, McNaughton finished the season as the club's top scorer with 22 goals. Kenny Thomson had the distinction for the fourth season running of never missing a first-team match. During the season, Thomson, as the club's longest serving player, captained his side against East Stirling on 6 September when he played his 302nd league game for the club and thus surpassed the old record held by George Peebles. At the AGM of the Scottish League in May, Dunfermline voted to revert to a two-league set-up of 18 and 20 clubs, but the motion failed.

Stanton was only too pleased to see the season end to give him time to prepare for the challenges ahead. His record of 11 points from 19 games, compared with the 16 points Melrose had accumulated over 20 games, suggested that he had plenty of homework to do.

SEASON 1981-82

For his first full season in charge at East End Park, Pat Stanton proved that he had been busy during the summer break by unveiling a whole batch of new signings to bring his squad up to 29, 11 of whom had just joined; no fewer than 15 players were beginning their first full season with the club. Though it was never publicised, the Board had their eyes on the Premier Division, and were, for the first time in many years, ready to spend substantial sums of money. The sale of the club house at Garvock Hill helped to finance the shopping bill which Stanton had drawn up to restore the club to its former glory.

George Young (31), the former Stirling Albion goal-keeper, cost £2,000 to bring from Ibrox to keep Hugh Whyte on his toes. For £5,000, Stanton acquired the services of Jim Brown (30), the former Hearts and Hibs player, and appointed him captain. £11,000 brought mid-field player, Hugh Hamill, from Hibs, while £7,000 was the sum required to secure the services of Aberdeen forward, Steve Morrison. Other signings included the Edinburgh twins, Robert and Stuart Dall (17), Gavin Tait (19), Rab Stewart (19) and Willie Blackie. The best bargain of all was negotiated when Norrie McCathie came to East End Park in August in a swap which sent McFarlane to Cowdenbeath. An old mate of Stanton, George Stewart, formerly of Dundee and Hibs, joined the club as coach. Colin O'Brien was transferred to East Fife while Mike Leonard, once the tormentor of Second Division defences in his prime, went to the junior club Pollok in Glasgow. Thus the teams which took the field in the pre-season friendlies

against Aberdeen (1–1), Dundee (1–1) and Keith (0–0) showed considerable alterations from the team that had played 12 months earlier.

In his remarks to the supporters in the first match programme, the chairman felt unusually optimistic about the prospects for the new season. He wrote: "I am going to stick my neck out by saying that there is going to be an undoubted upturn in the economy here and certainly something to build on at least. There seems to be a veritable whole new crop of very young and skilful talent."

The League Cup, reverting to its traditional form for the first time since 1976, gave the new look team a chance to knit together. Though the first game was lost to Hamilton, three successive victories against Montrose (twice) and East Stirling, gave Dunfermline a chance to overtake the section leaders, Hamilton, by beating them at East End Park. After an excellent start, the Pars allowed their concentration to lapse and, by losing 3–2 before 3,000 fans, went out of the Cup.

The prospect of Hearts crossing the Forth to Dunfermline always guaranteed a good gate. Interest in the opening game of the league programme was considerably heightened by the announcement that Stanton's latest signing, the 24-year-old Doug Considine, would play. Unable to command a regular place in a talented Aberdeen defence, the centre back from Banchory seized the chance to play for the Pars. When he scored the opening goal against Hearts and majestically took command at the back, it seemed that the expenditure of £43,000, an all-time record for the club, had been a wise investment. The Board were particularly pleased with the 4,300 crowd since a new ruling by the

The Dunfermline squad for 1981-82. Back row: B. Dall, Harris, Henderson, Tait, Blackie, Scullion, S. Dall, Wilcox, McGovern, Stewart, Thomson. Middle: Johnson, Stewart, Mercer, Leishman, Morrison, Young, Whyte, Robertson, Jenkins, Salton, Forrest, Thomson. Front: Nelson, Hegarty, Donnelly, Dunlop, Brown, Hamill, Hutt, Bowie, Stanton. (Inset: K. Thomson and McNaughton.) (Dunfermline Press)

Above: *Doug Considine*. (Dunfermline Press)

Top left: *George Young (left) and captain Jim Brown*. (Dunfermline Press)

Left: *Steve Morrison (left) and Hugh Hamill*. (Dunfermline Press)

Scottish League allowed the home club to retain all their gate receipts, a change from which a relatively well-supported club like Dunfermline could only benefit.

The following away victory over East Stirling was remarkable not just for the two valuable points collected, nor for the fact that the opposition was managed by another former East Ender, Martin Ferguson, but for the dropping from the team of Kenny Thomson, which brought his remarkable run of 227 consecutive games to an end. The last occasion on which he did not play for the Pars was on 11 September 1976 when his mates lost 3–0 to Stranraer.

A fairly good run, marred by a 4–1 defeat by Clydebank, kept Dunfermline up with the leaders. A great chance to cut Motherwell's lead at the top of the table was missed when the Lanarkshire club, reduced to 10 men, was allowed to snatch a last-minute winner and deprive the home side of precious points. Two victories and two draws still left the Pars in touch with the top of the league, and against St Johnstone at home they looked to be on their way further up the table. One goal up through a lovely shot from

Stewart, his first for the club, Dunfermline seemed to be in total control when full back Brown was carried off, crippled by a vicious tackle. Though the miscreant was sent off, and subsequently banned for the rest of the season, the rhythm of the home side was destroyed and the depleted Perth side went on not just to equalise, but to win the contest.

With the felling of Brown, who was never to play football again, Dunfermline's brave bid for promotion wilted. Although the team went on to record their first home win in the league, the following week on 7 November, against lowly East Stirling, the team were never again in the hunt. George Nicol (29), the former Stirling Albion player, was signed from Dundee United for £6,000 as a replacement for Brown, but failed to shore up a defence which lost six goals in successive Saturdays to Clydebank (home) and Motherwell (away) before losing at home to Kilmarnock on 5 December. Injury-prone John Salton, for whom the club had rejected a bid of £15,000 from Arbroath one year earlier, was given a free transfer.

Ice-bound pitches then forced Dunfermline to suspend their league programme for fully two months until February. In the interim, the third round of the Scottish Cup took the Pars to Clydebank. With only seconds left and a replay looking more and more likely, Young fluffed his goal-kick to allow the Bankies to slot home a dramatic winner.

On the resumption of league football, a single point from three games suggested that the club was going to have another struggle to steer clear of the relegation zone. Whyte took over from Young in goals and the team picked up eight points from the next five games to ease the pressure. With little now at stake the season quietly drew to a close with the Athletic occupying a safe, if unspectacular, 10th place, 12 points clear of relegation trouble, perhaps not a bad achievement for a team which had won only three of its home games. While fans switched their attention to the impending World Cup finals in Spain, Dunfermline had to be content with winning the Fife Cup in the year which marked the centenary of the Fife Football Association.

The end of the season brought a few nasty surprises. Kenny Thomson, who had joined the club in 1970, was shocked to receive a free transfer. He had played in no less than 348 league games, a record which is likely to stand for some time. He was soon snapped up by Alloa and later proved to his old club that he was far from a spent force. Bonar Mercer was also freed. McNaughton, the club's top scorer yet again with 16 goals, was put up for sale at his own request. Physiotherapist Jimmy Stevenson, whose association with the club began 27 years ago, retired to make way for the man who had stood in for him during his recent illness, Phil Yeates of the local rugby club.

SEASON 1982-83

More signings by Stanton made their appearance at East End Park for the start of the new season. The experienced midfield schemer, Bobby Ford, was bought from Raith Rovers but the accent was again on youth. Prominent among the new talent were Paul Crawford (18) from Leicester City, Trevor Smith, a schoolboy from Sauchie Juveniles, Colin Grant (19) from Linlithgow Rose and Kevin Hepburn (16) from Redding Juniors. Hugh Whyte, signed in May 1976, now became the club's longest-serving player. Doug Considine became the club captain. Two-thirds of the squad had been signed by Stanton and it was interesting to note that few of the squad had any local connections. Former player Jim Leishman rejoined the club in a coaching capacity. Andrew Watson, who had resigned from the Board at the last AGM after 30 years of dedicated service, was made the club's first honorary president. His place on the Board was taken by local businessman, Mr William Braisby (49), who was sponsoring the team for the third successive year.

The three pre-season friendlies at home against Dundee United (0–0), Sheffield United (0–2) and Sunderland (0–1) demonstrated that Stanton had yet to find the right blend, especially up front. The shortage of goals spilled over to the League Cup. At Parkhead, Dunfermline received a 6–0 mauling from Celtic and suffered just as disastrously in the return leg by going down 7–1 with the young Charlie Nicholas entertaining the 8,000 crowd with four goals. In the other matches, re-shuffled teams could only pick up two points from Alloa and one from Arbroath to end up at the foot of their section. After nine games, the Athletic had conceded 21 goals while scoring only three.

Across the Forth, a struggling Hibs side were doing little better and dispensed with their manager, Bertie Auld. Within a few days, the Easter Road Board had successfully enticed Stanton back to manage the club he had so gracefully served as a player. One of his last acts before he resigned on 2 September was to arrange the transfer of prolific scorer, Sandy McNaughton, to Ayr United for

All set for season 1982-83. Back row: O'Donnell, Stewart, Forrest, Morrison, Young, Whyte, McCathie, B. Dall, Nicol, Buckley. Middle: Yeates, McAuley, Ford, McNaughton, Hegarty, McGovern, Tait, Wilcox, Jenkins, Hepburn, Grant, Hamill, Leishman, Nelson. Front: Smith, Thomson, Black, Harris, Considine, Stanton, Stewart, Crawford, Blackie, S. Dall, Johnson, Bowie. (Absent: Robertson and Donnelly.) (Dunfermline Press)

£16,000. Coach Jimmy Thomson was appointed caretaker manager until a new appointment could be made. The Athletic could hardly have wished for a worse start to their league programme, but in spite of the obvious problems the side secured a creditable away draw against Partick Thistle and a disappointing home draw against newly promoted Clyde. Two defeats to Hamilton (away) and Raith (home) made the appointment of a manager even more urgent.

When it was announced that the former Motherwell and Rangers internationalist, Tom Forsyth, who had just retired at the age of 33 because of a recurrent knee injury, had been selected, the fans were surprised that the Board had gone for someone with no previous managerial experience. The "Iron Man's" reputation, however, as a tough, uncompromising defender led many to hope that some of his qualities, talents and undoubted experience would rub off on his new squad of players. Immediately after his appointment, as he watched his team from the stand go into the dressing-room at half-time trailing St Johnstone by 3–0, he was left in no doubt as to the magnitude of the task ahead of him. Jim Thomson followed George Stewart to join their former boss at Easter Road while Cammy Murray, the former St Mirren and Arbroath player, was brought from Motherwell to become first-team coach. Jim Leishman was put in charge of the reserves.

After giving the fans their first league win of the season on 25 September, against Ayr, the team were to become the favourites of the Pools' tipsters by drawing five of their next six games. Unhappy with the goalkeeping position, Forsyth dropped Young (who was soon to be transferred

to East Stirling), and for £10,000 bought Jim Moffat to challenge Whyte for the vital position between the posts. The 22-year-old PE student had once been on the books of Manchester City but had failed to make the grade and returned to Scotland to play for Montrose and Hamilton Accies. Another new signing was Ian Wildridge, a defender from Kelty Hearts.

Three disastrous defeats in November pushed Dunfermline to the bottom of the league with only 10 points from 16 games. A young blond-haired striker, Maurice Johnston, suggested that he was someone to watch for the future by scoring two of Partick's four goals in their defeat of Dunfermline. In the following week, the home fans had to suffer another humiliating defeat when a slick Dumbarton side went two goals up and despite having two of their players sent off, rallied to score a third goal with the home side unable to score. The club's surprise win over high-flying Airdrie in December was only their second victory of the season. Derek Rodier (23), the recent £6,000 buy from Hibs, made his debut and another new signing, Joe Smith (29), formerly of Aberdeen and Motherwell, appeared on the substitutes' bench.

The end of the year brought the final change to what had been a traumatic year for the club when Dr John Yellowley, the club's longest serving chairman, gave up the post after 12 difficult years which had seen the club's fortunes fluctuate considerably. In his valedictory address at the AGM, he spoke of "being very disenchanted at the state of affairs, if not very disillusioned. The previous season's dream of achieving Premier League status had all been swallowed up in the financial mire. In my experience

Top left: *Trevor Smith.*

Below: *Tom Forsyth in action for Rangers against Dunfermline, October 1974.* (Dunfermline Press)

Rab Stewart.

planning and success did not often go hand in hand in football, fate often played a bigger part." Yellowley remained a director with Mr Jimmy Watters becoming chairman and Mr Mel Rennie taking over as vice-chairman.

The New Year promised little better when Raith inflicted a 6–0 whitewash at Kirkcaldy in the derby game. Only three points out of a possible eight that month left the Pars at the foot of the table. Given such poor form many supporters anticipated the worst when Elgin City were drawn against their side in the third round of the Scottish Cup. Their fears were proved to be totally unfounded as the Highland League side, which had caused a few shocks in the past, were comprehensively beaten 5–0. Sponsorship from the Scottish Health Education Group brought Dunfermline £2,500 for participating and £500 for each goal scored. In the next round, the roles were to be reversed when the Athletic went to Parkhead to meet the side which had already taken 13 goals from them at the start of the season. Encouraged by a victory over league leaders Hearts, Dunfermline surprised the 12,000 crowd with their pluck and determination and for fully an hour held Celtic at bay. The full-time training of the home side began to tell and two goals from McGarvey and one from McCluskey on the stroke of time saw Celtic through. At the end of the month, the death of Andrew Watson robbed the club of one of its most ardent and hardworking supporters.

In the league campaign, the Pars continued to struggle to rise off the bottom berth. Against Clydebank it took a last-minute equaliser to give Dunfermline a share of the points.

Defeats by fellow strugglers, Hamilton and Clyde, deepened the gloom. Victory over Dumbarton on 12 March, the team's first away victory of the season, raised them two points above Queen's Park at the foot. Hopes of a revival were dashed when the next three games again resulted in draws when victories were essential. When the Pars scored all four goals in the 2–2 draw versus Raith, it seemed that luck had deserted them.

A surprise win at Somerset Park, the club's first success there for 36 years, followed by victory over Queen's Park, gave Dunfermline a chance to escape the drop if only they could produce their best form. While Queen's Park looked doomed, the Athletic had a chance of catching not only Ayr and Hamilton but possibly Clyde as well, especially since the Shawfield side were the next visitors to East End Park. Dunfermline should have had both points sewn up after a first half display which saw them do everything but put the ball in the net. In the end, a goalless draw suited Clyde more than Dunfermline.

A visit to Tynecastle where Hearts were just as desperate for points to secure promotion and the Championship, was a daunting prospect to say the least. Despite going twice behind by two goals and having a man sent off, the Pars turned on a magnificent performance to force a 3–3 draw to keep their slender hopes alive. Another draw against Falkirk, managed by Alex Totten, in the last home match left Dunfermline with the almost impossible task of beating First Division champions, St Johnstone, at Muirton Park, to have any chance of survival. A 1–0 defeat plunged the Athletic once again into the backwater of Second Division football.

The changeover of managers and coaching staff certainly contributed to Dunfermline's failure, especially when so many players had just joined the club and were trying to build up a new understanding. Significantly, 32 players were used over the 39 games. Considine's dispute with the club in January and his refusal to play for the club again did nothing to raise morale. One statistic more than anything else relegated Dunfermline – 17 draws out of 39 games, a record for the club. Their points total of 31 was the highest number of points to relegate a club. The Board accepted full responsibility for the gamble which they had taken to spend money to better the club and which had now apparently failed. Their accountants depressingly pointed out that while it cost over £150,000 to run the club, only £25,000 was taken in at the turnstiles.

Opposite: *Team photo of 1983-84. Back row: Tait, Hepburn, McCathie, Whyte, Moffat, Perry, Stuart Morrison, Steve Morrison. Middle: Yeates, R. Dall, Black, Bowie, Jenkins, Crawford, Donnelly, J. Smith, Forrest, Nelson. Front: Leishman, Stewart, Jim Smith, Rodier, Forsyth, Wilcox, T. Smith, Strachan, Murray. (Dundee Courier)*

SEASON 1983-84

Not for the first time the season opened with the pledge that the aim of the club was to gain promotion in one season. Tom Forsyth was confirmed as manager by the Board as the man to achieve it. Andy Young, the man who brought youngsters like Evans to East End Park more than a decade before, rejoined the club to help bring on its young talent. Hugh Hamill, a costly signing just two years ago, was surprisingly given a free transfer. The discontented Doug Considine was put up for sale though no offers were to be forthcoming and the club's massive investment wilted away in the north of Scotland. Terry Wilson and Joe Smith failed to report for training, were fined and duly left the club. The talented John Perry was brought on a free transfer from Falkirk and the experienced defender, John Lapsley, came from Partick Thistle. Centre half, Bobby Dall, sold only nine months earlier, rejoined the club. Hugh Whyte, who had recently seen off two challengers for his position, was appointed captain, a rare honour for a goalkeeper. During the close season, major repairs were yet again carried out on the pitch to solve the drainage problems which had caused so many postponements in the past. The whole turf was lifted, drainage channels inserted and the pitch immaculately relaid. This costly operation prevented the playing of any pre-season friendly games.

A solid 1-0 victory over Cowdenbeath at Central Park gave the Pars the perfect start to their league challenge. The following Wednesday took them to Tannadice to meet the league champions in the second round of the League Cup, played once again on a knock-out basis over two legs. A 6-1 thrashing by Jim McLean's men in the first leg made the second leg little more than a practice game. Another victory, though in a game that was much more evenly contested, saw Dundee United through on an 8-1 aggregate.

In the more important business of the league, a disappointing 1-1 draw with East Fife at home followed by a defeat at Palmerston Park showed that Dunfermline could not expect promotion to come gift-wrapped. The hospitalisation of the manager in the first week of September did not help matters as the team served up one indifferent display after another which was reflected in home gates well below the 2,000 mark. Attempts to strengthen the squad by signing either Herd (Falkirk), Pettigrew (Hearts) or Sullivan (ex-Celtic) came to nothing.

When Forfar visited East End Park on 28 September they topped the league and led Dunfermline by five points after only six games. Excellent goalkeeping from Kennedy, formerly of Dunfermline and Rangers, helped the visitors to beat the Pars 2-1 and to move even further ahead. On 15 October, another home defeat, by Arbroath, left Dunfermline in eighth position and persuaded Forsyth and his assistant that the time had come to resign. Forsyth had obviously found it difficult to make the transition from the full-time set-up and glamour of Premier Division Rangers to the part-time frugal situation of Second Division football at East End Park. A return trip of 80 miles per day from his Lanarkshire home did not make the task any easier for him.

In the meantime, reserve coach, Jim Leishman, was appointed caretaker manager while the Board sifted through 40 applications. While Leishman was empowered to make two new signings – the experienced central defender Alan Forsyth from Raith Rovers for £2,300 and the youngster Ian Heddle from Dunfermline Railway FC – the team lost at Hampden and could only draw with East Stirling at home before a crowd of not much more than a thousand.

On 31 October, the 29-year-old former player was confirmed as manager, the fourth incumbent in three years. Leishman had first joined the club as a 14-year-old and could remember walking from his home in Lochgelly to watch the Pars play their European matches at East End Park. A double fracture to his leg cut short a promising career with Dunfermline and after a short spell with Cow-

Above: *A young Jim Leishman.* (Dunfermline Press)

Below: *Relaxing in the bath at Lin-lor, a health and beauty salon.* (Dundee Courier)

Opposite: *The formidable striking force of Grant Jenkins (left), Norrie McCathie and John Watson.*

denbeath he gave up playing to manage the junior club, Kelty Hearts. After that he returned to Central Park to assist manager Andy Rolland before accepting an invitation from Stanton to return to East End Park. For the first time since the war the manager's job became a part-time one with Leishman continuing to work at a local job centre. As one of the last full-time players in 1976, Leishman fervently hoped to restore the club to its rightful place at the top of Scottish football. He wrote in the match programme following his appointment – "There is no one more keen to see these halcyon days return to East End Park . . . Promotion is certainly not an impossibility." Bill Baxter, formerly of Ipswich, was appointed to look after the club's youth policy and a new wave of enthusiasm and bustle swept through the corridors of the stadium.

The next two months, however, confirmed that Leishman would have no fairytale start to his new job. Only one victory through the dark months of November and December destroyed any faltering hopes of promotion that Dunfermline might have harboured. The collapse of a local printing company even deprived the home fans of their match programme for some time. Across in Edinburgh former player, Jim Brown, who had sued John Pelosi of St Johnstone in the Court of Session for prematurely ending his career two years earlier through a crippling tackle, was awarded £30,000 in an out-of-court settlement which was seen as a test case for other players. The end of another traumatic year saw the departure of Rodier to Berwick Rangers and Moffat to Forfar for £1,000 each. A new forward, the 25-year-old red-haired John Watson, was signed from Hong Kong.

The best the New Year could offer the Athletic was a good run in the Scottish Cup. A bye in the first round gave them a home draw against Forfar and the chance to avenge two earlier defeats by the league leaders. In an evenly contested match on the evening of 9 January, Dunfermline just squeezed through by a single goal from Stewart to gain a plum tie against Rangers in the third round. It was over 20

years since the Pars had last met the Light Blues in the Scottish Cup – in the semi-finals in March 1964 to be exact.

Thanks to undersoil heating at Ibrox, the game went ahead as scheduled on 28 January before a crowd of 18,000. During the first half, Dunfermline belied their lowly position in the Second Division and went into the dressing-room at half-time on equal terms. Early in the second half, Stewart sent the loyal band of Pars fans wild by putting his side into a shock lead. As the minutes ticked away it seemed that Dunfermline might inflict a defeat even greater than the one Rangers suffered at Berwick in 1967. With only nine minutes left, centre half Colin McAdam brought sighs of relief to the Ibrox faithful by snatching the equaliser. Rangers continued to pile on the pressure and a second goal from McCoist killed off any hopes of a lucrative replay at East End Park. Afterwards, manager Jock Wallace admitted that "I was worried." Dunfermline received a cheque for more than £10,000 and Steve Morrison was chosen by the Cup's sponsors, the Scottish Health Education Group, as 'Mr Superfit', for overall stamina and physical fitness.

The club was brought back down to earth in their next game when they could only draw at home against bottom of the table Montrose. In the same month, Gregor Abel (35), who had recently resigned the manager's post at Brockville after three months, was appointed coach. His first game with his new club saw them record their first home league victory for over three months against Stranraer on 25 February. Indifferent and inconsistent form from the team as they played out their remaining fixtures made for a disappointing end to the season. Indeed, three defeats were sustained in the last four games of what can only be described as the club's worst season for 30 years as they languished in ninth position in the Second Division beneath 32 other league clubs. Morrison, top scorer with 10 goals, was put up for transfer as was one of the club's most promising youngsters, Rab Stewart. There was certainly no chance of Leishman being allowed to spend the £100,000 which his two immediate predecessors had squandered on players, only one of whom could now command a first-team place.

SEASON 1984–85

The disappointments of the old season were soon forgotten as the Pars prepared for the new season with the added incentive of gaining promotion in the club's centenary year, 1985. Missing from the line-up was Stewart who was sold to Motherwell for just over £10,000. In the opening game of the season, a meagre crowd of 1,000 turned up to see the Athletic take on Stranraer against whom Leishman fielded his three close season signings: Rowan Hamilton (midfield) from Dundee FC; Paul Rodgers (midfield) from Hong Kong and former Celtic centre half, Dave Young, freed by Arbroath. Four goals from Watson and one from Jenkins gave the Pars the perfect start to the league campaign. Afterwards the unsettled Paul Donnelly was transferred to Partick Thistle for £6,000.

The goal-scoring machine was again in action four days later when a burst of four goals in 20 minutes demolished Arbroath at East End Park in the first round of the Skol League Cup to give Dunfermline a money-spinning home draw against Celtic. By the time that game was played a sound 3–1 away victory over Raith Rovers put the Athletic firmly at the top of the table. "I honestly cannot remember," wrote the manager in the programme, "of the club having a better start to the season in all my long years connected with Dunfermline Athletic both as player and backroom boy."

The appearance of Celtic and a bumper crowd on Wednesday 22 August certainly brought "the Good Old Days" back to East End Park and when Watson sent his side into the dressing-room at half-time with a one-goal lead, a Cup upset looked possible. Constant pressure, however, from Celtic was finally rewarded when two goals inside as many minutes put the Glasgow side ahead. Almost immediately the Pars shocked everyone in the stadium by storming back and equalising through Watson. With extra time looming, Celtic's superior fitness and skill paid dividends when McClair scored his second goal of the night to edge a plucky Pars side out of the competition.

Encouraged by their very creditable performance, Dunfermline picked themselves up to resume their promotion campaign with a tricky fixture at Montrose who were already shaping up as serious challengers. Another fine victory (4–2) with two goals apiece from Watson and Jenkins kept Dunfermline in top position. John Watson's goal-scoring feats were rewarded when he was nominated "Player of the Month" for August by Scottish Brewers. September began in equally fine fashion with further victories over Stirling at home (1–0), Berwick away (1–0) and Cowdenbeath at home (2–1) before a crowd of 3,500. Leishman strengthened his squad by signing Colin McGlashan, a full-time forward with Dundee, for £5,000. With six victories recorded out of six, Dunfermline supporters were jubilant and looked with confidence not just to promotion but even to the championship itself.

The bubble burst, as it had to one day, on 22 September when the Pars stumbled, not for the first time, at Ochilview by the only goal of the game, scored three minutes from time. Before that, Morrison had been sent off for retaliation and Stenhousemuir had missed a penalty. At the end of the game, the referee was jostled and barracked as he left the field, causing the chairman to issue stern words of warning to the fans as to their future behaviour.

The squad which almost took Dunfermline into the First Division in their centenary year. Back row: Strachan, Forsyth, Wilcox, Jenkins, Hamilton, Donnelly. Middle: Pryde, Black, Morrison, McGregor, Rodgers, O'Hara, Bowie. Front: Abel, Smith, Watson, Whyte, Heddle, Forrest, Leishman. (Dundee Courier)

Watson opens the scoring against Celtic in the Skol Cup. (Dunfermline Press)

A 1–1 draw with Queen of the South at home gave fans the jitters, but three fine wins against Arbroath away (2–0), Queen's Park at home (4–0) and Albion Rovers away (2–0) in the opening weeks of October restored confidence. The next game on 27 October, against second placed Alloa at East End Park, drew the amazingly large gate for a Second Division match of 4,404 patrons, one of the highest crowds in Scotland that day. Despite going one goal up through Jenkins, the Pars let the Wasps off the hook and allowed them to go into a 2–1 lead. The home fans were content to settle for a point when Watson equalised near the end which was enough to keep Dunfermline at the top of the table.

Another setback occurred in the first Saturday of November when Dunfermline delivered one of their worst performances of the season in torrential rain to lose 2–0 against East Stirling at Firs Park, the first home league win for the Falkirk club since February which allowed Alloa to push Dunfermline into second spot for the first time. The following week a home draw against Berwick Rangers gave the Pars the point they needed to go joint top with rivals Alloa and Montrose, also on the 23 point mark from 15 games. A goal by Watson against Cowdenbeath at Central Park kept Dunfermline in top spot. On the last Saturday of November, Stenhousemuir, only four points behind, did further damage to the Pars' hopes by forcing home an equaliser against the home side five minutes from time in a game which Dunfermline should have won easily. New signing, Ian Gordon, a midfield player from Broomfield, scored Dunfermline's goal and looked a good prospect for the future.

December brought a dramatic slump in form beginning with the first home defeat (2–1) against lowly Arbroath, a side they had comprehensively beaten twice already. Worse was to come the following week at East End Park when East Stirling recorded their second victory (3–1) over the Pars, this time in the first round of the Scottish Cup. Thus for only the second time in 25 years the Athletic's name would not go onto the lucrative third-round draw with the chance to meet a top club. A few days later, Martin Sisman, the director who had done so much to raise money through his money-spinning East End Enterprises, shocked the club by announcing his resignation, "for personal reasons". Three more draws, against Queen of the South, Montrose and Stirling, completed a depressing month for the Pars who were now pushed into third place behind Alloa and Montrose.

The New Year could not have produced a worse start with the derby game against Raith resulting in a 2–1 home defeat. Their programme for the rest of the month was postponed because of ground conditions, causing the Pars to slip further behind while Stenhousemuir and Cowdenbeath showed that they were far from out of the race by picking up valuable points. Leishman strengthened his squad with two new signings – Frank Liddell (31), the former Hearts and Alloa centre half, and Derek O'Connor (30), a proven goal-scorer with Hearts. The injection of new blood failed to save the club from their heaviest defeat of the season – a 4–1 drubbing at Hampden by Queen's Park on 2 February; a 1–1 draw the following week against lowly Albion Rovers left fans wondering if their team could ever make up the nine-point gap which now separated them from top placed Alloa.

Against Stirling Albion the rot continued. Provisional signing Willie Callaghan (17), son of the illustrious sixties star of the same name, made his first-team debut. After giving the visitors a two-goal lead, the Pars fought back through Young and Liddell to level the score. In the last minute a penalty miss by Morrison marred a magnificent fight back and put Dunfermline further adrift of Alloa and Montrose. Leishman was appointed full-time commercial manager and launched Pars Pools Promotions to raise the extra revenue that the club so desperately required.

Morrison soon made amends for his slip-up by scoring the only goal at Stair Park in the next game. An even more important away win was recorded three days later when a large travelling support journeyed to Alloa to see two goals from Morrison help defeat the league leaders 3–1. This fine form away from home was soon nullified yet again by another poor performance in front of the home support. Despite going one goal up against Cowdenbeath, the Pars let their rivals off the hook and slack defensive work allowed Cowdenbeath to score twice to deprive the home side of two vital points. Away from home, Dunfermline continued to do well, beating Arbroath 3–1 and drawing 1–1 with Queen's Park. Liddell was released and McGlashan was transferred to Cowdenbeath for £3,000.

A rearranged fixture against East Stirling on Tuesday 19 March gave Dunfermline their first home victory since 13 October though it took a cracker of an own-goal to help the home side to their 2–0 win. New signing, David Moyes (29), bought earlier in the day from Meadowbank, made a promising debut in midfield. Once again the momentum

was not maintained when Dunfermline disappointed their fans by dropping yet another point at home to Stenhousemuir in a 0–0 draw. To freshen up his side, Leishman bought former Scottish Youth goalkeeper, Ian Westwater (21), from Hearts for £4,000 and brought Ian Campbell, a former colleague in the mid-seventies, back to East End Park from Brechin in a straight swap involving Perry and O'Connor. Both players travelled to Stranraer on 3 April and helped their new mates to a fine 2–0 win.

A tremendous boost was given to the Pars' promotion hopes when Raith defeated Alloa which reduced the once massive gap to a mere three points with Dunfermline having a game in hand and a match against the leaders still to come. It was at this point that Dunfermline stumbled once again, drawing 0–0 with East Stirling and 1–1 with Albion Rovers, both away from home.

As the season drew to a tremendous climax, Dunfermline had another excellent chance of improving their position when league leaders, Montrose, visited East End Park on 20 April. In a dour, uninspiring struggle both sides played out an unexciting goalless draw which, thanks to East Stirling's shock defeat of Alloa, sent Dunfermline back into second top position due to their superior goal difference. On the following Tueday, Dunfermline failed to consolidate their position when they disappointingly lost 3–2 at home in a thrilling match to Raith Rovers, then enjoying one of their best ever runs in league football.

Although this was undoubtedly a setback, Dunfermline showed no signs of giving up the struggle and a few days

The Dunfermline players who took part in a "fun run" to help the Iain Skinner Appeal. (Dundee Courier)

later they ran up their highest victory of the year by trouncing Queen of the South 4–0. With only two games left, the scene was set for a nail-biting finish to one of the most exciting contests for years. The top of the table showed that while Montrose were certain to be promoted, the second berth could go to either Alloa, Dunfermline or possibly, Cowdenbeath:

	P	W	D	L	F	A	Pts
Montrose	37	21	8	8	54	39	50
Alloa	37	19	9	9	57	40	47
Dunfermline	37	16	14	7	59	35	46
Cowdenbeath	37	17	11	9	66	37	45

As fate would have it, the penultimate game sent the Pars to Recreation Park to do battle with second placed Alloa. A crowd of over 4,000 spectators, mostly from Dunfermline, turned up on the sunny afternoon of 4 May to witness what promised to be a titanic struggle. However, with each side determined not to lose a goal, the match failed to live up to expectations and play was anything but spectacular. The best chance fell to the visitors 19 minutes from the end when a handling offence rewarded them with a penalty. Sadly, there was no Andy Rolland available on this occasion and a weakly struck kick by Morrison was saved by the 'keeper. The game ended in a goalless draw, a result which obviously delighted the Wasps, but left the Pars dejected.

With only one game to go, the best the Pars could hope was to win their fixture at home against second bottom Berwick, while praying that foot-of-the-table Arbroath might take a point at Gayfield from Alloa. The English side proved to be awkward opponents and it took a penalty, coolly converted by Trevor Smith, to break the deadlock. However, as they had done so often during the season after taking the lead, the Pars let their concentration wander and almost immediately allowed the visitors to equalise just before the interval. To make matters worse, the half-time score from Gayfield announced that Alloa were one goal up. Undeterred, the Pars plodded on against a packed Berwick defence and after missing several excellent chances were duly rewarded in the 83rd minute with a second penalty award. Once again, no one envied Smith his task as he placed the ball on the spot. The youngster was equal to the occasion and brought the house down with another well-struck shot to the same corner of the net.

What then followed was unprecedented in the whole hundred years of football at East End Park. No sooner had the game re-started than a rumour, based on a radio report, started in the west enclosure and spread like wildfire throughout the stadium to the effect that Alloa were now only drawing with their hosts. As the final whistle sounded the park was engulfed in a sea of supporters who believed that their heroes had finally managed to overhaul Alloa and gain promotion. There were scenes of great jubilation as fans congratulated each other and applauded the players. Sadly, the news began to percolate through that Alloa had, in fact, beaten Arbroath (1–0) and they, not Dunfermline, were to be promoted. "It was like winning the pools," a dejected Jim Leishman explained, "and then finding out your coupon had not been posted."

Smith coolly fires home the first of his two penalties against Berwick. (Dunfermline Press)

Jubilant fans thought their team had won promotion. (Dunfermline Press)

As he looked back over the season, the manager must have wondered how his team had allowed promotion, not to mention the championship, to slip away. As in recent seasons, the team's performance at home left a lot to be desired – only seven wins were recorded. On the other hand, no fewer than 10 games ended in draws. Figures released by the Scottish League showed that lack of support was certainly not to blame. No fewer than 46,576 fans cheered on Dunfermline, a figure which only Motherwell could better out of the 28 clubs outwith the Premier League. Perhaps the whole matter was put in perspective that evening. As television viewers watched Manchester City fans celebrate their promotion, the screen also carried pictures of the horrific fire which engulfed the stand of Bradford City Football Club causing the deaths of 56 supporters.

The dream of this historian – to record Dunfermline's overdue promotion in their centenary year – was not to be realised. Dunfermline's history over the last century, as these pages have hopefully set out, has been a chequered one. From humble, inauspicious beginnings and with an often uncertain future, the club has survived the advent of professionalism, two world wars, various economic blizzards and several league reconstructions to fill an honourable and, at times, memorable place in the annals of Scottish football history. Few clubs outwith the Old Firm have

enjoyed such a purple patch in their history as Dunfermline experienced in the Glorious Sixties. Sadly, Dunfermline have joined that illustrious list of proud, provincial clubs like Dundee, Motherwell, Kilmarnock and others who have found it well nigh impossible to keep together successful teams for more than a few years, or to maintain their excellent standards when a highly successful manager departs. It will be the task of future historians to note whether the New Firm of Aberdeen and Dundee United can sustain their challenge for much longer.

Today, the situation at East End Park is not as depressing or forlorn as the club's lowly status might indicate. The club has a stadium which is undoubtedly one of the best in Scotland, an ambitious and hard-working Board of Directors, one of the most energetic and enthusiastic managers for years and potentially the largest support of any club outside the Premier League. To imagine how Dunfermline Athletic will develop in the next hundred years in an ever-changing society would require a crystal ball of amazing clarity; I would wager, however, that Dunfermline will be Fife's first representatives in the Top Ten where their rightful place amongst the leaders of Scottish football will once again be secured.

Here's to the next hundred years. Up the Pars!

LOOKING FORWARD! *The 1985-86 squad. Back row: Strachan, Forrest, Jenkins, Bowie, Campbell, McGinlay, Houston, Foggo, Lobban. Middle: Nelson, Gordon, Smith, Whyte, Westwater, McGregor, Grant, Young, Jobson. Front: McCathie, Hamilton, Pryde, Leishman, Irvine, Heddle, Watson. (Absent: Abel [coach], Forsyth, Morrison, Moyes and Robertson.)* (Dundee Courier)

LOOKING BACK! *STV kindly donating their tapes of the club's exploits in the 1960s. From left: A. Edwards, A. Smith, H. Melrose, R. Mailer, G. Peebles, G. Miller (hidden), B. Paton, J. McConville, A. Montford, Rita Henderson (tea lady for 25 years), M. Sisman, M. Allan, W. Cunningham, Sheila Peters (office secretary), J. Stein, J. Watters, J. Leishman, W. Rennie, W. Braisby.* (Dunfermline Press)

Before the centenary match against Aberdeen on Wednesday 7 August, former players and managers gathered together to be presented to the crowd. In the centre of the group is 89-year-old Jimmy Tonner who played for the club in 1912!

The club also used the occasion to publicise its new fund-raising venture, the Centenary Club, which, it is hoped, will bring in the cash to restore the club to its former glory. (Dunfermline Press)

For the Record

CHAIRMEN

(from 1919, the formation of the club into a company)

ALEX MITCHELL	1919
JOHN FRASER	1923
WILLIAM WHYTE	1930
MARTIN PORTER	1933
JAMES ANDERSON	1935
MARTIN PORTER	1936
ROBERT WYLIE	1939
GEORGE ROBB	1943
TOM GIBSON	1947
GEORGE ROBB	1950
HUGH McMILLAN	1951
JOHN SPEARS	1955
DAVID THOMSON	1957
ANDREW WATSON	1963
LEONARD JACK	1970
JOHN YELLOWLEY	1971
JAMES WATTERS	1982

MANAGERS

WILLIE KNIGHT	1922-25
SANDY PATERSON	1925-30
WILLIE KNIGHT	1930-36
DAVID TAYLOR	1936-38
PETER WILSON	1938-39
SANDY ARCHIBALD	1939-46
WILLIAM McANDREW	Feb-Aug 1947
BOBBY CALDER	1947-48
SANDY TERRIS, Director	1948-49
WEBBER LEES	1949-51
TOM YOUNGER, Director	1951-52
BOBBY ANCELL	1952-55
ANDY DICKSON	1955-60
JOCK STEIN	1960-64
WILLIE CUNNINGHAM	1964-67
GEORGE FARM	1967-70
ALEC WRIGHT	1970-72
GEORGE MILLER	1972-75
HARRY MELROSE	1975-80
PAT STANTON	1980-82
TOM FORSYTH	1982-83
JIM LEISHMAN	1983-

Stein with the Scottish Cup in 1961.

JOCK STEIN, 1922-85

No one was to know that this was to be Jock Stein's last visit to East End Park before his untimely death one month later after the crucial Wales-Scotland World Cup qualifying match at Ninian Park on Tuesday 10 September 1985. It has often been said that Jock Stein put Dunfermline Athletic on the football map, but he was always the first to point out that it was also the club which made Jock Stein and brought him to national prominence. He always had a special regard for East End Park and his Cup success in 1961 was one of his proudest moments.

After leaving Dunfermline to join Hibs in 1964, he returned one year later to Parkhead to guide Celtic to eight victories in the Scottish Cup, six in the League Cup in addition to a record-breaking nine successive League Championships. The highlight of his career was, of course, in steering Celtic to success in the European Cup in Lisbon against Inter Milan in 1967.

Stein left Parkhead in 1978 to become manager of Leeds United, but after 45 days he found irresistible the summons to manage the Scottish national team, still smarting from a disappointing performance in the World Cup Finals in Argentina. Under Stein's careful guidance the team qualified for the Finals in Spain in 1982 where they were only prevented from going further in the tournament by goal difference. At the moment of his death it seemed as though he had directed his country to qualifying for the 1986 Finals in Mexico.

The Big Man will certainly be missed.

HONOURS

Scottish Cup	Winners	1961 and 1968
	Runners-up	1965
Qualifying Cup	Winners	1911-12
Central League	Champions	1910-11; 1911-12
League, Division 2	Champions	1925-26
	Runners-up	1912-13; 1933-34; 1954-55; 1957-58; 1972-73; 1978-79
League, Division 1	Best position	3rd 49pts 1964-65
		3rd 45pts 1968-69
League Cup	Runners-up	1949-50
Europe	Semi-finals	Cup Winners' Cup 1968-69

GOALS

Record win	Early days	15-1(h) v Dunfermline		1886-87
	Division 2	11-2(h) v Stenhousemuir		1930-31
	Division 1	10-1(h) v Partick Thistle		1958-59
	Scottish Cup	9-0(h) v Wigtown & Blad.		1961-62
	Europe	10-1(h) v Apoel		1968-69
Record defeat	Early days	2-17(h) v Clackmannan		1891-92
	Division 2	0-10(a) v Dundee		1947-48
	Division 1	0-9(a) v Celtic		1927-28
	Scottish Cup	0-7(a) v Airdrie		1954-55
		1-11(h) v Hibs		1889-90
	Europe	0-4(a) v Valencia		1962-63
Overall record total	C. Dickson	240		1955-64
League total	C. Dickson	154		1955-64
Division 1	A. Ferguson	31		1965-66
(also joint highest for Scottish First Division that season)				
Division 2	R. Skinner	53		1925-26
(also the highest in Scottish League football that season)				
Most League goals	Division 1	94		1965-66
	Division 2	120		1957-58
Most goals in a Senior game	C. Dickson	6 v St Mirren		1961-62
	H. Melrose	6 v Partick Thistle		1958-59
Fastest goal	C. Dickson	10 seconds v Celtic		1959-60

ATTENDANCES

Highest pre-war crowd	16,611	v Alloa	1938-39
League	27,816	v Celtic	1967-68
Scottish Cup	24,377	v Rangers	1957-58
Europe	25,000	v West Bromwich	1968-69
New Second Division	5,955	v Falkirk	1978-79
Best supported season	750,000		1964-65
Largest crowd	113,228	Hampden	April 1961
Cup Final campaigns	282,764		1960-61
	172,977		1964-65
	158,165		1967-68

APPEARANCES

Longest serving player	J. Baird		1913-26
	R. Mailer		1951-64
Most league appearances	K. Thomson	348	1970-82
	G. Peebles	301	1955-66
Most consecutive appearances	K. Thomson	227	1976-81
Most European games	W. Callaghan	34	
Youngest player	A. Edwards	16 yrs 5 days	
(This would have been a Scottish record but for R. Simpson's appearance in 1945 at the age of 14 yrs 304 days.)			
Most expensive player	D. Considine	£43,000+VAT	1982
Most expensive transfer	A. Ferguson	£60,000	1967
Most capped player	A. Wilson	6 (12 in all)	
Other internationalists	E. Connachan, W. Callaghan, W. Cunningham, G. Karlsen.		

MISCELLANEOUS

Pitch	115 yards × 71 yards		
Best run of successive	Division 1	7	1961-62
League victories	Division 2	8	1957-58
Best undefeated run in	Division 2	16	1978-79
League	Division 2	15	1925-26
	Division 1	12	1961-62
Most League points	Division 2	59	1925-26
	Division 1	49	1964-65

SCOTTISH CUP

(Results from the institution of the Qualifying Cup in 1895–96.)

Season	Round	Opponents	Result
			(Dunfermline score first)
1905–6	1	Aberdeen (a)	0–3
1911–12	1	Celtic (a)	0–1
1912–13	1	Hearts (a)	1–3
World War One and rebel Central League			
1921–22	1	Stevenson United (h)	3–1
	2	East Stirling (a)	1–2
1922–23	1	Dumbarton (a)	1–0
	2	Clydebank (h)	1–0
	3	Raith (h)	0–3
1923–24	1	Arbroath (h)	0–1
1924–25	1	Arbroath (h)	1–1
	Replay	Arbroath (a)	0–1
1925–26	1	Clyde (a)	0–3
1926–27	1	Bathgate (a)	2–2
	Replay	Bathgate (h)	5–2
	2	Airdrie (h)	2–1
	3	East Fife (a)	0–2
1927–28	1	Clydebank (a)	3–0
	2	Leith (h)	3–1
	3	Dundee (a)	2–1
	Quarter-Final	Hibs (h)	0–4
1928–29	1	Cowdenbeath (h)	1–3
1929–30	1	Airdrie (a)	1–3
1930–31	1	Airdrie (h)	2–2
	Replay	Airdrie (a)	1–6
1931–32	1	East Stirling (h)	5–2
	2	Dundee (h)	1–0
	3	Bye	
	Quarter-Final	Kilmarnock (h)	1–3
1932–33	1	Celtic (h)	1–7
1933–34	1	Ayr (a)	0–2
1934–35	1	Hamilton (h)	1–2
1935–36	1	Brechin (h)	6–2
	2	Galston (h)	5–2
	3	Bye	

Season	Round	Opponents	Result
	Quarter-Final	Falkirk (a)	0–5
1936–37	1	Arbroath (h)	0–0
	Replay	Arbroath (a)	0–1
1937–38	1	St Mirren (h)	0–1
1938–39	1	Morton (h)	5–2
	2	Duns (h)	2–0
	3	Alloa (h)	1–1
	Replay	Alloa (a)	2–3
World War Two			
1946–47	1	East Fife (a)	2–6
1947–48	1	Bye	
	2	Clyde (a)	1–2
1948–49	1	Stenhousemuir (h)	3–3
	Replay	Stenhousemuir (a)	0–2
1949–50	1	Forfar (h)	5–3
	2	Albion Rovers (a)	2–1
	3	Stenhousemuir (h)	1–4
1950–51	1	Clyde (h)	0–3
1951–52	1	Bye	
	2	Clyde (a)	4–3
	3	Motherwell (h)	1–1
	Replay	Motherwell (a)	0–4
1952–53	1	Morton (a)	1–3
1953–54	1	Stranraer (a)	4–1
	2	Motherwell (a)	2–5
1954–55	5	Partick Thistle (h)	4–2
	6	Airdrie (a)	0–7
1955–56	5	Clyde (a)	0–5
1956–57	5	Morton (h)	3–0
	6	St Mirren (a)	0–1
1957–58	1	Alloa (a)	2–0
	2	St Mirren (a)	4–1
	3	Rangers (h)	1–2
1958–59	1	Cowdenbeath (a)	2–2
	Replay	Cowdenbeath (h)	4–1
	2	Montrose (a)	1–0
	3	Ayr (h)	2–1
	Quarter-Final	St Mirren (a)	1–2
1959–60	1	St Johnstone (h)	1–1

Opposite: *Edwards and Cruickshank duel for this cross in the 1968 Cup Final.*   Below: *Stevenson discusses tactics with his players.*

Season	Round	Opponents	Result (Dunfermline score first)		Season	Round	Opponents	Result (Dunfermline score first)
	Replay	St Johnstone (a)	4-1		1967-68	1	Celtic (a)	2-0
	2	Stenhousemuir (h)	2-3			2	Aberdeen (h)	2-1
1960-61	1	Berwick (a)	4-1			Quarter-Final	Partick Thistle (h)	1-0
	2	Stranraer (a)	3-1			Semi-Final (Tynecastle)	St Johnstone	1-1
	3	Aberdeen (a)	6-3			Replay (Tynecastle)	St Johnstone	2-1
	Quarter-Final	Alloa (h)	4-0			FINAL (Hampden)	Hearts	3-1
	Semi-Final (Tynecastle)	St Mirren	0-0		1968-69	1	Raith (a)	2-0
	Replay (Tynecastle)	St Mirren	1-0			2	Aberdeen (a)	2-2
	FINAL (Hampden)	Celtic	0-0			Replay	Aberdeen (h)	0-2
	Replay (Hampden)	Celtic	2-0		1969-70	3	Celtic (a)	1-2
1961-62	1	Forfar (h)	5-1		1970-71	3	Arbroath (h)	3-1
	2	Wigtown & Bladnoch (h)	9-0			4	Celtic (a)	1-1
	3	Stenhousemuir (h)	0-0			Replay	Celtic (h)	0-1
	Replay	Stenhousemuir (a)	3-0		1971-72	3	Raith (a)	0-2
	Quarter-Final	St Mirren (a)	0-1		1972-73	3	Dundee (h)	0-3
1962-63	1	Bye			1973-74	3	Falkirk (a)	2-2
	2	Cowdenbeath (a)	3-2			Replay	Falkirk (h)	1-0
	3	Aberdeen (a)	0-4			4	Queen of the South (h)	1-0
1963-64	1	Bye				5	Dundee United (h)	1-1
	2	Fraserburgh (h)	7-0			Replay	Dundee United (a)	0-4
	3	East Stirling (a)	6-1		1974-75	3	Clydebank (a)	1-2
	Quarter-Final	Ayr (h)	7-0		1975-76	3	Hibs (a)	2-3
	Semi-Final (Hampden)	Rangers	0-1		1976-77	3	Aberdeen (h)	0-1
1964-65	1	Queen of the South (a)	2-0		1977-78	1	Clyde (h)	0-0
	2	Third Lanark (a)	1-1			Replay	Clyde (a)	3-0
	Replay	Third Lanark (h)	2-2			2	Brechin (a)	0-1
	2nd Replay (Tynecastle)	Third Lanark	4-2		1978-79	1	Albion Rovers (h)	2-2
	3	Stirling Albion (h)	2-0			Replay	Albion Rovers (a)	3-2
	Semi-Final (Tynecastle)	Hibs	2-0			2	Stranraer (a)	1-1
	FINAL (Hampden)	Celtic	2-3			Replay	Stranraer (h)	1-0
1965-66	1	Partick Thistle (h)	3-1			3	Hibs (h)	1-1
	2	Stirling Albion (a)	0-0			Replay	Hibs (a)	0-2
	Replay	Stirling Albion (h)	4-1		1979-80	3	Buckie Thistle (h)	2-0
	Quarter-Final	Kilmarnock (h)	2-1			4	Morton (a)	0-5
	Semi-Final (Ibrox)	Celtic	0-2		1980-81	3	Hibs (a)	1-1
1966-67	1	Kilmarnock (a)	2-2			Replay	Hibs (h)	1-2
	Replay	Kilmarnock (h)	1-0		1981-82	3	Clydebank (a)	1-2
	2	Partick Thistle (a)	1-1		1982-83	3	Elgin City (h)	5-0
	Replay	Partick Thistle (h)	5-1			4	Celtic (a)	0-3
	3	Dundee United (a)	0-1		1983-84	1	Bye	
						2	Forfar (h)	1-0
						3	Rangers (a)	1-2
					1984-85	1	East Stirling (h)	1-3

Melrose heads for goal in Dunfermline's record win of 9–0 over Wigtown and Bladnoch. (Dunfermline Press)

LEAGUE CUP *(Compiled by Mark Gribbin.)*

Dunfermline score first. *Qualifying team.

Season	Team	H.	A.
1945–46	Airdrie*	0–0	1–5
	St Johnstone	2–0	0–1
	Albion Rovers	3–1	0–3
1946–47	East Fife*	0–2	0–7
	St Johnstone	3–2	2–6
	Alloa	3–1	1–2
1947–48	Hamilton*	1–3	2–3
	Raith Rovers	0–2	1–6
	Alloa	1–0	1–1
1948–49	Raith Rovers*	1–0	1–2
	Stirling Albion	1–1	3–4
	Cowdenbeath	3–2	2–0
1949–50	Queen's Park	3–0	1–0
	Kilmarnock	5–1	4–2
	St Johnstone	1–2	3–2
	Airdrie (Quarter-Final)	0–0	4–3
	Hibs (Semi-Final)	2–1 (at Tynecastle)	
	East Fife (Final)	0–3 (at Hampden)	
1950–51	Ayr*	2–5	0–1
	Kilmarnock	5–4	1–3
	Dumbarton	4–1	1–1
1951–52	Queen's Park	2–1	0–2
	Alloa	4–1	2–2
	Hamilton	3–0	4–1
	Rangers (Quarter-Final)	1–0	1–3
1952–53	Kilmarnock*	3–4	2–3
	Alloa	4–3	2–2
	Arbroath	3–1	5–0
1953–54	Arbroath	2–1	1–3
	Forfar	3–0	1–2
	Dumbarton	6–1	3–1
	East Fife (Quarter-Final)	2–3	2–6
1954–55	Ayr*	4–0	1–3
	Brechin	2–1	1–1
	Dundee United	3–1	1–3
1955–56	Aberdeen*	2–2	2–3
	Hibs	1–3	1–3
	Clyde	4–2	2–3
1956–57	St Mirren	2–0	0–2
	Queen of the South	2–1	1–1
	Kilmarnock	5–1	0–0
	Celtic (Quarter-Final)	3–0	0–6
1957–58	Brechin*	3–1	1–2
	Ayr	3–0	1–4
	Cowdenbeath	1–1	5–2
1958–59	East Fife	5–2	3–1
	Stirling	6–1	3–1
	Brechin	4–1	2–1
	Kilmarnock (Quarter-Final)	3–3	1–4
1959–60	Third Lanark*	2–3	1–6
	Clyde	1–4	0–0
	St Mirren	3–0	2–1
1960–61	Kilmarnock*	2–0	1–2
	Hibs	3–1	0–3
	Airdrie	5–2	2–4
1961–62	Motherwell*	2–0	1–1
	Dundee United	3–0	0–0
	Aberdeen	1–2	0–0
1962–63	Kilmarnock*	3–3	2–3
	Raith Rovers	1–1	2–2
	Airdrie	4–1	4–2
1963–64	Dundee*	3–4	1–4
	Third Lanark	2–3	3–0
	Airdrie	3–2	1–0
1964–65	Hibs	2–0	1–1
	Third Lanark	3–1	1–0
	Airdrie	3–0	4–1
	Rangers (Quarter-Final)	0–3	2–2
1965–66	Kilmarnock*	1–3	1–0
	St Johnstone	5–1	1–3
	Partick	6–2	0–0
1966–67	Motherwell	2–1	3–4
	Partick	3–2	3–0
	Falkirk	2–2	2–1
	Celtic (Quarter-Final)	1–3	3–6
1967–68	Kilmarnock*	1–3	2–2
	Airdrie	2–1	3–2
	Partick	1–1	2–3
1968–69	Clyde*	2–1	0–3
	Dundee United	3–2	1–2
	Aberdeen	1–2	0–1
1969–70	Aberdeen*	0–1	2–2
	Hibs	3–1	0–2
	Clyde	0–0	0–0
1970–71	Rangers*	0–6	1–4
	Morton	0–2	2–3
	Motherwell	1–1	0–3
1971–72	St Johnstone*	0–2	1–1
	Hearts	1–0	0–4
	Airdrie	2–1	0–1
1972–73	Dundee United*	0–1	0–2
	Stenhousemuir	2–2	2–5
	Kilmarnock	1–0	1–2
1973–74	St Mirren*	5–1	1–2
	Berwick	3–2	2–1
	Stenhousemuir	2–2	0–1
1974–75	Hearts*	2–1	3–2
	Aberdeen	1–1	0–3
	Morton	1–1	1–1
1975–76	Hibs*	0–4	0–3
	Ayr United	1–1	2–2
	Dundee	1–1	0–4
1976–77	Clydebank*	0–1	0–2
	Alloa Athletic	3–0	0–4
	Queen of the South	0–0	0–1
1977–78	Clyde (Second Round)	2–1	0–0
	Clydebank (Third Round)	2–0	2–2
	Rangers (Quarter-Final)	1–3	1–3
1978–79	Airdrie (Second Round)	0–3	0–5
1979–80	Stranraer (First Round)	2–4	0–0
1980–81	Kilmarnock (Second Round)	1–2	0–0
1981–82	Hamilton*	2–3	0–2
	Montrose	2–1	1–0
	East Stirling	2–1	1–0
1982–83	Celtic*	1–7	0–6
	Arbroath	0–0	0–1
	Alloa Athletic	2–1	0–3
1983–84	Dundee United (Second Round)	0–2	1–6
1984–85	Arbroath (First Round)	4–0	
	Celtic (Second Round)	2–3	

EUROPE

Season	Round	Opponents	Result
			(Dunfermline score first)

RESULTS
European Cup Winners' Cup

Season	Round	Opponents	Result
1961–62	1	St Patrick's (Eire)	4–1 (h)
			4–0 (a)
	2	Vardar (Yugoslavia)	5–0 (h)
			0–2 (a)
	Quarter-Final	Ujpest Dozsa (Hungary)	3–4 (a)
			0–1 (h)
1968–69	1	Apoel (Cyprus)	10–1 (h)
			2–0 (a)
	2	Olympia (Greece)	4–0 (h)
			0–3 (a)
	Quarter-Final	West Bromwich (England)	0–0 (a)
			1–0 (h)
	Semi-Final	Slovan Bratislava (Czechoslovakia)	1–1 (h)
			0–1 (a)

Inter-Cities Fairs Cup

Season	Round	Opponents	Result
1962–63	1	Everton (England)	0–1 (a)
			2–0 (h)
	2	Valencia (Spain)	0–4 (a)
			6–2 (h)
			0–1 †
1964–65	1	Orgryte (Sweden)	4–2 (h)
			0–0 (a)
	2	VFB Stuttgart (West Germany)	1–0 (h)
			0–0 (a)
	3	Atletico Bilbao (Spain)	0–1 (a)
			1–0 (h)
			1–2 (a)
1965–66	1	Bye	
	2	Boldklub (Denmark)	5–0 (h)
			4–2 (a)
	3	Spartak Brno (Czechoslovakia)	2–0 (h)
			0–0 (a)
	Quarter-Final	Real Zaragoza (Spain)	1–0 (h)
			2–4 (a)
1966–67	1	FC Frigg (Norway)	3–1 (a)
			3–1 (h)
	2	Dynamo Zagreb (Yugoslavia)	4–2 (h)
			0–2 (a)*
1969–70	1	Girondins Bordeaux (France)	4–0 (h)
			0–2 (a)
	2	Gwardia Warsaw (Poland)	2–1 (h)
			1–0 (a)
	3	Anderlecht (Belgium)	0–1 (a)
			3–2 (h)*

*Dismissed on away goals rule.   †Neutral ground.
Thus, in 20 European matches at home, Dunfermline won 17 games, drew 2 and lost only one.

APPEARANCES

Figures in brackets refer to *additional* appearances as a substitute.

BAILLIE	6
BARRY	10
CALLAGHAN, T.	12(+2)
CALLAGHAN, W.	34
CONNACHAN	6
COWAN	0(+1)
CUNNINGHAM	11
DELANEY	4
DICKSON	9
DUFF	8
DUFFY	1
EDWARDS	30
FERGUSON, A.	13
FERGUSON, E.	0(+1)
FLEMING	8
FRASER, C.	5
FRASER, J.	7
GARDNER	14
GILLESPIE	1
HERRIOT	12
KILGANNON	3
LISTER	5(+1)
LUNN	29
McDONALD	6
McGARTY	5
McKIMMIE	1(+2)
McLAREN	2
McLAUGHLIN	5
McLEAN, G.	6
McLEAN, J.	21
McLINDON	3
McNICOLL	2
MAILER	6
MARTIN	16
MELROSE	15
MILLER	13
MITCHELL	9
PATON	20
PEEBLES	16
RENTON	12
ROBERTSON	16(+1)
SINCLAIR	7
SMITH	23
THOMSON	22(+1)
TOTTEN	2(+1)
WILLIAMSON	5
WILSON	1

GOALSCORERS

BERT PATON	7
ALEX FERGUSON	6
TOM CALLAGHAN	5
CHARLIE DICKSON	5
ALEC EDWARDS	5
PAT GARDNER	5
GEORGE PEEBLES	5
ALEX SMITH	5
JIM FLEMING	4
HARRY MELROSE	4
JACKIE SINCLAIR	4
WILLIE CALLAGHAN	3
TOMMY McDONALD	3
PAT DELANEY	3
GEORGE McLEAN	3
BARRIE MITCHELL	3
HUGH ROBERTSON	3
WILLIE RENTON	3
JIM FRASER	2
JOHN McLAUGHLIN	2
ROY BARRY	1
JIM McLEAN	1
GEORGE MILLER	1

A. Edwards, G. Miller and J. Herriot in Norway, May 1962.

SCOTTISH DIVISION 2 1912-13

1	Ayr*	26	13	8	5	45:19	34
2	Dunfermline	26	13	7	6	45:27	33
3	E. Stirlingshire	26	12	8	6	43:27	32
4	Abercorn	26	12	7	7	33:31	31
5	Cowdenbeath	26	12	6	8	36:27	30
6	Dumbarton*	26	12	5	9	39:30	29
7	St Bernard's	26	12	3	11	36:34	27
8	Johnstone	26	9	6	11	31:43	24
9	Albion	26	10	3	13	38:40	23
10	Dundee Hibs	26	6	10	10	34:43	22
11	St Johnstone	26	7	7	12	29:38	21
12	Vale of Leven	26	8	5	13	28:45	21
13	Arthurlie	26	7	5	14	37:49	19
14	Leith	26	5	8	13	26:47	18

* Promoted

SCOTTISH DIVISION 2 1913-14

1	Cowdenbeath	22	13	5	4	34:17	31
2	Albion	22	10	7	5	38:33	27
3	Dunfermline	22	11	4	7	46:28	26
4	Dundee Hibs	22	11	4	7	36:31	26
5	St Johnstone	22	9	5	8	48:38	23
6	Abercorn	22	10	3	9	32:32	23
7	St Bernard's	22	8	6	8	39:31	22
8	E. Stirlingshire	22	7	8	7	40:36	22
9	Arthurlie	22	8	4	10	35:37	20
10	Leith	22	5	9	8	31:37	19
11	Vale of Leven	22	5	3	14	23:47	13
12	Johnstone	22	4	4	14	20:55	12

SCOTTISH DIVISION 2 1914-15

1	Cowdenbeath‡	26	16	5	5	49:17	37
2	Leith‡	26	15	7	4	54:31	37
3	St Bernard's‡	26	18	1	7	66:34	37
4	E. Stirlingshire	26	13	5	8	53:46	31
5	Clydebank	26	13	4	9	68:37	30
6	Dunfermline	26	13	2	11	49:39	28
7	Johnstone	26	11	5	10	41:52	27
8	St Johnstone	26	10	6	10	56:53	26
9	Albion	26	9	7	10	37:42	25
10	Lochgelly	26	9	3	14	44:60	21
11	Dundee Hibs	26	8	3	15	48:61	19
12	Abercorn	26	5	7	14	35:65	17
13	Arthurlie	26	6	4	16	36:66	16
14	Vale of Leven	26	4	5	17	33:66	13

‡Played each other to determine top 3 placings at end of season; Cowdenbeath declared champions

SCOTTISH DIVISION 2 1921-22

1	Alloa*	38	26	8	4	81:32	60
2	Cowdenbeath	38	19	9	10	56:30	47
3	Armadale	38	20	5	13	64:49	45
4	Vale of Leven	38	17	10	11	56:43	44
5	Bathgate	38	16	11	11	56:41	43
6	Bo'ness	38	16	7	15	57:49	39
7	Broxburn	38	14	11	13	43:43	39
8	Dunfermline	38	14	10	14	56:42	38
9	St Bernard's	38	15	8	15	50:49	38
10	Stenhousemuir	38	14	10	14	50:51	38
11	Johnstone	38	14	10	14	46:59	38
12	East Fife	38	15	7	16	55:54	37
13	St Johnstone	38	12	11	15	41:52	35
14	Forfar	38	11	12	15	44:53	34
15	E. Stirlingshire	38	12	10	16	43:60	34
16	Arbroath	38	11	11	16	45:56	33
17	King's Park	38	10	12	16	47:65	32
18	Lochgelly	38	11	9	18	46:56	31
19	Dundee Hibs	38	10	8	20	47:65	28
20	Clackmannan	38	10	7	21	41:75	27

SCOTTISH DIVISION 2 1922-23

1	Queen's Park*	38	24	9	5	73:31	57
2	Clydebank*	38	21	10	7	69:29	52
3	St Johnstone§	38	19	12	7	60:39	48
4	Dumbarton	38	17	8	13	61:40	42
5	Bathgate	38	16	9	13	67:55	41
6	Armadale	38	15	11	12	63:52	41
7	Bo'ness	38	12	17	9	48:46	41
8	Broxburn	38	14	12	12	40:43	40
9	East Fife	38	16	7	15	48:42	39
10	Lochgelly	38	16	5	17	41:64	37
11	Cowdenbeath§	38	16	6	16	56:52	36
12	King's Park	38	14	6	18	46:60	34
13	Dunfermline	38	11	11	16	47:44	33
14	Stenhousemuir	38	13	7	18	53:67	33
15	Forfar	38	13	7	18	51:73	33
16	Johnstone	38	13	6	19	41:62	32
17	Vale of Leven	38	11	8	19	50:59	30
18	St Bernard's§	38	8	15	15	39:50	29
19	E. Stirlingshire	38	10	8	20	48:69	28
20	Arbroath	38	8	12	18	45:69	28

§two points deducted for fielding an ineligible player

SCOTTISH DIVISION 2 1923-24

1	St Johnstone*	38	22	12	4	79:33	56
2	Cowdenbeath*	38	23	9	6	78:33	55
3	Bathgate	38	16	12	10	58:49	44
4	Stenhousemuir	38	16	11	11	58:45	43
5	Albion	38	15	12	11	67:53	42
6	King's Park	38	16	10	12	67:56	42
7	Dunfermline	38	14	11	13	52:45	39
8	Johnstone	38	16	7	15	60:56	39
9	Dundee United	38	12	15	11	41:41	39
10	Dumbarton	38	17	5	16	55:58	39
11	Armadale	38	16	6	16	56:63	38
12	East Fife	38	14	9	15	54:47	37
13	Bo'ness	38	13	11	14	45:52	37
14	Forfar	38	14	7	17	43:68	35
15	Broxburn	38	13	8	17	50:56	34
16	Alloa	38	14	6	18	44:53	34
17	Arbroath	38	12	8	18	49:51	32
18	St Bernard's	38	11	10	17	49:54	32
19	Vale of Leven	38	11	9	18	41:67	31
20	Lochgelly	38	4	4	30	20:86	12

SCOTTISH DIVISION 2 1924-25

1	Dundee U *	38	20	10	8	58:44	50
2	Clydebank*	38	20	8	10	65:42	48
3	Clyde	38	20	7	11	72:39	47
4	Alloa	38	17	11	10	57:33	45
5	Arbroath	38	16	10	12	47:46	42
6	Bo'ness	38	16	9	13	71:48	41
7	Broxburn	38	16	9	13	48:54	41
8	Dumbarton	38	15	10	13	45:44	40
9	East Fife	38	17	5	16	66:58	39
10	King's Park	38	15	8	15	54:46	38
11	Stenhousemuir	38	15	7	16	51:58	37
12	Arthurlie	38	14	8	16	56:60	36
13	Dunfermline	38	14	7	17	62:57	35
14	Armadale	38	15	5	18	55:62	35
15	Albion	38	15	5	18	46:61	35
16	Bathgate	38	12	10	16	58:74	34
17	St Bernard's	38	14	4	20	52:70	32
18	E. Stirlingshire	38	11	8	19	58:72	30
19	Johnstone	38	12	4	22	53:85	28
20	Forfar	38	10	7	21	46:67	27

SCOTTISH DIVISION 2 1925-26

1	Dunfermline*	38	26	7	5	109:43	59
2	Clyde*	38	24	5	9	87:51	53
3	Ayr	38	20	12	6	77:39	52
4	East Fife	38	20	9	9	98:73	49
5	Stenhousemuir	38	19	10	9	74:52	48
6	Third Lanark	38	19	8	11	72:47	46
7	Arthurlie	38	17	5	16	81:75	39
8	Bo'ness	38	17	5	16	65:70	39
9	Albion	38	16	6	16	78:71	38
10	Arbroath	38	17	4	17	80:73	38
11	Dumbarton	38	14	10	14	54:78	38
12	Nithsdale	38	15	7	16	79:82	37
13	King's Park	38	14	9	15	67:73	37
14	St Bernard's	38	15	5	18	86:82	35
15	Armadale	38	14	5	19	82:101	33
16	Alloa	38	11	8	19	54:63	30
17	Queen o' South	38	10	8	20	64:88	28
18	E. Stirlingshire	38	10	7	21	59:89	27
19	Bathgate	38	7	6	25	60:105	20
20	Broxburn	38	4	6	28	55:126	14

SCOTTISH DIVISION 1 1926-27

1	Rangers	38	23	10	5	85:41	56
2	Motherwell	38	23	5	10	81:52	51
3	Celtic	38	21	7	10	101:55	49
4	Airdrie	38	18	9	11	97:64	45
5	Dundee	38	17	9	12	77:51	43
6	Falkirk	38	16	10	12	77:60	42
7	Cowdenbeath	38	18	6	14	74:60	42
8	Aberdeen	38	13	14	11	73:72	40
9	Hibernian	38	16	7	15	62:71	39
10	St Mirren	38	16	5	17	78:76	37
11	Partick	38	15	6	17	89:74	36
12	Queen's Park	38	15	6	17	74:84	36
13	Hearts	38	12	11	15	65:64	35
14	St Johnstone	38	13	9	16	55:69	35
15	Hamilton	38	13	9	16	60:85	35
16	Kilmarnock	38	12	8	18	54:71	32
17	Clyde	38	10	9	19	54:85	29
18	Dunfermline	38	10	8	20	53:85	28
19	Morton†	38	12	4	22	56:101	28
20	Dundee U.†	38	7	8	23	56:101	22

SCOTTISH DIVISION 1 1927-28

1	Rangers	38	26	8	4	109:36	60
2	Celtic	38	23	9	6	93:39	55
3	Motherwell	38	23	9	6	92:46	55
4	Hearts	38	20	7	11	89:50	47
5	St Mirren	38	18	8	12	77:76	44
6	Partick	38	18	7	13	85:67	43
7	Aberdeen	38	19	5	14	71:61	43
8	Kilmarnock	38	15	10	13	68:78	40
9	Cowdenbeath	38	16	7	15	66:68	39
10	Falkirk	38	16	5	17	76:69	37
11	St Johnstone	38	14	8	16	66:67	36
12	Hibernian	38	13	9	16	73:75	35
13	Airdrie	38	12	11	15	59:69	35
14	Dundee	38	14	7	17	65:80	35
15	Clyde	38	10	11	17	46:72	31
16	Queen's Park	38	12	6	20	69:80	30
17	Raith	38	11	7	20	60:89	29
18	Hamilton	38	11	6	21	67:86	28
19	Bo'ness†	38	9	8	21	48:86	26
20	Dunfermline†	38	4	4	30	41:126	12

SCOTTISH DIVISION 2 1928-29

1	Dundee U.*	36	24	3	9	99:55	51
2	Morton*	36	21	8	7	85:49	50
3	Arbroath	36	19	9	8	90:60	47
4	Albion	36	18	8	10	95:67	44
5	Leith	36	18	7	11	78:56	43
6	St Bernard's	36	16	9	11	77:55	41
7	Forfar	35	14	10	11	69:75	38
8	East Fife	35	15	6	14	88:77	36
9	Queen o' South	36	16	4	16	86:79	36
10	Bo'ness	35	15	5	15	62:62	35
11	Dunfermline	36	13	7	16	66:72	33
12	E. Stirlingshire	36	14	4	18	71:75	32
13	Alloa	36	12	7	17	64:77	31
14	Dumbarton	36	11	9	16	59:78	31
15	King's Park	36	8	13	15	60:84	29
16	Clydebank	36	11	5	20	70:86	27
17	Arthurlie‡	32	9	7	16	51:73	25
18	Stenhousemuir	35	9	6	20	52:90	24
19	Armadale	36	8	7	21	47:99	23
20	Bathgate resigned during the season						

‡Arthurlie resigned with four games to play, leaving matches against Forfar, East Fife, Bo'ness and Stenhousemuir unplayed

SCOTTISH DIVISION 2 1929-30

1	Leith*	38	23	11	4	92:42	57
2	East Fife*	38	26	5	7	114:58	57
3	Albion	38	24	6	8	101:60	54
4	Third Lanark	38	23	6	9	92:53	52
5	Raith	38	18	8	12	94:67	44
6	King's Park	38	17	8	13	109:80	42
7	Queen o' South	38	18	6	14	65:63	42
8	Forfar	38	18	5	15	98:95	41
9	Arbroath	38	16	7	15	83:87	39
10	Dunfermline	38	16	6	16	99:85	38
11	Montrose	38	14	10	14	79:87	38
12	E. Stirlingshire	38	16	4	18	83:75	36
13	Bo'ness	38	15	4	19	67:95	34
14	St Bernard's	38	13	6	19	65:65	32
15	Armadale	38	13	5	20	56:91	31
16	Dumbarton	38	14	2	22	77:95	30
17	Stenhousemuir	38	11	5	22	75:108	27
18	Clydebank	38	7	10	21	66:92	24
19	Alloa	38	9	6	23	55:104	24
20	Brechin	38	7	4	27	57:125	18

SCOTTISH DIVISION 2 1930-31

1	Third Lanark*	38	27	7	4	107:42	61
2	Dundee U.*	38	21	8	9	93:54	50
3	Dunfermline	38	20	7	11	83:50	47
4	Raith	38	20	6	12	93:72	46
5	Queen o' South	38	18	6	14	83:66	42
6	St Johnstone	38	18	6	14	76:64	42
7	E. Stirlingshire	38	17	7	14	85:74	41
8	Montrose	38	19	3	16	75:90	41
9	Albion	38	14	11	13	80:83	39
10	Dumbarton	38	15	8	15	73:72	38
11	St Bernard's	38	14	9	15	85:66	37
12	Forfar	38	15	6	17	78:83	36
13	Alloa	38	15	5	18	65:87	35
14	King's Park	38	14	6	18	78:70	34
15	Arbroath	38	15	4	19	83:94	34
16	Brechin	38	13	7	18	52:84	33
17	Stenhousemuir	38	13	6	19	78:98	32
18	Armadale	38	13	2	23	74:99	28
19	Clydebank	38	10	2	26	61:108	22
20	Bo'ness	38	9	4	25	54:100	22

SCOTTISH DIVISION 2 1931-32

1	E. Stirlingshire*	38	26	3	9	111:55	55
2	St Johnstone*	38	24	7	7	102:52	55
3	Raith	38	20	6	12	83:65	46
4	Stenhousemuir	38	19	8	11	88:76	46
5	St Bernard's	38	19	7	12	81:62	45
6	Forfar	38	19	7	12	90:79	45
7	Hibernian	38	18	8	12	73:52	44
8	East Fife	38	18	5	15	107:77	41
9	Queen o' South	38	18	5	15	99:91	41
10	Dunfermline	38	17	6	15	78:73	40
11	Arbroath	38	17	5	16	82:78	39
12	Dumbarton	38	14	10	14	70:68	38
13	Alloa	38	14	7	17	73:74	35
14	Bo'ness	38	15	4	19	70:103	34
15	King's Park	38	14	5	19	97:93	33
16	Albion	38	13	2	23	81:104	28
17	Montrose	38	11	6	21	60:96	28
18	Armadale	38	10	5	23	68:102	25
19	Brechin	38	9	7	22	52:97	25
20	Edinburgh C.	38	5	7	26	78:146	17

SCOTTISH DIVISION 2 1932-33

1	Hibernian*	34	25	4	5	80:29	54
2	Queen o' South*	34	20	9	5	93:59	49
3	Dunfermline	34	20	7	7	89:44	47
4	Stenhousemuir	34	18	6	10	67:58	42
5	Albion	34	19	2	13	82:57	40
6	Raith	34	16	4	14	83:67	36
7	East Fife	34	15	4	15	85:71	34
8	King's Park	34	13	8	13	85:80	34
9	Dumbarton	34	14	6	14	69:67	34
10	Arbroath	34	14	5	15	65:62	33
11	Alloa	34	14	5	15	60:58	33
12	St Bernard's	34	13	6	15	67:64	32
13	Dundee U.	34	14	4	16	65:67	32
14	Forfar	34	12	4	18	68:87	28
15	Brechin	34	11	4	19	65:95	26
16	Leith	34	10	5	19	43:81	25
17	Montrose	34	8	5	21	63:89	21
18	Edinburgh C.	34	4	4	26	39:133	12

19 Bo'ness were expelled in Nov 1932 being unable to meet match guarantees

SCOTTISH DIVISION 2 1933-34

1	Albion*	34	20	5	9	74:47	45
2	Dunfermline*	34	20	4	10	90:52	44
3	Arbroath	34	20	4	10	83:53	44
4	Stenhousemuir	34	18	4	12	70:73	40
5	Morton	34	17	5	12	67:64	39
6	Dumbarton	34	17	3	14	67:68	37
7	King's Park	34	14	8	12	78:70	36
8	Raith	34	15	5	14	71:55	35
9	E. Stirlingshire	34	14	7	13	65:74	35
10	St Bernard's	34	15	4	15	75:56	34
11	Forfar	34	13	7	14	77:71	33
12	Leith	34	12	8	14	63:60	32
13	East Fife	34	12	8	14	71:76	32
14	Brechin	34	13	5	16	60:70	31
15	Alloa	34	11	9	14	55:68	31
16	Montrose	34	11	4	19	53:81	26
17	Dundee U.	34	10	4	20	81:88	24
18	Edinburgh C.	34	4	6	24	37:111	14

SCOTTISH DIVISION 1 1934-35

1	Rangers	38	25	5	8	96:46	55
2	Celtic	38	24	4	10	92:45	52
3	Hearts	38	20	10	8	87:51	50
4	Hamilton	38	19	10	9	87:67	48
5	St Johnstone	38	18	10	10	66:46	46
6	Aberdeen	38	17	10	11	68:54	44
7	Motherwell	38	15	10	13	83:64	40
8	Dundee	38	16	8	14	63:63	40
9	Kilmarnock	38	16	6	16	76:68	38
10	Clyde	38	14	10	14	71:69	38
11	Hibernian	38	14	8	16	59:70	36
12	Queen's Park	38	13	10	15	61:80	36
13	Partick	38	15	5	18	61:68	35
14	Airdrie	38	13	7	18	64:72	33
15	Dunfermline	38	13	5	20	56:96	31
16	Albion	38	10	9	19	62:77	29
17	Queen o' South	38	11	7	20	52:72	29
18	Ayr	38	12	5	21	61:112	29
19	St Mirren†	38	11	5	22	49:70	27
20	Falkirk†	38	9	6	23	58:82	24

SCOTTISH DIVISION 1 1935-36

1	Celtic	38	32	2	4	115:33	66
2	Rangers	38	27	7	4	110:43	61
3	Aberdeen	38	26	9	3	96:50	61
4	Motherwell	38	18	12	8	77:58	48
5	Hearts	38	20	7	11	88:55	47
6	Hamilton	38	15	7	16	77:74	37
7	St Johnstone	38	15	7	16	70:81	37
8	Kilmarnock	38	14	7	17	69:64	35
9	Partick	38	12	10	16	64:72	34
10	Dunfermline	38	13	8	17	73:92	34
11	Third Lanark	38	14	5	19	63:71	33
12	Arbroath	38	11	11	16	46:69	33
13	Dundee	38	11	10	17	67:80	32
14	Queen's Park	38	11	10	17	58:75	32
15	Queen o' South	38	11	9	18	54:72	31
16	Albion	38	13	4	21	69:92	30
17	Hibernian	38	11	7	20	56:82	29
18	Clyde	38	10	8	20	63:84	28
19	Airdrie†	38	9	9	20	68:91	27
20	Ayr†	38	11	3	24	53:98	25

SCOTTISH DIVISION 1 1936-37

1	Rangers	38	26	9	3	88:32	61
2	Aberdeen	38	23	8	7	89:44	54
3	Celtic	38	22	8	8	89:58	52
4	Motherwell	38	22	7	9	96:54	51
5	Hearts	38	24	3	11	99:60	51
6	Third Lanark	38	20	6	12	79:61	46
7	Falkirk	38	19	6	13	98:66	44
8	Hamilton	38	18	5	15	91:96	41
9	Dundee	38	12	15	11	58:69	39
10	Clyde	38	16	6	16	59:70	38
11	Kilmarnock	38	14	9	15	60:70	37
12	St Johnstone	38	14	8	16	74:68	36
13	Partick	38	11	12	15	73:68	34
14	Arbroath	38	13	5	20	57:84	31
15	Queen's Park	38	9	12	17	51:77	30
16	St Mirren	38	11	7	20	68:81	29
17	Hibernian	38	6	13	19	54:83	25
18	Queen o' South	38	8	8	22	49:95	24
19	Dunfermline†	38	5	11	22	65:98	21
20	Albion†	38	5	6	27	53:116	16

SCOTTISH DIVISION 2 1937-38

1	Raith*	34	27	5	2	142:54	59
2	Albion*	34	20	8	6	97:50	48
3	Airdrie	34	21	5	8	100:53	47
4	St Bernard's	34	20	5	9	75:49	45
5	East Fife	34	19	5	10	104:61	43
6	Cowdenbeath	34	17	9	8	115:71	43
7	Dumbarton	34	17	5	12	85:66	39
8	Stenhousemuir	34	17	5	12	87:78	39
9	Dunfermline	34	17	5	12	82:76	39
10	Leith	34	16	5	13	71:56	37
11	Alloa	34	11	4	19	78:106	26
12	King's Park	34	11	4	19	64:96	26
13	E. Stirlingshire	34	9	7	18	55:95	25
14	Dundee U.	34	9	5	20	69:104	23
15	Forfar	34	8	6	20	67:100	22
16	Montrose	34	7	8	19	56:88	22
17	Edinburgh C.	34	7	3	24	77:135	17
18	Brechin	34	5	2	27	53:139	12

SCOTTISH DIVISION 2 1938-39

1	Cowdenbeath*	34	28	4	2	120:45	60
2	Alloa*	34	22	4	8	91:46	48
3	East Fife	34	21	6	7	99:61	48
4	Airdrie	34	21	5	8	85:57	47
5	Dunfermline	34	18	5	11	99:78	41
6	Dundee	34	15	7	12	99:63	37
7	St Bernard's	34	15	6	13	79:79	36
8	Stenhousemuir	34	15	5	14	74:69	35
9	Dundee U.	34	15	3	16	78:69	33
10	Brechin	34	11	9	14	82:106	31
11	Dumbarton	34	9	12	13	68:76	30
12	Morton	34	11	6	17	74:88	28
13	King's Park	34	12	2	20	87:92	26
14	Montrose	34	10	5	19	82:96	25
15	Forfar	34	11	3	20	74:138	25
16	Leith	34	10	4	20	57:83	24
17	E. Stirlingshire	34	9	4	21	89:130	22
18	Edinburgh C.	34	6	4	24	58:119	16

SCOTTISH DIVISION 2‡ 1946-47

1	Dundee*	26	21	3	2	113:30	45
2	Airdrie*	26	19	4	3	78:38	42
3	East Fife	26	12	7	7	58:39	31
4	Albion	26	10	7	9	50:54	27
5	Alloa	26	11	5	10	51:57	27
6	Raith	26	10	6	10	45:52	26
7	Stenhousemuir	26	8	7	11	43:53	23
8	Dunfermline	26	10	3	13	50:72	23
9	St Johnstone	26	9	4	13	45:47	22
10	Dundee U.	26	9	4	13	53:60	22
11	Ayr	26	9	2	15	56:73	20
12	Arbroath	26	7	6	13	42:63	20
13	Dumbarton	26	7	4	15	41:54	18
14	Cowdenbeath	26	6	6	14	44:77	18

‡Division 1 was called 'A' and Division 2 was called 'B' from 1946–47 to 1955–56 inclusive

SCOTTISH DIVISION 2‡ 1947-48

1	East Fife*	30	25	3	2	103:36	53
2	Albion*	30	19	4	7	58:49	42
3	Hamilton	30	17	6	7	75:45	40
4	Raith	30	14	6	10	83:66	34
5	Cowdenbeath	30	12	8	10	56:53	32
6	Kilmarnock	30	13	4	13	72:62	30
7	Dunfermline	30	13	3	14	72:71	29
8	Stirling A.	30	11	6	13	85:66	28
9	St Johnstone	30	11	5	14	69:63	27
10	Ayr	30	9	9	12	59:61	27
11	Dumbarton	30	9	7	14	66:79	25
12	Alloa§	30	10	6	14	53:77	24
13	Arbroath	30	10	3	17	55:62	23
14	Stenhousemuir	30	6	11	13	53:83	23
15	Dundee U.	30	10	2	18	58:88	22
16	Leith	30	6	7	17	45:84	19

§two points deducted for fielding unregistered players

SCOTTISH DIVISION 2‡ 1948-49

1	Raith*	30	20	2	8	80:44	42
2	Stirling A.*	30	20	2	8	71:47	42
3	Airdrie	30	16	9	5	76:42	41
4	Dunfermline	30	16	9	5	80:58	41
5	Queen's Park	30	14	7	9	66:49	35
6	St Johnstone	30	14	4	12	58:51	32
7	Arbroath	30	12	8	10	62:56	32
8	Dundee U.	30	10	7	13	60:67	27
9	Ayr	30	10	7	13	51:70	27
10	Hamilton	30	9	8	13	48:57	26
11	Kilmarnock	30	9	7	14	58:61	25
12	Stenhousemuir	30	8	8	14	50:54	24
13	Cowdenbeath	30	9	5	16	53:58	23
14	Alloa	30	10	3	17	42:85	23
15	Dumbarton	30	8	6	16	52:79	22
16	E. Stirlingshire	30	6	6	18	38:67	18

SCOTTISH DIVISION 2‡ 1949-50

1	Morton*	30	20	7	3	77:33	47
2	Airdrie*	30	19	6	5	79:40	44
3	Dunfermline	30	16	4	10	71:57	36
4	St Johnstone	30	15	6	9	64:56	36
5	Cowdenbeath	30	16	3	11	63:56	35
6	Hamilton	30	14	6	10	57:44	34
7	Dundee U.	30	14	5	11	74:56	33
8	Kilmarnock	30	14	5	11	50:43	33
9	Queen's Park	30	12	7	11	63:59	31
10	Forfar	30	11	8	11	53:56	30
11	Albion	30	10	7	13	49:61	27
12	Stenhousemuir	30	8	8	14	54:72	24
13	Ayr	30	8	6	16	53:80	22
14	Arbroath	30	5	9	16	47:69	19
15	Dumbarton	30	6	4	20	39:62	16
16	Alloa	30	5	3	22	47:96	13

SCOTTISH DIVISION 2‡ 1950-51

1	Queen o South*	30	21	3	6	69:35	45
2	Stirling A.*	30	21	3	6	78:44	45
3	Ayr	30	15	6	9	64:40	36
4	Dundee U.	30	16	4	10	78:58	36
5	St Johnstone	30	14	5	11	68:53	33
6	Queen's Park	30	13	7	10	56:53	33
7	Hamilton	30	12	8	10	65:49	32
8	Albion	30	14	4	12	56:51	32
9	Dumbarton	30	12	5	13	52:53	29
10	Dunfermline	30	12	4	14	58:73	28
11	Cowdenbeath	30	12	3	15	61:57	27
12	Kilmarnock	30	8	8	14	44:49	24
13	Arbroath	30	8	5	17	46:78	21
14	Forfar	30	9	3	18	43:76	21
15	Stenhousemuir	30	9	2	19	51:80	20
16	Alloa	30	7	4	19	58:98	18

SCOTTISH DIVISION 2 ‡ 1951-52

1	Clyde*	30	19	6	5	100:45	44
2	Falkirk*	30	18	7	5	80:34	43
3	Ayr	30	17	5	8	55:45	39
4	Dundee U.	30	16	5	9	75:60	37
5	Kilmarnock	30	16	2	12	62:48	34
6	Dunfermline	30	15	2	13	74:65	32
7	Alloa	30	13	6	11	55:49	32
8	Cowdenbeath	30	12	8	10	66:67	32
9	Hamilton	30	12	6	12	47:51	30
10	Dumbarton	30	10	8	12	51:57	28
11	St Johnstone	30	9	7	14	62:68	25
12	Forfar	30	10	4	16	59:97	24
13	Stenhousemuir	30	8	6	16	57:74	22
14	Albion	30	6	10	14	39:57	22
15	Queen's Park	30	8	4	18	40:62	20
16	Arbroath	30	6	4	20	40:83	16

SCOTTISH DIVISION 2 ‡ 1952-53

1	Stirling A.*	30	20	4	6	64:43	44
2	Hamilton*	30	20	3	7	72:40	43
3	Queen's Park	30	15	7	8	70:46	37
4	Kilmarnock	30	17	2	11	74:48	36
5	Ayr	30	17	2	11	76:56	36
6	Morton	30	15	3	12	79:57	33
7	Arbroath	30	13	7	10	52:57	33
8	Dundee U.	30	12	5	13	52:56	29
9	Alloa	30	12	5	13	63:68	29
10	Dumbarton	30	11	6	13	58:67	28
11	Dunfermline	30	9	9	12	51:58	27
12	Stenhousemuir	30	10	6	14	56:65	26
13	Cowdenbeath	30	8	7	15	37:54	23
14	St Johnstone	30	8	6	16	41:63	22
15	Forfar	30	8	4	18	54:88	20
16	Albion	30	5	4	21	44:77	14

SCOTTISH DIVISION 2 ‡ 1953-54

1	Motherwell*	30	21	3	6	109:43	45
2	Kilmarnock*	30	19	4	7	71:39	42
3	Third Lanark	30	13	10	7	78:48	36
4	Stenhousemuir	30	14	8	8	66:58	36
5	Morton	30	15	3	12	85:65	33
6	St Johnstone	30	14	3	13	80:71	31
7	Albion	30	12	7	11	55:63	31
8	Dunfermline	30	11	9	10	48:57	31
9	Ayr	30	11	8	11	50:56	30
10	Queen's Park	30	9	9	12	56:51	27
11	Alloa	30	7	10	13	50:72	24
12	Forfar	30	10	4	16	38:69	24
13	Cowdenbeath	30	9	5	16	67:81	23
14	Arbroath	30	8	7	15	53:67	23
15	Dundee U.	30	8	6	16	54:79	22
16	Dumbarton	30	7	8	15	51:92	22

SCOTTISH DIVISION 2 ‡ 1954-55

1	Airdrie*	30	18	10	2	103:61	46
2	Dunfermline*	30	19	4	7	72:40	42
3	Hamilton	30	17	5	8	74:51	39
4	Queen's Park	30	15	5	10	65:36	35
5	Third Lanark	30	13	7	10	63:49	33
6	Stenhousemuir	30	12	8	10	70:51	32
7	St Johnstone	30	15	2	13	60:51	32
8	Ayr	30	14	4	12	61:73	32
9	Morton	30	12	5	13	58:69	29
10	Forfar	30	11	6	13	63:80	28
11	Albion	30	8	10	12	50:69	26
12	Arbroath	30	8	8	14	55:72	24
13	Dundee U.	30	8	6	16	55:70	22
14	Cowdenbeath	30	8	5	17	55:72	21
15	Alloa	30	7	6	17	51:75	20
16	Brechin	30	8	3	19	53:89	19

SCOTTISH DIVISION 1 ‡ 1955-56

1	Rangers	34	22	8	4	85:27	52
2	Aberdeen	34	18	10	6	87:50	46
3	Hearts	34	19	7	8	99:47	45
4	Hibernian	34	19	7	8	86:50	45
5	Celtic	34	16	9	9	55:39	41
6	Queen o South	34	16	5	13	69:73	37
7	Airdrie	34	14	8	12	85:96	36
8	Kilmarnock	34	12	10	12	52:45	34
9	Partick	34	13	7	14	62:60	33
10	Motherwell	34	11	11	12	53:59	33
11	Raith	34	12	9	13	58:75	33
12	East Fife	34	13	5	16	61:69	31
13	Dundee	34	12	6	16	56:65	30
14	Falkirk	34	11	6	17	58:75	28
15	St Mirren	34	10	7	17	57:70	27
16	Dunfermline	34	10	6	18	42:82	26
17	Clyde†	34	8	6	20	50:74	22
18	Stirling A.†	34	4	5	25	23:82	13

SCOTTISH DIVISION 1 1956-57

1	Rangers	34	26	3	5	96:48	55
2	Hearts	34	24	5	5	81:48	53
3	Kilmarnock	34	16	10	8	57:39	42
4	Raith	34	16	7	11	84:58	39
5	Celtic	34	15	8	11	58:43	38
6	Aberdeen	34	18	2	14	79:59	38
7	Motherwell	34	16	5	13	72:66	37
8	Partick	34	13	8	13	53:51	34
9	Hibernian	34	12	9	13	69:56	33
10	Dundee	34	13	6	15	55:61	32
11	Airdrie	34	13	4	17	77:89	30
12	St Mirren	34	12	6	16	58:72	30
13	Queen's Park	34	11	7	16	55:59	29
14	Falkirk	34	10	8	16	51:70	28
15	East Fife	34	10	6	18	59:82	26
16	Queen o' South	34	10	5	19	54:96	25
17	Dunfermline†	34	9	6	19	54:74	24
18	Ayr†	34	7	5	22	48:89	19

SCOTTISH DIVISION 2 1957-58

1	Stirling A.*	36	25	5	6	105:48	55
2	Dunfermline*	36	24	5	7	120:42	53
3	Arbroath	36	21	5	10	89:72	47
4	Dumbarton	36	20	4	12	92:57	44
5	Ayr	36	18	6	12	98:81	42
6	Cowdenbeath	36	17	8	11	100:85	42
7	Brechin	36	16	8	12	80:81	40
8	Alloa	36	15	9	12	88:78	39
9	Dundee U.	36	12	9	15	81:77	33
10	Hamilton	36	12	9	15	70:79	33
11	St Johnstone	36	12	9	15	67:85	33
12	Forfar	36	13	6	17	70:71	32
13	Morton	36	12	8	16	77:83	32
14	Montrose	36	13	6	17	55:72	32
15	E. Stirlingshire	36	12	5	19	55:79	29
16	Stenhousemuir	36	12	5	19	68:98	29
17	Albion	36	12	5	19	53:79	29
18	Stranraer	36	9	7	20	54:83	25
19	Berwick	36	5	5	26	37:109	15

SCOTTISH DIVISION 1 1958-59

1	Rangers	34	21	8	5	92:51	50
2	Hearts	34	21	6	7	92:51	48
3	Motherwell	34	18	8	8	83:50	44
4	Dundee	34	16	9	9	61:51	41
5	Airdrie	34	15	7	12	64:62	37
6	Celtic	34	14	8	12	70:53	36
7	St Mirren	34	14	7	13	71:74	35
8	Kilmarnock	34	13	8	13	58:51	34
9	Partick	34	14	6	14	59:66	34
10	Hibernian	34	13	6	15	68:70	32
11	Third Lanark	34	11	10	13	74:83	32
12	Stirling A.	34	11	8	15	54:64	30
13	Aberdeen	34	12	5	17	63:66	29
14	Raith	34	10	9	15	60:70	29
15	Clyde	34	12	4	18	62:66	28
16	Dunfermline	34	10	8	16	68:87	28
17	Falkirk†	34	10	7	17	58:79	27
18	Queen o' South†	34	6	6	22	38:101	18

SCOTTISH DIVISION 1 1959-60

1	Hearts	34	23	8	3	102:51	54
2	Kilmarnock	34	24	2	8	67:45	50
3	Rangers	34	17	8	9	72:38	42
4	Dundee	34	16	10	8	70:49	42
5	Motherwell	34	16	8	10	71:61	40
6	Clyde	34	15	9	10	77:69	39
7	Hibernian	34	14	7	13	106:85	35
8	Ayr	34	14	6	14	65:73	34
9	Celtic	34	12	9	13	73:59	33
10	Partick	34	14	4	16	54:78	32
11	Raith	34	14	3	17	64:62	31
12	Third Lanark	34	13	4	17	75:83	30
13	Dunfermline	34	10	9	15	72:80	29
14	St Mirren	34	11	6	17	78:86	28
15	Aberdeen	34	11	6	17	54:72	28
16	Airdrie	34	11	6	17	56:80	28
17	Stirling A.†	34	7	8	19	55:72	22
18	Arbroath†	34	4	7	23	38:106	15

SCOTTISH DIVISION 1 1960-61

1	Rangers	34	23	5	6	88:46	51
2	Kilmarnock	34	21	8	5	77:45	50
3	Third Lanark	34	20	2	12	100:80	42
4	Celtic	34	15	9	10	64:46	39
5	Motherwell	34	15	8	11	70:57	38
6	Aberdeen	34	14	8	12	72:72	36
7	Hearts	34	13	8	13	51:53	34
8	Hibernian	34	15	4	15	66:69	34
9	Dundee U.	34	13	7	14	60:58	33
10	Dundee	34	13	6	15	61:53	32
11	Partick	34	13	6	15	59:69	32
12	Dunfermline	34	12	7	15	65:81	31
13	Airdrie	34	10	10	14	61:71	30
14	St Mirren	34	11	7	16	53:58	29
15	St Johnstone	34	10	9	15	47:63	29
16	Raith	34	10	7	17	46:67	27
17	Clyde†	34	6	11	17	55:77	23
18	Ayr†	34	5	12	17	51:81	22

SCOTTISH DIVISION 1 1961-62

1	Dundee	34	25	4	5	80:46	54
2	Rangers	34	22	7	5	84:31	51
3	Celtic	34	19	8	7	81:37	46
4	Dunfermline	34	19	5	10	77:46	43
5	Kilmarnock	34	16	10	8	74:58	42
6	Hearts	34	16	6	12	54:49	38
7	Partick	34	16	3	15	60:55	35
8	Hibernian	34	14	5	15	58:72	33
9	Motherwell	34	13	6	15	65:62	32
10	Dundee U.	34	13	6	15	70:71	32
11	Third Lanark	34	13	5	16	59:60	31
12	Aberdeen	34	10	9	15	60:73	29
13	Raith	34	10	7	17	51:73	27
14	Falkirk	34	11	4	19	45:68	26
15	Airdrie	34	9	7	18	57:78	25
16	St Mirren	34	10	5	19	52:80	25
17	St Johnstone†	34	9	7	18	35:61	25
18	Stirling A.†	34	6	6	22	34:76	18

SCOTTISH DIVISION 1 1962-63

1	Rangers	34	25	7	2	94:28	57
2	Kilmarnock	34	20	8	6	92:40	48
3	Partick	34	20	6	8	66:44	46
4	Celtic	34	19	6	9	76:44	44
5	Hearts	34	17	9	8	85:59	43
6	Aberdeen	34	17	7	10	70:47	41
7	Dundee U.	34	15	11	8	67:52	41
8	Dunfermline	34	13	8	13	50:47	34
9	Dundee	34	12	9	13	60:49	33
10	Motherwell	34	10	11	13	60:63	31
11	Airdrie	34	14	2	18	52:76	30
12	St Mirren	34	10	8	16	52:72	28
13	Falkirk	34	12	3	19	54:69	27
14	Third Lanark	34	9	8	17	56:68	26
15	Queen o' South	34	10	6	18	36:75	26
16	Hibernian	34	8	9	17	47:67	25
17	Clyde†	34	9	5	20	49:83	23
18	Raith†	34	2	5	27	35:118	9

SCOTTISH DIVISION 1 1963-64

1	Rangers	34	25	5	4	85:31	55
2	Kilmarnock	34	22	5	7	77:40	49
3	Celtic	34	19	9	6	89:34	47
4	Hearts	34	19	9	6	74:40	47
5	Dunfermline	34	18	9	7	64:33	45
6	Dundee	34	20	5	9	94:50	45
7	Partick	34	15	5	14	55:54	35
8	Dundee U.	34	13	8	13	65:49	34
9	Aberdeen	34	12	8	14	53:53	32
10	Hibernian	34	12	6	16	59:66	30
11	Motherwell	34	9	11	14	51:62	29
12	St Mirren	34	12	5	17	44:74	29
13	St Johnstone	34	11	6	17	54:70	28
14	Falkirk	34	11	6	17	54:84	28
15	Airdrie	34	11	4	19	52:97	26
16	Third Lanark	34	9	7	18	47:74	25
17	Queen o' South†	34	5	6	23	40:92	16
18	E. Stirlingshire†	34	5	2	27	37:91	12

SCOTTISH DIVISION 1 1964-65

1	Kilmarnock	34	22	6	6	62:33	50
2	Hearts	34	22	6	6	90:49	50
3	Dunfermline	34	22	5	7	83:36	49
4	Hibernian	34	21	4	9	75:47	46
5	Rangers	34	18	8	8	78:35	44
6	Dundee	34	15	10	9	86:63	40
7	Clyde	34	17	6	11	64:58	40
8	Celtic	34	16	5	13	76:57	37
9	Dundee U.	34	15	6	13	59:51	36
10	Morton	34	13	7	14	54:54	33
11	Partick	34	11	10	13	57:58	32
12	Aberdeen	34	12	8	14	59:75	32
13	St Johnstone	34	9	11	14	57:62	29
14	Motherwell	34	10	8	16	45:54	28
15	St Mirren	34	9	6	19	38:70	24
16	Falkirk	34	7	7	20	43:85	21
17	Airdrie†	34	5	4	25	48:110	14
18	Third Lanark†	34	3	1	30	22:99	7

SCOTTISH DIVISION 1 1965-66

1	Celtic	34	27	3	4	106:30	57
2	Rangers	34	25	5	4	91:29	55
3	Kilmarnock	34	20	5	9	73:46	45
4	Dunfermline	34	19	6	9	94:55	44
5	Dundee U	34	19	5	10	79:51	43
6	Hibernian	34	16	6	12	81:55	38
7	Hearts	34	13	12	9	56:48	38
8	Aberdeen	34	15	6	13	61:54	36
9	Dundee	34	14	6	14	61:61	34
10	Falkirk	34	15	1	18	48:72	31
11	Clyde	34	13	4	17	62:64	30
12	Partick	34	10	10	14	55:64	30
13	Motherwell	34	12	4	18	52:69	28
14	St Johnstone	34	9	8	17	58:81	26
15	Stirling A.	34	9	8	17	40:68	26
16	St Mirren	34	9	4	21	44:82	22
17	Morton†	34	8	5	21	42:84	21
18	Hamilton†	34	3	2	29	27:117	8

SCOTTISH DIVISION 1 1966-67

1	Celtic	34	26	6	2	111:33	58
2	Rangers	34	24	7	3	92:31	55
3	Clyde	34	20	6	8	64:48	46
4	Aberdeen	34	17	8	9	72:38	42
5	Hibernian	34	19	4	11	72:49	42
6	Dundee	34	16	9	9	74:51	41
7	Kilmarnock	34	16	8	10	59:46	40
8	Dunfermline	34	14	10	10	72:52	38
9	Dundee U	34	14	9	11	68:62	37
10	Motherwell	34	10	11	13	59:60	31
11	Hearts	34	11	8	15	39:48	30
12	Partick	34	9	12	13	49:68	30
13	Airdrie	34	11	6	17	41:53	28
14	Falkirk	34	11	4	19	33:70	26
15	St Johnstone	34	10	5	19	53:73	25
16	Stirling A.	34	5	9	20	31:85	19
17	St Mirren†	34	4	7	23	25:81	15
18	Ayr†	34	1	7	26	20:86	9

SCOTTISH DIVISION 1 1967-68

1	Celtic	34	30	3	1	106:24	63
2	Rangers	34	28	5	1	93:34	61
3	Hibernian	34	20	5	9	67:49	45
4	Dunfermline	34	17	5	12	64:41	39
5	Aberdeen	34	16	5	13	63:48	37
6	Morton	34	15	6	13	57:53	36
7	Kilmarnock	34	13	8	13	59:57	34
8	Clyde	34	15	4	15	55:55	34
9	Dundee	34	13	7	14	62:59	33
10	Partick	34	12	7	15	51:67	31
11	Dundee U.	34	10	11	13	53:72	31
12	Hearts	34	13	4	17	56:61	30
13	Airdrie	34	10	9	15	45:58	29
14	St Johnstone	34	10	7	17	43:52	27
15	Falkirk	34	7	12	15	36:50	26
16	Raith	34	9	7	18	58:86	25
17	Motherwell†	34	6	7	21	40:66	19
18	Stirling A.†	34	4	4	26	29:105	12

SCOTTISH DIVISION 1 1968-69

1	Celtic	34	23	8	3	89:32	54
2	Rangers	34	21	7	6	81:32	49
3	Dunfermline	34	19	7	8	63:45	45
4	Kilmarnock	34	15	14	5	50:32	44
5	Dundee U.	34	17	9	8	61:49	43
6	St Johnstone	34	16	5	13	66:59	37
7	Airdrie	34	13	11	10	46:44	37
8	Hearts	34	14	8	12	52:54	36
9	Dundee	34	10	12	12	47:48	32
10	Morton	34	12	8	14	58:68	32
11	St Mirren	34	11	10	13	40:54	32
12	Hibernian	34	12	7	15	60:59	31
13	Clyde	34	9	13	12	35:50	31
14	Partick	34	9	10	15	39:53	28
15	Aberdeen	34	9	8	17	50:59	26
16	Raith	34	8	5	21	45:67	21
17	Falkirk†	34	5	8	21	33:69	18
18	Arbroath†	34	5	6	23	41:82	16

SCOTTISH DIVISION 1 1969-70

1	Celtic	34	27	3	4	96:33	57
2	Rangers	34	19	7	8	67:40	45
3	Hibernian	34	19	6	9	65:40	44
4	Hearts	34	13	12	9	50:36	38
5	Dundee U.	34	16	6	12	62:64	38
6	Dundee	34	15	6	13	49:44	36
7	Kilmarnock	34	13	10	11	62:57	36
8	Aberdeen	34	14	7	13	55:45	35
=9	Dunfermline	34	15	5	14	45:45	35
=9	Morton	34	13	9	12	52:52	35
11	Motherwell	34	11	10	13	49:51	32
12	Airdrie	34	12	8	14	59:64	32
13	St Johnstone	34	11	9	14	50:62	31
14	Ayr	34	12	6	16	37:52	30
15	St Mirren	34	8	9	17	39:54	25
16	Clyde	34	9	7	18	34:56	25
17	Raith†	34	5	11	18	32:67	21
18	Partick†	34	5	7	22	41:82	17

SCOTTISH DIVISION 1 1970-71

1	Celtic	34	25	6	3	89:23	56
2	Aberdeen	34	24	6	4	68:18	54
3	St Johnstone	34	19	6	9	59:44	44
4	Rangers	34	16	9	9	58:34	41
5	Dundee	34	14	10	10	53:45	38
6	Dundee U.	34	14	8	12	53:54	36
7	Falkirk	34	13	9	12	46:53	35
8	Morton	34	13	8	13	44:44	34
9	Airdrie	34	13	8	13	60:65	34
10	Motherwell	34	13	8	13	43:47	34
11	Hearts	34	13	7	14	41:40	33
12	Hibernian	34	10	10	14	47:53	30
13	Kilmarnock	34	10	8	16	43:67	28
14	Ayr	34	9	8	17	37:54	26
15	Clyde	34	8	10	16	33:59	26
16	Dunfermline	34	6	11	17	44:56	23
17	St Mirren†	34	7	9	18	38:56	23
18	Cowdenbeath†	34	7	3	24	33:77	17

SCOTTISH DIVISION 1 1971-72

1	Celtic	34	28	4	2	96:28	60
2	Aberdeen	34	21	8	5	80:26	50
3	Rangers	34	21	2	11	71:38	44
4	Hibernian	34	19	6	9	62:34	44
5	Dundee	34	14	13	7	59:38	41
6	Hearts	34	13	13	8	53:49	39
7	Partick	34	12	10	12	53:54	34
8	St Johnstone	34	12	8	14	52:58	32
9	Dundee U.	34	12	7	15	55:70	31
10	Motherwell	34	11	7	16	49:69	29
11	Kilmarnock	34	11	6	17	49:64	28
12	Ayr	34	9	10	15	40:58	28
13	Morton	34	10	7	17	46:52	27
14	Falkirk	34	10	7	17	44:60	27
15	Airdrie	34	7	12	15	44:76	26
16	East Fife	34	5	15	14	34:61	25
17	Clyde†	34	7	10	17	33:66	24
18	Dunfermline†	34	7	9	18	31:50	23

SCOTTISH DIVISION 2 1972-73

1	Clyde*	36	23	10	3	68:28	56
2	Dunfermline*	36	23	6	7	95:32	52
3	Raith	36	19	9	8	73:42	47
4	Stirling A.	36	19	9	8	70:39	47
5	St Mirren	36	19	7	10	79:50	45
6	Montrose	36	18	8	10	82:58	44
7	Cowdenbeath	36	14	10	12	57:53	38
8	Hamilton	36	16	6	14	67:63	38
9	Berwick	36	16	5	15	45:54	37
10	Stenhousemuir	36	14	8	14	44:41	36
11	Queen o' South	36	13	8	15	45:52	34
12	Alloa	36	11	11	14	45:49	33
13	E. Stirlingshire	36	12	8	16	52:69	32
14	Queen's Park	36	9	12	15	44:61	30
15	Stranraer	36	13	4	19	56:78	30
16	Forfar	36	10	9	17	38:66	29
17	Clydebank	36	9	6	21	48:72	21
18	Albion	36	5	8	23	35:83	18
19	Brechin	36	5	4	27	46:99	14

SCOTTISH DIVISION 1 1973-74

1	Celtic	34	23	7	4	82:27	53
2	Hibernian	34	20	9	5	75:42	49
3	Rangers	34	21	6	7	67:34	48
4	Aberdeen	34	13	16	5	46:26	42
5	Dundee	34	16	7	11	67:48	39
6	Hearts	34	14	10	10	54:43	38
7	Ayr	34	15	8	11	44:40	38
8	Dundee U.	34	15	7	12	55:51	37
9	Motherwell	34	14	7	13	45:40	35
10	Dumbarton	34	11	7	16	43:58	29
11	Partick	34	9	10	15	33:46	28
12	St Johnstone	34	9	10	15	41:60	28
13	Arbroath	34	10	7	17	52:69	27
14	Morton	34	8	10	16	37:49	26
15	Clyde	34	8	9	17	29:65	25
16	Dunfermline	34	8	8	18	43:65	24
17	East Fife†	34	9	6	19	26:51	24
18	Falkirk†	34	4	14	16	33:58	22

SCOTTISH DIVISION 1‡ 1974-75

1	Rangers	34	25	6	3	86:33	56
2	Hibernian	34	20	9	5	69:37	49
3	Celtic	34	20	5	9	81:41	45
4	Dundee U.	34	19	7	8	72:43	45
5	Aberdeen	34	16	9	9	66:43	41
6	Dundee	34	16	6	12	48:42	38
7	Ayr	34	14	8	12	50:61	36
8	Hearts	34	11	13	10	47:52	35
9	St Johnstone	34	11	12	11	41:44	34
10	Motherwell	34	14	5	15	52:57	33
11	Airdrie	34	11	9	14	43:55	31
12	Kilmarnock	34	8	15	11	52:68	31
13	Partick	34	10	10	14	48:62	30
14	Dumbarton	34	7	10	17	44:55	24
15	Dunfermline	34	7	9	18	46:66	23
16	Clyde	34	6	10	18	40:63	22
17	Morton	34	6	10	18	31:62	22
18	Arbroath	34	5	7	22	34:66	17

‡First 10 clubs formed new Premier Division; bottom 8 clubs plus top 6 from Division 2 formed new Division 1

SCOTTISH DIVISION 1 1975-76

1	Partick*	26	17	7	2	47:19	41
2	Kilmarnock*	26	16	3	7	44:29	35
3	Montrose	26	12	6	8	53:43	30
4	Dumbarton	26	12	4	10	35:46	28
5	Arbroath	26	11	4	11	41:39	26
6	St Mirren	26	9	8	9	37:37	26
7	Airdrie	26	7	11	8	44:41	25
8	Falkirk	26	10	5	11	38:35	25
9	Hamilton	26	7	10	9	37:37	24
10	Queen o' South	26	9	6	11	41:47	24
11	Morton	26	7	9	10	31:40	23
12	East Fife	26	8	7	11	39:53	23
13	Dunfermline†	26	5	10	11	30:51	20
14	Clyde†	26	5	4	17	34:52	14

SCOTTISH DIVISION 2 1976-77

1	Stirling A.*	39	22	11	6	59:29	55
2	Alloa*	39	19	13	7	73:45	51
3	Dunfermline	39	20	10	9	52:36	50
4	Stranraer	39	20	6	13	74:53	46
5	Queens Park	39	17	11	11	65:51	45
6	Albion	39	15	12	12	74:61	42
7	Clyde	39	15	11	13	68:64	41
8	Berwick	39	13	10	16	37:51	36
9	Stenhousemuir	39	15	5	19	38:49	35
10	E. Stirlingshire	39	12	8	19	47:63	32
11	Meadowbank	39	8	16	15	41:57	32
12	Cowdenbeath	39	13	5	21	46:64	31
13	Brechin	39	7	12	20	51:77	26
14	Forfar	39	7	10	22	43:68	24

SCOTTISH DIVISION 2 1977-78

1	Clyde*	39	21	11	7	71:32	53
2	Raith*	39	19	15	5	63:34	53
3	Dunfermline	39	18	12	9	64:41	48
4	Berwick	39	16	16	7	68:51	48
5	Falkirk	39	15	14	10	51:46	44
6	Forfar	39	17	8	14	61:55	42
7	Queen's Park	39	13	15	11	52:51	41
8	Albion	39	16	8	15	68:68	40
9	East Stirlingshire	39	15	8	16	55:65	38
10	Cowdenbeath	39	13	8	18	75:78	34
11	Stranraer	39	13	7	19	54:63	33
12	Stenhousemuir	39	10	10	19	43:67	30
13	Meadowbank	39	6	10	23	43:89	22
14	Brechin	39	7	6	26	45:73	20

SCOTTISH DIVISION 2 1978-79

1	Berwick*	39	22	10	7	82:44	54
2	Dunfermline*	39	19	14	6	66:40	52
3	Falkirk	39	19	12	8	66:37	50
4	East Fife	39	17	9	13	64:53	43
5	Cowdenbeath	39	16	10	13	63:58	42
6	Alloa	39	16	9	14	57:62	41
7	Albion	39	15	10	14	57:56	40
8	Forfar	39	13	12	14	55:52	38
9	Stranraer	39	18	2	19	52:66	38
10	Stenhousemuir	39	12	8	19	54:58	32
11	Brechin	39	9	14	16	49:65	32
12	E. Stirlingshire	39	12	8	19	61:87	32
13	Queen's Park	39	8	12	19	46:57	28
14	Meadowbank	39	8	8	23	37:74	24

SCOTTISH DIVISION 1 1979-80

1	Hearts*	39	20	13	6	58:39	53
2	Airdrie*	39	21	9	9	78:47	51
3	Ayr	39	16	12	11	64:51	44
4	Dumbarton	39	19	6	14	59:51	44
5	Raith	39	14	15	10	59:46	43
6	Motherwell	39	16	11	12	59:48	43
7	Hamilton	39	15	10	14	60:59	40
8	Stirling A.	39	13	13	13	40:40	39
9	Clydebank	39	14	8	17	58:57	36
10	Dunfermline	39	11	13	15	39:57	35
11	St Johnstone	39	12	10	17	57:74	34
12	Berwick	39	8	15	16	57:64	31
13	Arbroath†	39	9	10	20	50:79	28
14	Clyde†	39	6	13	20	43:69	25

SCOTTISH DIVISION 1 1980-81

1	Hibernian*	39	24	9	6	67:24	57
2	Dundee*	39	22	8	9	64:40	52
3	St Johnstone	39	20	11	8	64:45	51
4	Raith	39	20	10	9	49:32	50
5	Motherwell	39	19	11	9	65:51	49
6	Ayr	39	17	11	11	59:42	45
7	Hamilton	39	15	7	17	61:57	37
8	Dumbarton	39	13	11	15	49:50	37
9	Falkirk	39	13	8	18	39:52	34
10	Clydebank	39	10	13	16	48:59	33
11	E. Stirlingshire	39	6	17	16	41:56	29
12	Dunfermline	39	10	7	22	41:58	27
13	Stirling†	39	6	11	22	18:48	23
14	Berwick†	39	5	12	22	31:82	22

SCOTTISH DIVISION 1					1981-82	
1	Motherwell	39	26	9	4	92:36	61
2	Kilmarnock	39	17	17	5	60:29	51
3	Hearts	39	21	8	10	65:37	50
4	Clydebank	39	19	8	12	61:53	46
5	St Johnstone	39	17	8	14	69:60	42
6	Ayr U.	39	15	12	12	56:50	42
7	Hamilton	39	16	8	15	52:49	40
8	Queen's Park	39	13	10	16	41:41	36
9	Falkirk	39	11	14	14	49:52	36
10	Dunfermline	39	11	14	14	46:56	36
11	Dumbarton	39	13	9	17	49:61	35
12	Raith Rovers	39	11	7	21	31:59	29
13	E. Stirlingshire	39	7	10	2	38:77	24
14	Queen o' South	39	4	10	25	44:93	18

SCOTTISH DIVISION 2					1983-84	
1	Forfar	39	27	9	3	73:31	63
2	East Fife	39	20	7	12	57:42	47
3	Berwick	39	16	11	12	60:38	43
4	Stirling A.	39	14	14	11	51:42	42
5	Arbroath	39	18	6	15	51:46	42
6	Queen o' South	39	16	10	13	51:46	42
7	Stenhousemuir	39	14	11	14	47:57	39
8	Stranraer	39	13	12	14	47:47	38
9	Dunfermline	39	13	10	16	44:45	36
10	Queen's Park	39	14	8	17	58:63	36
11	E. Stirlingshire	39	10	11	18	51:66	31
12	Montrose	39	12	7	20	36:59	31
13	Cowdenbeath	39	10	9	20	44:58	29
14	Albion	39	8	11	20	46:76	27

SCOTTISH DIVISION 1					1982-83	
1	St Johnstone	39	25	5	9	59:37	55
2	Hearts	39	22	10	7	79:38	54
3	Clydebank	39	20	10	9	72:49	50
4	Partick Thistle	39	20	9	10	66:45	49
5	Airdrie	39	16	7	16	62:46	39
6	Alloa	39	14	11	14	52:52	39
7	Dumbarton	39	13	10	16	50:59	36
8	Falkirk	39	15	6	18	45:55	36
9	Raith Rovers	39	13	8	18	64:63	34
10	Clyde	39	14	6	19	55:66	34
11	Hamilton	39	11	12	16	54:66	34
12	Ayr U.	39	12	8	19	45:61	32
13	Dunfermline	39	7	17	15	39:69	31
14	Queen's Park	39	6	11	22	44:80	23

SCOTTISH DIVISION 2					1984-85	
1	Montrose	39	22	9	8	57:40	53
2	Alloa	39	20	10	9	58:40	50
3	Dunfermline	39	17	15	7	61:36	49
4	Cowdenbeath	39	18	11	10	68:39	47
5	Stenhousemuir	39	15	15	9	45:43	45
6	Stirling A.	39	15	13	11	62:47	43
7	Raith Rovers	39	18	6	15	69:57	42
8	Queen o' South	39	10	14	15	42:56	34
9	Albion	39	13	8	18	49:72	34
10	Queen's Park	39	12	9	18	48:55	33
11	Stranraer	39	13	6	20	52:67	32
12	E. Stirlingshire	39	8	15	16	38:53	31
13	Berwick	39	8	12	19	36:49	28
14	Arbroath	39	9	7	23	35:66	25

Charlie Dickson heading for goal against Aberdeen. Jim Clunie looks on in dismay. Late 1950s.

Congratulations
to
Dunfermline Athletic
Football Club
on your
Centenary.

The Royal Bank of Scotland plc

Registered Office: 36 St. Andrew Square, Edinburgh EH2 2YB. Registered in Scotland No. 90312.

Training in the public park, July 1971. (M. Allan)

Thomson (No. 9) is congratulated on scoring the opening goal of the 1961 Final.

184

Another hat-trick from Mike Leonard wins his club three crates of whisky. (Dunfermline Press)

The end of an era: McLean scores Dunfermline's third goal against Anderlecht – their last in Europe. (Dundee Courier)

Training session in the gym supervised by coach Gregor Abel and Jim Leishman, November 1984. (Dundee Courier)

Above: Goalkeeper Connachan is carried off the field at Hampden Park by his jubilant team-mates after Dunfermline had won the Cup in 1961. (Daily Record)

DISPENSES WITH FORMALITIES AT OVER 2,500 CASH DISPENSERS ALL OVER BRITAIN

Clydesdale AutoBank

MR JOHN SMITH

Expires end	Code Number	Account Number	Card
JUN.88	820000	40800018	1

The Clydesdale AutoBank card allows personal current account customers the use of AutoBank facilities at over 2,500 cash dispensers operated by Clydesdale Bank, Midland Bank and National Westminster Bank the length and breadth of Britain and in Ireland by Northern Bank.

Another example of how the Clydesdale Bank is nearer your needs — wherever you are.

Clydesdale Bank

THERE WHEN YOU NEED US

An aerial view of East End Park, 1966.

AUTOGRAPHS